ARISTOCRACY AND ATHLETICS IN ARCHAIC AND CLASSICAL GREECE

Athletics represented an important institution through which the Greek aristocracies sought to maintain their privileged political position. Victory, however, had always involved the use of others, such as charioteers, jockeys, and trainers, and in the late archaic and early classical period, the relationship between the victors and these helpers changed radically. This threatened the political value of athletics and thus undermined the utility of the institution for aristocrats. Nigel Nicholson examines how aristocrats responded to these changes through a study of victory memorials. New Historicist in method, the book draws on odes, dedications, vases, and coins, as well as anecdotes about the victors. It asks how the vulgar details of winning are represented by the memorials, and it assumes that the value of athletics was always under threat, from groups both inside and outside the elite. The result is a fascinating look at one area of social struggle in ancient Greece.

Nigel James Nicholson is the Walter Mintz Associate Professor of Classics at Reed College. He has contributed to *Classical World, Arethusa, Phoenix, Classical Journal*, and *Intertexts* and was named Oregon Professor of the Year for 2004 by the Carnegie Foundation for the Advancement of Teaching.

ARISTOCRACY AND ATHLETICS IN ARCHAIC AND CLASSICAL GREECE

NIGEL JAMES NICHOLSON

Reed College

CAMBRIDGE
UNIVERSITY PRESS

CAMBRIDGE UNIVERSITY PRESS
Cambridge, New York, Melbourne, Madrid, Cape Town, Singapore, São Paulo

Cambridge University Press
40 West 20th Street, New York, NY 10011-4211, USA

www.cambridge.org
Information on this title: www.cambridge.org/9780521845229

First published 2005

Printed in the United States of America

A catalog record for this publication is available from the British Library.

Library of Congress Cataloging in Publication Data

Nicholson, Nigel James.
Aristocracy and athletics in Archaic and Classical Greece / Nigel James Nicholson.
p. cm.
Includes bibliographical references and index.
ISBN 0-521-84522-X (hardback)
1. Sports – Greece – History – To 1500 – Sources. 2. Athletes in literature.
3. Athletes – Social conditions – Greece. 4. Greece – Social conditions – To
146 B.C. – Sources. I. Title.
GV21.N53 2006
796′.0938 – dc22 2005000126

ISBN-13 978-0-521-84522-9 hardback
ISBN-10 0-521-84522-X hardback

Magistris Wiccamicis

CONTENTS

ILLUSTRATIONS

ABBREVIATIONS

The abbreviations of *L'annee philologique* are used for journal titles, while those of the *Oxford Classical Dictionary* or H. G. Liddell, R. Scott, and H. Stuart Jones, *A Greek-English Lexicon*, are used for ancient authors and works, with the following additions or exceptions:

ABV	John Davidson Beazley. 1956. *Attic Black-Figure Vase-Painters.* Oxford: Oxford University Press.
ARV^2	John Davidson Beazley. 1963. *Attic Red-Figure Vase-Painters.* 2nd ed. Oxford: Oxford University Press.
Ba.	Bacchylides
DP	Dittenberger, Wilhelm, and Karl Purgold. 1966. *Olympia: Die Ergebnisse der von dem Deutschen Reich veranstalteten Ausgrabung.* Vol. 5. *Die Inschriften von Olympia.* Ed. Ernst Curtius and Friedrich Adler. Amsterdam: Hakkert.
Is.	Isthmian Odes
Ne.	Nemean Odes
Ol.	Olympian Odes
Py.	Pythian Odes
Sim.	Simonides

ACKNOWLEDGMENTS

In a book that presumes that memorials advance certain political interests through what they include and what they exclude, the acknowledgments may come to seem more of a tool for promoting a particular ideology of academic production than a chance to thank the people and institutions that made the book possible. Fortunately, the stakes are rather lower here than they were with victory memorials.

Let me begin by acknowledging the central role played by my institution, Reed College. Through its paid leave and sabbatical programs, Reed provided a year and a half of paid leave between 1999 and 2003, and through the Levine Fund, the Stillman Drake Fund, and the Dean's Summer Fund, it supported various research expenses, including visits to museums in Europe, the costs of the photographs and permissions for this book, and student assistance in the preparation of the manuscript. Most important, the college allowed the project to develop in its own time.

Reed also provided me with stimulating and helpful colleagues; Walter Engert, Ellen Millender, Alex Nice, Geoffrey Schmalz, Joel Robbins, and Rupert Stasch deserve special thanks. My students, too, played a large part in the development of the theoretical framework for this book, particularly the students in my classes on literary theory and the victory ode.

Reed cannot take all the credit, and I owe a great debt to two scholars who promoted the application of New Historicism to Archaic Greece, Leslie Kurke and Carol Dougherty, the latter a colleague at Wellesley in 1994–5. I am also grateful to Jeff Carnes, Mark Golden,

Tom Hubbard, Sarah Harrell, and Malcolm Bell III for sharing their work with me and commenting so thoughtfully on my own.

The move into material culture presented various problems, which another Wellesley colleague, Miranda Marvin, did much to resolve. Thanks also to Ben David, Tony Iaccarino, Sam Danon, Franco Sgariglia, two Reed students, Charlie Stein and Alexandra Manglis, and especially Pericles Manglis, for helping me obtain authorization to reproduce some of the artworks that appear here.

Beatrice Rehl and Cambridge University Press were professional, sympathetic, and efficient throughout the publication process. Thanks also to the Press for giving me permission to reuse, for various parts of Chapters 1, 2, and 3, much of my piece, "Aristocratic Victory Memorials and the Absent Charioteer," from *The Cultures within Greek Culture: Contact, Conflict, Collaboration*, edited by Leslie Kurke and Carol Dougherty and published by Cambridge University Press in 2003. Last, but not least, many thanks to Jessica Rossknecht for her help in preparing the manuscript.

INTRODUCTION

The memorial of Polydamas of Scotussa, victor in the pancration in 408, seems to have been a favorite with visitors to Olympia in the imperial period. Polydamas' statue was made by Lysippus and was one of the tallest at Olympia, but the monument's draw lay elsewhere. Many thought it would cure their fever, but many others stopped to look at the large pedestal, where, in the inscription and in relief, were narrated many of the victor's colorful feats. Polydamas, it was said, had killed a lion bare-handed, stopped a speeding chariot by grabbing it as it went by, killed three of the Persian king's bodyguards whom he had challenged to fight him three against one, and held onto the hoof of a bucking bull until it came away in his hands.[1]

Polydamas' memorial may suggest that almost anything could be included in a victory memorial, but the content of these memorials was in almost all cases carefully controlled. Everything had to support an aristocratic ideology of athletics – Polydamas' memorial, with its list of his Herculean labors, elevates the victorious athlete to the status of a hero – and what did not support this ideology was rigorously excluded. These exclusions are of as much interest as the inclusions, and this study examines one of them, the exclusion from victory memorials in the late archaic and early classical periods of some of the personnel involved in the victories. For although these victory memorials could speak of the victors at length, they were almost entirely silent concerning the drivers, jockeys, and athletic trainers who helped them win.

The root cause of this silence was the lack of a real relationship between the patrons who sought the victories and the charioteers, jockeys, and trainers who were instrumental to their quest. In the late archaic and early classical periods, few of these sportsmen had any lasting relationship with their patrons; they were unlikely to have known them before the period of their service and had little expectation that their connection would continue once that service was over. Most sold their services to a number of patrons over their careers, and some trainers must have sold their services to several patrons concurrently. They were, in short, professionals; what relationship they had with their patrons was constituted by a commodity exchange, the exchange of their labor for a wage.

The use of professional charioteers, jockeys, and trainers to secure victory in the various events posed two significant problems for the aristocratic patrons who won the great majority of the victories.[2] First, the aristocrats' reliance on professionals to secure their victories undermined a central tenet of aristocratic ideology, that the qualities necessary for victory – the favor of the gods, determination, character, the intelligent application of wealth, and, in the gymnastic events (that is, the athletic, as opposed to equestrian or musical events), strength, endurance, and skill – were mostly the exclusive possessions of a few aristocratic families, whose new members possessed these qualities primarily by virtue of their birth into these families, and not because they had learned or invented them.[3] As professionals, however, the charioteers, jockeys, and athletic trainers circulated with little restraint, and so exposed as false the idea that the qualities needed for victory were anchored within these few families; what was crucial now appeared to be the right personnel, not the right character, talent, or divine favor, and this personnel was clearly mobile, available to anyone who could pay their wages, not only to the aristocratic clans. This revelation had repercussions far beyond stadia and hippodromes, since the privileged political and social position of these clans was justified in part by identifying the qualities necessary for athletic victory with the qualities necessary for the exercise of political power.[4] If these qualities were not the exclusive preserve of these clans, then there was no reason they should have a greater share of that power or a superior social position.

Second, aristocrats regularly denounced commodity exchange.[5] Indeed, their opposition to this mode of exchange was so central to their identity that their use of professionals to secure athletic victories must have generated something of a crisis in their self-understanding. Their denunciations of commodity exchange were not without reason: the spread of commodity exchange did, in fact, threaten their power, since it allowed individuals to bypass the traditional networks of reciprocity and redistribution that the aristocrats largely controlled, and so weakened their control of society and of the movement of goods and services within it.[6]

The services of charioteers, jockeys, and trainers had not always been commodified; in the earlier part of the sixth century and before, these services must have been typically supplied by family members, friends, slaves, bondsmen, or other members of the patron's estate. But as the services become increasingly available for purchase, the aristocratic clans that had a tradition of competing in the games were confronted with a difficult problem. On one hand, the use of professionals was extremely awkward; on the other hand, the commodification of these services offered buyers access to a much larger pool of experienced and skilled sportsmen, so that to keep aloof from such exchanges meant that patrons would in most cases have to compete at a disadvantage. Those aristocrats who were not lucky enough to have one of the leading charioteers within their circle of family or friends or on their estates had only two real options. They could simply withdraw from such competition and focus their energies on other forms of display that could justify their position in society, as King Agesilaus of Sparta was to do in the fourth century;[7] or, as most of them did with trade more generally, they could make the most of the benefits of commodification, but make use of whatever resources were at their disposal to disguise their engagement in such exchanges.

One especially suitable resource was the victory memorial, which developed during the sixth century, presumably to meet the aristocrats' demands for media through which to represent their newly problematic victories in ways that made them accord with aristocratic ideology. Ironically, the poets, sculptors, and vase makers who produced the memorials were also largely professionals from the late archaic period on,[8] so that the victors found themselves engaged in the rather contradictory activity of hiring professionals to disguise their hiring of other professionals. Typically, the disguise took the form of a simple erasure: the memorials removed the professionals from the victory by ignoring (or trivializing) the role these sportsmen played in the victories. The fact that charioteers, jockeys, and athletic trainers were not named in victory memorials was thus not the result of their poverty so much as of the ideological battles in which their patrons were involved.

Almost all the competitors in the equestrian and gymnastic contests relied on others in some significant way to secure their victories. In the sixth century, there were only two equestrian events at Olympia, the horse race and the four-horse chariot race, but at smaller festivals there were probably many more options: in the early fourth century a two-horse chariot race and a four-foal chariot race were added to the Olympic program, races for mares only were held at various local festivals, and the Panathenaia offered a sequence of races for some sort of cart other than a chariot.[9] In the horse races owners never rode their horses (youths served as jockeys), and in the chariot races it was rare for owners to drive. Some owners did drive, however, and some met with success, especially in the minor festivals, where there was a greater variety of races and the fields were smaller and less competitive: in the first part of the fifth century, Herodotus of Thebes won six local victories, all in four-horse chariot races, serving as his own driver,[10] and in the early fourth century Damonon of Sparta won forty-three local victories, twelve in the four-horse chariot race and thirty-one in the chariot race for full-grown mares, clearly something of a specialty.[11] To judge by the memorials from the late archaic period, however, victories at the major contests were extremely rare: memorials make it clear when a victor drove his own chariot, but only Herodotus of Thebes, in a victory at the Isthmian games, is explicitly credited with driving his own chariot.[12] Damonon had no success at the Panhellenic venues.

At the beginning of the fifth century two further equestrian events were introduced at Olympia, the mule-cart race and the mares' trotting race, the *kalpe*. Both events seem never to have been fully accepted and were discontinued half a century later.[13] The mule-cart race certainly followed the pattern of the chariot race, with owners employing drivers, while the obscure *kalpe* probably resembled the Olympic horse race, rather than the *apobates* race at the Panathenaea, which did require the competitors to take part.[14] Both races involved a mix of riding and running, but there the similarities end: in the *kalpe*, only one person was involved, and he rode the horse and then held its bridle as he ran to the finish, while the *apobates* was a chariot race, involving a charioteer and a second athlete, dressed as a hoplite, who dismounted from the chariot and ran to the finish.[15] Moreover, the festivals in which the two events were held must be sharply distinguished: unlike the Olympics, the Panathenaea was located in a particular city and explicitly promoted its interests; the *apobates* race was, in fact, one of several equestrian events at the festival restricted to Athenian citizens.[16] Such events were opposed to the traditional equestrian contests open to all Greek competitors: whereas the open contests did not concern themselves with the physical abilities of the competitors, the citizen-only contests sought to demonstrate the city's martial prowess.

In the gymnastic events, that is, the combat events (boxing, wrestling, and pancration), the running events (the stadion; the *diaulos*, or two-length race; the *hippios*, or horse-course race; the *dolichos*, or long race; and the hoplite race), and the pentathlon,[17] trainers provided invaluable assistance. All these events required a technical mastery that would be hard, if not impossible, to develop or sustain on one's own; moreover, trainers, at least on occasion, traveled with the athletes to competitions and attended their events.[18] It is generally accepted that the youths who sought to compete in the combat sports used trainers, but it is rarely admitted that other athletes used them too. Chapter 6 argues, however, that not only did youths use trainers for the other events, but most athletes continued to use them when they graduated to the open contests.[19]

We should not imagine some Edenic time early in the history of Greek athletics when competitors drove their own chariots and had no need of trainers; the use of drivers, jockeys, and trainers had always been an integral part of the different events for most competitors. This is clearest for the horse race, in which youths served as the jockeys, but there are also early references to the use of specialist charioteers in chariot races: although in the *Iliad* the leaders drive their own chariots during the funeral games of Patroclus, elsewhere Nestor speaks of a team of horses that Neleus had sent off with a charioteer to compete in some games (and which Augeias impounded) and Agamemnon's horses seem to have been winning prizes without him.[20] Further, the social function of equestrian competition seems to have been precisely to allow those from the elite who were too old to compete as athletes to continue to compete.[21] As for trainers, the earliest to be recorded, a pancration trainer named Eryxias, is linked to a victory in 564,[22] and, although this is recorded only in a late source, trainers must always have been a prerequisite for success in the combat sports, even if they may have been less crucial in the running events.

It would thus be odd if the use of drivers, jockeys, and trainers constituted a problem in itself; yet in the late archaic and early classical periods, 550 to 440, these figures were indeed a locus of concern. What generated this concern was the general commodification of their services during this time, combined with a general perception that these services were central to success in the event in question. The process of commodification should be traced not so much in the objects used to remunerate the charioteer or trainer as in the nature of his relationship with his patron. Certain forms of remuneration, such as a wage, strongly suggest that the object of exchange has been commodified but cannot be taken as definitive of this.[23] Rather, commodity exchange is defined by the lack of an enduring relationship between the parties to the exchange. In gift exchange, in principle, no transaction is singular or complete but is always made in the expectation of continued exchanges; it establishes a relation between the subjects of the exchange, not the objects.[24] Commodity exchange, however, implies the reduction of such personal costs; there is no expectation that a lasting relationship is established. What must primarily be examined to judge the commodification of the work of trainers, jockeys, and charioteers is, therefore, the depth of the relationship between these figures and their patrons.

Trainers certainly received wages for their work in Athens by at least the 450s: Plato records that Thucydides, the son of Melesias, spent money on the trainers Xanthias and Eudorus for his sons, who must have been born around 470.[25] What is more significant is that the relation between the trainers and their charges appears tenuous throughout the fifth century. There is no suggestion that Xanthias and Eudorus were chosen because they were friends or relatives of Thucydides; indeed, Plato suggests that their qualification was simply their quality as wrestlers. This is all the more surprising given that

Thucydides' family probably had a fine pedigree in coaching wrestlers: his father, Melesias, a succesful pancratiast in his own right, should probably be identified with the Melesias celebrated by Pindar in 460 for having guided his charges to thirty wins, a large proportion, apparently, in wrestling contests,[26] and Thucydides himself may have been a good wrestler.[27] Melesias offers an excellent illustration more generally of the shallow relation between patron and trainer in this period: he must have worked for a large number of families to amass such a record, and it is not likely that he was closely connected to them all. Pindar tells us of three different clans that he worked for, the Blepsiads, Bassids, and Theandrids; all are Aeginetan.[28] There is some reason to believe that Thucydides, Melesias' son, had a close relationship with the Aeginetan aristocracy, perhaps as a proxenos of Aegina,[29] but there is no reason to believe that this relationship with the island preceded his father's coaching activity there. Rather, it seems more likely that Melesias was drawn to the island by the Aeginetan clans' demand for high-quality coaching in wrestling and pancration and their willingness to pay handsomely for it, and that this initiated relations between his family and Aegina. Consequently, although Thomas Figueira sees Melesias' training as a form of patronage of the Aeginetan aristocracy (and thus, presumably, not a paid activity), other scholars view him as a professional, although perhaps one that was not denigrated as a wage earner.[30]

A second Athenian trainer employed in Aegina is also recorded, Menander, and in praising him Pindar suggests that Athens provided the lion's share of the coaches of combat sports in this period, which implies that the coaches had little or no prior relationship with the patrons for whom they worked.[31] Bacchylides, in his ode for the same victory, claims that Menander's charges have had frequent successes at Olympia;[32] such a record at Olympia can only have been achieved by coaching youths from a number of families in Aegina and Attica, and Menander cannot have been connected to them all.[33]

Some training was surely done in-house, by friends or family members with the appropriate skills and experience, but in the late archaic and early classical period, it must have been rare for athletes to find success at the major festivals without having availed themselves of the services of a professional trainer, just as it was rare for successful competitors in the chariot races at such festivals to drive their own chariots. Consequently, the majority opinion that successful athletes hired trainers in the late archaic and early classical period should be upheld.[34]

For the commodification of charioteers there is less evidence. Just as it was rare for owners to drive their own chariots in the major games, it also seems to have been rare for friends or family to drive: as with the owners, memorials seem to have taken some trouble to make it clear when this happens, but only two such memorials remain, suggesting that the vast majority of chariots were not driven by friends or family.[35] This leaves members of the owner's estate or hired drivers, and at least in the second half of the fifth century the latter seems to have been the norm: according to Plato, Lysis' father, Democrates, who was part of one of the most successful chariot-racing families in Athens in the fifth century, with victories at the Pythian, Isthmian, and Nemean games, employed a hired charioteer, something Plato presents as entirely to be expected.[36] The practice, evident in the last quarter of the fifth century, of entering multiple chariot teams in a single competition also suggests that it was usual to hire charioteers: as the example of Alcibiades' massive entry in the Olympics of 416 demonstrates, some of these teams were purchased from far afield, rather than bred in-house, and it is a fair assumption that charioteers came with them.[37] There is no evidence that multiple entries were made earlier in the century,[38] but one of the factors that prepared the ground for this practice was surely the ready availability of drivers, generated by their commodification. From the late archaic period itself, the only direct testimony for the relationship between a charioteer and his patron is Pindar's *Isthmian* 2. Pindar describes a charioteer, Nicomachus, who drove for more than one patron, but the patrons he speaks of, Theron and Xenocrates, are brothers, so that Nicomachus' circulation follows the tracks of kinship.[39] Pindar's potrait is, however, likely to be a mystification of the circumstances of Nicomachus' employment; the charioteer was almost certainly a professional who worked for a number of other patrons also, although the scholiast's claim that he was Athenian is fabricated.[40]

There is thus little to go on with charioteers because, unlike the trainers, they were carefully ignored in almost all our sources. Yet there are good reasons to accept that charioteers sold their services. For something to become a commodity, as Arjun Appadurai argues, there must be a context, such as a market, where it can be converted into a commodity, and there must be a general perception that it is appropriate for that thing to become a commodity[41]; both conditions are satisfied for competitive chariot driving. First, the games themselves provided an excellent venue for the charioteers to sell their services: owners, or their representatives, would regularly congregate at a place where the charioteers displayed their abilities. Second, it is clear that a general perception that athletic services could be bought and sold had developed by the late archaic period; not only were trainers selling their training in this period, but some athletes were selling their services also. After winning victories in the Olympic stadion and diaulos in 488, Astylus, the most successful Olympic athlete in the fifth century, was induced by Gelon or Hieron to change his civic affiliation from Croton to Syracuse; as a Syracusan, he won two more double victories in the stadion and *diaulos*, as well as at least one victory in the hoplite race.[42] Another highly successful runner, Ergoteles, may also have been tempted by the wealth of the Sicilian tyrants: after being exiled from Cnossos, he settled in Himera, a town apparently under Theron's control;[43] it is unclear whether he had already established himself as a leading runner, but at Olympia he proclaimed himself a native of Himera on the memorial recording his eight Panhellenic victories in the long race, two at each festival.[44] Given these developments in the way in which athletics was valued, and given the potential of the games to serve as a market, the opinion of many scholars that in the late archaic period the majority of charioteers was hired can be accepted.[45]

Whether there were contexts in which a jockey's services could be bought and sold is less clear. The fact that youths took the role of the jockeys meant that jockeys had only brief careers, which meant that there would have been little point in scouting out the most experienced jockeys at the major festivals. This in turn suggests that victors were constrained to draw on local resources, especially their own estates. There is no reason to expect all aspects of athletics to become commodified at roughly the same time; indeed, the horses themselves only become commodified in the late fifth century.[46] Yet the prestige of a victory in the horse race, although not equal to that of a victory in the chariot race, was so significant that it is hard to imagine that the same owners who hired the best charioteers in their bid for chariot victories would not have employed similar methods in their bid for glory in the horse race. Moreover, it is clear from the memorials themselves that jockeys, like charioteers and trainers, were a source of considerable anxiety to the victors, which points to some sort of implication in commodity exchange, with either their services or themselves for sale. We should perhaps imagine a more localized market for jockeys than for the charioteers, restricted in size by the speed with which the information about the jockeys became out-of-date. There were so many local competitions each year that a successful jockey would certainly have had plenty of opportunities to catch an owner's eye before he became too large for a racehorse.

There are, therefore, compelling reasons to conclude that the services of athletic trainers, charioteers, and jockeys became increasingly commodified in the late archaic period. In their increasing circulation, these athletes thus mirrored the artists who commemorated the victories they helped their patrons win. Artists like Pindar, Simonides, and Pythagoras of Rhegium were not tied to a single patron or his family for any length of time, but served many patrons over their careers, often commemorating several victories concurrently[47]; and just as, prior to the commodification of their services, most poets must have been drawn from among each patron's family, clan, friends, household, and estate, so, in the first half of the sixth century, must have most trainers, jockeys, and charioteers. The bulk of the charioteers were probably drawn from the slaves, debt bondsmen, and tenant farmers on the aristocrat's estate, and most of the trainers probably came from his family or friends, since they had themselves probably been competitors, or at least potential competitors. Traces of this earlier use of friends and kinsmen as trainers (and as poets) survive in the ideology of Pindar's odes.[48]

Many developments created the conditions in which the services these sportsmen provided could be commodified: the spread of trade fostered the propensity to view things as commodities, the increased availability of coinage allowed wealth to be transported more easily,[49] and the increasing numbers of athletic festivals offered convenient markets. The transformation was not, however, smooth or uniform.

Commodification encroached more quickly and more thoroughly into athletic competition, as into society more generally, in certain parts of the Greek world, such as Athens, Aegina, and Croton, than in others, such as Sparta,[50] and it affected local contests much less than the crown-bearing ones.[51] Yet despite this varied landscape, there can be no doubt that commodification was one of the dominant forces shaping Greek athletic competition in the late archaic and early classical periods. Most competitors simply could not ignore the opportunities it afforded or fail to recognize the challenges it posed.

For those who competed, it was crucial that commodity exchange not be perceived as central to their victories, and victory memorials proved an excellent tool for fixing the meaning of victory to their advantage. There were three main types of memorial to choose from: victory odes, dedications, and vases.

The victory ode flourished under the hands of Pindar, Simonides, and Bacchylides in the latter part of the sixth century and the first half of the fifth, although odes were produced by other poets as well.[52] The odes were performed mainly in the victor's city of residence, although other locations, including the site of the victory, were possible[53] and were usually commissioned by the victor, or, in the case of victories by youths, by the youth's father or the head of his clan, although again departures from this norm were possible.[54] The odes would have been sung and sometimes accompanied by music and dancing,[55] but after their initial performance they would have been kept in the aristocratic community's memory primarily through solo reperfomance at symposia.[56] They varied in length, but were all complex works of art that required some knowledge of the genre's rules for a good understanding.[57] This must have restricted their reach to the elites, but it is clear from their content, as well as from the testimony that Pindar's ode to Diagoras of Rhodes was dedicated in the temple of Lindian Athena that they were directed to members of the victor's city, not just his friends and clan.[58]

Statues and other dedications such as tripods or bowls certainly provided the poets with competition. These were set up both at the site of the victory and in the victor's hometown, in temples or other civic spaces, where they were especially open to the view of all parts of the population. They were usually accompanied by an inscription, which revealed the details of the victor and his victory. Dedications made at Olympia seem to have been regulated with regard to style and content, and this may also have been true for other sites.[59] Like the victory odes, dedications were primarily commissioned by the victor, his father, or the head of his clan, but there are also examples of civic dedications for victorious youths or long-dead stars.[60] Pausanias is the primary source for these dedications, but fragmentary remains have also been uncovered, especially at Olympia and Delphi and on the Athenian acropolis, and they affirm Pausanias' reliability.[61]

Vases were also specially commissioned to commemorate victories. Like odes, they were presumably intended for celebratory symposia and commissioned by the victors or their family and friends. Few examples remain that unambiguously declare someone a victor,[62] but a satirical hydria from the late sixth or early fifth century that was found in the Athenian agora suggests that vases with a brief inscription declaring someone a victor were common memorials, at least in Athens. Certainly, the vase's inscription seems to mock such a practice, for it begins by naming a Titas, declares him an Olympic victor, but then concludes with an insult: Τίτας ὀλυ<μ>πιον̣[ί]κ̣ος καταπύγον.[63]

Beyond unambiguous examples, there is a mass of possibilities. First, there is a great number of uninscribed vases that depict victorious athletes.[64] Various signs, such as Nikai, tripods, crowns, and even the shape of the vase, indicate that victory is being pictured, but, without an inscription, such vases are unlikely to be special commissions. Indeed, it would be rash to assume that they were even primarily intended for purchase by victors because the scenes are mostly highly formulaic and seem simply to have been a popular decorative motif. Not all such vases are so formulaic, however; one makes such a thoughtful departure from the usual practice of representing chariot races that, although not a special commission, it seems to have been intended to appeal specifically to an aristocratic victor in such a race.[65]

A second, small group consists of unusual prize Panathenaic amphoras. As one might expect, given that the city was responsible for commissioning the vases, the typical prize Panathenaic amphora is designed to glorify the city and pays little attention to the ideological interests of potential aristocratic patrons. In the center, on the front, appeared Athena in warrior garb together with an inscription declaring that the vase was "one of the prizes from Athens" (τõν Αθένεθεν ἄθλον), and the back indicated the event in which the victory had been won with a representation of such an event in progress and thus did not picture victors in the open equestrian events.[66] A few exceptional amphoras, although still commissioned by the city, do not conform to this pattern, however, and reflect some concern for the interests of the probable eventual owner of the prize.[67]

A final group of possible victory memorials consists of inscribed vases that represent athletic scenes but that are not unambiguously marked as victory memorials by their inscriptions. One such vase names a famous Athenian victor,[68] but without independent information on the person named, it is impossible to know whether he was a victor or just someone unconnected with the race, such as the intended recipient of the vase. Moreover, in the case of chariot races, a name placed near a charioteer may refer to the charioteer himself, rather than the victor.[69] It is surely possible that victory vases may have been commissioned by someone other than a victor or his family or friends, and thus that they may have promoted the ideology of some other constituency: after all, vases offered a much cheaper and less narrowly controlled medium of commemoration than dedications and victory odes and may thus have been within the reach of a wider class of patron.[70] While it is unclear whether any charioteers are named on vases, a number of trainers certainly are, and such vases (which do not depict a victory) may have been commissioned by the trainers themselves.[71]

In addition to the three major media – vases, statuary, and odes – there is a fourth, very small group of memorials that is distinct from the other three: three coin issues make reference to specific equestrian victories, issues from the Chersonese under Miltiades, Syracuse under Gelon, and Rhegium and Messana under Anaxilas.[72] Such memorials were only open to tyrants or kings and were further restricted by a certain tendency to maintain the broad outlines of traditional coin designs.[73] It was not the restrictiveness of the medium so much as its usage, however, that marks the coins as different from the other memorials. Coins were not produced for a victory celebration; in fact, they did not name the victor, even when they named the city of issue. Such a lack of reference to the victor indicates that the references to victory represented not so much an effort to secure the value of the victory for the victor as an effort to secure this value for the currency itself; Olympic success served as a token of the divine favor enjoyed by the city that issued the coins.[74]

These various types of victory memorial either emerge or at least undergo significant developments in their form around the middle of the sixth century.[75] The invention of epinician is traditionally associated with Simonides, but papyrus finds have shown that poets were composing lyric odes for athletic victors in the fifty years before Simonides.[76] Dedications had long been made at Olympia, but, according to Pausanias, their form changed radically in the third quarter of the sixth century when, for the first time, statues of the athletes were dedicated, initially in wood.[77] Pausanias' dating of this innovation may be conservative, but, either way, it must have followed the dedication of such statues elsewhere: the pancratiast Arrhichion, who won three Olympic titles but died while winning his third crown in 564, was commemorated by a kouros-like statue in the marketplace of Phigalia.[78] The use of vases as victory memorials is first attested for the third quarter of the sixth century;[79] this is a plausible date for this development because such a use for vases must have been not only encouraged by the Panathenaea's practice of putting the oil awarded to victors in prize vases, but also intended as a response to the civic ideology encoded on them, and this practice was solidified only around 566.[80]

The emergence around 550 of these new possibilities for commemorating victories defines the upper limit of the period covered by this study. The continuous exploitation of these possibilities over the next hundred years shows that there was a real continuity across the late archaic and early classical periods in the culture of commemoration (many artists in fact served patrons in both periods),[81] but there is a clear break in the 440s, the lower limit of the study, when the market for victory odes all but collapsed.[82] This collapse marks a change in the goals of commemoration, as athletic, and especially equestrian, victories increasingly ceased to offer a viable route to political advancement and their commemoration became a more private matter.[83]

The emergence of these different types of victory memorials should be seen as a response to social and political developments that threatened the meaning of aristocratic participation in competitive athletics in the late archaic period. The meaning of an athletic victory was neither self-evident nor uncontested: that it was the pinnacle of human achievement, a sign of supreme virtue and divine favor, and a boon to the victor's civic community had to be established, and had to be established against very different versions of its meaning. Some of these versions survive – such as the elegies of Xenophanes of Colophon and Tyrtaeus of Sparta that deny the usefulness of a champion athlete to the good government and military security of his city, or the vases that ridicule the aristocratic ideals of fairness and nobility by depicting pancratiasts gouging their opponents' eyes and boxers punching their opponents' genitals[84] – but such evidence only hints at the size of the crisis threatening aristocratic athletics. What makes the size of this crisis clear is rather the radical innovations in commemorative practice that, along with the boom in athletic festivals themselves,[85] made possible the consequent explosion of memorials.

This struggle for the meaning of athletics was just one part of the larger struggle for power that shaped the sixth and fifth centuries. As Ian Morris argues, the latter part of the sixth century witnessed a general surge in the belief that the opinions of the larger community were valid and could not be ignored. The fearless aloofness of many aristocratic groups in the early part of the century was no longer acceptable, and instead aristocrats had to address themselves to the wider community and justify their privileged political position in its terms, in particular, as Morris shows, through embracing a rhetoric that validated the middle against the extremes.[86] The wider community consisted of many groups, but the most important were the peasant farmers, colonists, and traders who were wealthy enough to serve as hoplites and to challenge the power of the old aristocratic clans. In addition, there were also many among the aristocrats who needed persuading. Some, such as the displaced intellectual Xenophanes of

Colophon, were outspoken in their opposition to many aristocratic practices, but many supported these practices and just needed some affirmation of their beliefs.[87]

As a whole, the aristocratic clans attempted both to mark themselves out as superior to the broader community (and thus as qualified to rule it) and to prove this superiority in that community's terms. On one hand, through involvement in cult and athletics and through the promotion of the exclusive culture of the symposium and its particular art forms, the aristocrats sought to link themselves to groups outside of their civic community, to gods, to heroes, and to other Greek aristocrats. On the other hand, they set themselves up as patrons of the wider community by covering the costs of public sacrifices, embassies, entertainment, and poor relief, while representing their other activities as no threat to the good order of their cities.[88] For Morris, epinician poetry was typical of this double movement: as Leslie Kurke has shown, victory odes sought not only to prove the existence of a genuine aristocracy by articulating a set of practices that would define it, but also to represent these practices as serving the wider community and promoting its values.[89] All victory memorials were, in fact, engaged in this double project: it was the need to justify the continuing political power of the aristocrats to both the aristocrats themselves and the wider community that generated their boom.

The memorials must, therefore, be treated as representations; they are not unmediated reflections of reality, but attempts to corral that reality down certain interested paths. When an ode represents a trainer as a highly respected friend of an aristocratic family or when a vase or dedication represents a racehorse as doing the winning, we must not accept these pictures as statements of fact, but interrogate them as representations.

Moreover, these representations must be seen as responding to specific challenges posed to the meaning of athletics, as engaging in a kind of argument in which the prize is the authority to fix that meaning. Little remains of the other sides of the argument, but they can be discovered in the memorials themselves, since they provide the opposing views against which the memorials mobilize and around which they are structured.[90] Because these views leave traces in the memorials, they can be differentiated from other potential concerns that were not part of the argument. For example, one significant factor in the aristocrats' success in gymnastic competitions must have been their superior diet, but there is no evidence that this was ever a significant issue in the struggles for the meaning of athletic victory. Although special diets are mentioned in the odd anecdote,[91] no memorial can be said to have been constructed as an answer to the questions unequal diets might have posed. By contrast, professional charioteers were clearly a significant locus of ideological struggle because numerous memorials offer specific substitutes for professional charioteers.

In reconstructing these struggles, it is crucial to examine the full range of available sources. This means, first of all, examining all victory memorials, not just the literary remains;[92] the victors themselves did not use only victory odes, and all the memorials were produced within the same political and social context. It also means examining other sources about victors and victory, in particular, the anecdotes that survive in later, often imperial writings. Although their roots in the period can rarely be proven, anecdotes are nevertheless a rich source for the discourse of athletics in the late archaic and early classical periods.[93] Some anecdotes reproduce the tropes and ideologies of the memorials, but others stand in opposition to them; their lack of poetic form and the contexts in which they have been preserved (collections of anecdotes, travel guides, and scholia) seem to have allowed their oppositional attitudes to survive without interference. Yet others, as the story about the boxer Glaucus of Carystus beginning life on a farm,[94] seem to occupy a strange hinterland where they seem capable of supporting opposing ideologies: Glaucus' story could be a refutation of stories that attribute divine parentage to famous athletes[95] or a demonstration that it is natural talent, and not wealth or privilege, that determines athletic victory.

It is one of the premises of this study that the victory memorials can be understood within the larger narrative of the aristocrats' struggle to defend their power, but this very effort to impose a unitary narrative on the memorials has significant dangers. Although the various memorials shared the same broad concerns, they cannot be thought of as uniform: many were surely also engaged in local contests, and these may have taken precedence over the struggle to defend aristocratic privilege against the increasing claims of those outside the elite.[96] The state of our sources makes such local contests difficult to detect, but it is likely that in many cases a jockeying for power between rival aristocratic clans was the most significant force shaping the memorial. This is perhaps especially true for memorials for victors from Aegina, where at least eleven clans seem to have competed for prestige in the realm of athletics,[97] and Cyrene, where resentment among some of the other aristocrats at their exclusion from power seems to have been considerable.

Above all, the memorials must be treated with suspicion, as calculated moves in a high-stakes chess game. They are tools for advancing their patrons' interests, not transparent records of athletic achievement. This is not to disrespect the artistic qualities of these memorials, but rather to recognize their full power, the power to shape and establish as reality an imaginative idea of how a given victory was won and of what constituted victory in general. Indeed, it is through the successful exercise of this power that producers of memorials, such as Pindar, Pythagoras of Rhegium, or the Mastos Painter, prove themselves superior at their craft. These are great artists not simply because of the beauty and economy of their work, but because of the creativity and effectiveness with which their designs constitute a reality that supports the interests of their aristocratic patrons.

Although the spread of commodification through athletics posed general problems for all competitors, because of their different structures, it affected the various events in different ways. Accordingly, this book is broadly organized by event: its first part examines memorials for equestrian victories, and its second part memorials for gymnastic victors. The opening chapter of Part I traces the absence of charioteers and mule-cart drivers from equestrian memorials and argues that they are not simply passed over, but purposefully excluded. Such memorials are, in fact, organized around the exclusion of the drivers – sometimes the charioteer is replaced by the victor; sometimes charioteers are missing from depictions of victory parades and from mythical narratives where elsewhere they have a role; often the focus is somewhere other than the race itself – but in each case the driver is the central silence that organizes the representation of the victory.

The following three chapters trace the representation of those drivers that are included. Chapter 2 examines the praise accorded a charioteer, Carrhotus, by Pindar's *Pythian* 5, and uses this to argue that the usual exclusion of charioteers is motivated by the fact that most charioteers had no enduring relationship with the victors. Carrhotus is an exceptional charioteer: he is not a professional, but a kinsman of the victor, and as his kinsman, he does not threaten the value of his victory, but actually enhances it. This conclusion is supported by three more memorials: a dedication at the Ptoion, *SEG* XXIII.38, which praises a charioteer seemingly for similar reasons, and an ode and a vase, Pindar's *Pythian* 6 and Copenhagen 109, which falsely represent their charioteers as friends or relatives of the victor.

Chapter 3 examines Pindar's *Isthmian* 2 and argues that the charioteer who appears there, Nicomachus, is a professional charioteer from outside the elite who has gained prominence through his success in chariot racing. *Isthmian* 2 is focused on commodification, and the commodification of chariot driving in particular. It carefully avoids representing Nicomachus as hired, but his very inclusion, as well as the particulars of his representation, require explanation. The chapter argues that Nicomachus was given such prominence because he had won such fame and wealth by his driving that a memorial that recorded the highly prestigious Olympic victory of 476 in which he drove could not convincingly praise the victor for the victory without mentioning the charioteer. The remainder of the chapter considers how far such successful charioteers were themselves able to commemorate their own achievements in the various media available.

Chapter 4 examines memorials for mule-cart races, and in particular Pindar's *Olympian* 6, which names a driver, Phintis. Although the representation of Phintis mirrors that of Nicomachus in *Isthmian* 2, his inclusion is motivated not by any particular prominence achieved by the mule-cart driver, but by the victor's domestic political concerns. Phintis is used, just as the mule-cart race itself was often used, to articulate the relationship between the victor, Hagesias of Syracuse, and his tyrant, Hieron.

Chapter 5 concludes the equestrian section by examining memorials for horse races. Whether vases, odes, or dedications, these follow different patterns in their representation of their event to memorials for chariot races: while some exclude the jockey, most include the jockey but trivialize his work by making the racehorse the primary agent of the victory. Although the treatment of jockeys differs from that of drivers, the way in which their contribution is represented indicates that they, too, were professional in some way, even though the jockeys were all youths: the elevation of the horse in place of the jockey allows gift exchange to remain central to the victory. The differences in the representation of horse races also demonstrate how sensitive the memorials' representations were to the different possibilities or problems presented by the particular structure of each event.

Chapter 6 opens the second part of the book by examining the absence of athletic trainers from memorials for gymnastic victors and arguing, much as Chapter 1 argues, that these people were not beneath the notice of artists and patrons, but were excluded from these memorials. The exclusion of the trainers leaves less obvious traces than the exclusion of the horsemen but is made clear by their prominence in other discourses, as well as by an anecdote from Pausanias that implies that they were excluded from Olympic dedications.

Chapter 7 examines the representation of the trainer Melesias to demonstrate that the reason trainers were excluded from memorials generally was that they were professionals and as such seemed to render portable those qualities crucial to victory that the aristocrats wanted to represent as inherited. The three odes in which he appears, Pindar's *Olympian* 8 and *Nemeans* 4 and 6, consistently represent Melesias as bound to the victor in an enduring relationship of gift exchange; in addition, they portray his teaching as anything but the introduction into a pupil of external abilities and either suppress the importance of skill to victory or represent it as an inherited ability. Melesias must have enjoyed an unusual prominence, whether because of his record or his family; but the similar treatments of the trainers Ilas and Orseas in *Olympian* 10 and *Isthmian* 4 demonstrate that it was his training that generated anxiety. That professional trainers are accorded a greater status than professional drivers is to be explained by differences in their relationships with their patrons: although hired, aspects of these relationship were easily assimilated to a gift exchange relationship.

Chapter 8 examines the odes concerning the children of Lampon and the trainer Menander. Pindar's *Nemean* 5 and Bacchylides 13 both treat Menander, while *Isthmians* 5 and 6 represent a family member as the victor's trainer. Together, the odes confirm the conclusions of the previous chapter: first, that what motivated anxiety about professional trainers was that, by appearing to add new abilities such as skill to their pupils, they threatened the idea that the qualities on which victory depended were inherited, and, second, that, while the training was traded as a commodity, the relationship between trainer and patron was sufficiently complex that to represent it in other terms was convincing. In addition, Bacchylides' ode offers clear evidence that a highly successful trainer like Menander was able to insist on a prominent part in the celebrations of his pupils' victories. As a group, therefore, these four odes offer a vivid picture of an aristocrat engaging in certain compromises to increase his own prestige through athletic success.

The final chapter, Chapter 9, uses three odes that do not name trainers, Pindar's *Nemean* 3 and *Olympians* 7 and 13, to demonstrate that professional trainers were such a source of anxiety that they also shaped memorials in which they were not named: even though they do not name a trainer, the odes spend considerable resources constructing models for training and for the acquisition of skill that do not conflict with the idea that those qualities important for success are inherited. This anxiety was not restricted to youth victories, but *Pythian* 9 and various anecdotes suggest that it was focused on victors in the combat sports and the pentathlon: success in the running events was more generally perceived as the result of inherited talent rather than special training. This underlines how important it is to consider the mechanics of the event in which victory is won: although the memorials may seem to occupy a space far removed from the vulgar details of competition, the picture of the victory that they promote is carefully calibrated to the challenges and opportunities posed by those details.

PART I

CHARIOTEERS, MULE-CART DRIVERS, AND JOCKEYS

I

MISSING PERSONS

Μεγαλοπόλιες ὦ Συράκοσαι, βαθυπολέμου
τέμενος Ἄρεος, ἀνδρῶν ἵππων τε σιδαροχαρ-
μᾶν δαιμόνιαι τροφοί,
ὔμμιν τόδε τᾶν λιπαρᾶν ἀπὸ Θηβᾶν φέρων
μέλος ἔρχομαι ἀγγελίαν τετραορίας ἐλελίχθονος,
εὐάρματος Ἱέρων ἐν ᾇ κρατέων
τηλαυγέσιν ἀνέδησεν Ὀρτυγίαν στεφάνοις,
ποταμίας ἕδος Ἀρτέμιδος, ἇς οὐκ ἄτερ
κείνας ἀγαναῖσιν ἐν χερσὶ ποικιλα-
νίους ἐδάμασσε πώλους.
ἐπὶ γὰρ ἰοχέαιρα παρθένος χερὶ διδύμᾳ
ὅ τ' ἐναγώνιος Ἑρμᾶς αἰγλάεντα τίθησι κόσ-
μον, ξεστὸν ὅταν δίφρον
ἔν θ' ἅρματα πεισιχάλινα καταζευγνύῃ
σθένος ἵππιον, ὀρσοτρίαιναν εὐρυβίαν καλέων θεόν.[1]

Great city of Syracuse, precinct of Ares deep-in-war, godlike nurse of men and horses that fight in iron, I come from wealthy Thebes, bearing this song to you, a message of an earth-shaking four-horse car, in which Hieron of the fine chariot conquered and bound Ortygia with far-shining crowns, the seat of Artemis of the river, not without whom he mastered those fillies with their embroidered reins in his gentle hands. For with each hand the maiden who showers arrows, and Hermes who watches over the games, place shining glory[2] on him whenever he yokes the strong horses to the polished car and the chariot that obeys the bridle, calling on the wide-mighted god who wields the trident.

(*Py.* 2.1–12)

Pindar's *Pythian* 2 opens with a romantic portrait of equestrian competition. It represents the owner, Hieron, as driving his own horses in his recent victory in the Ioleia in Thebes,[3] yoking the horses to the chariot before the race and then skillfully using the reins to guide them to the finish. Yet although it was more common for owners to drive their own chariots at local contests,[4] we cannot accept that Hieron drove in this victory.[5] The two memorials, including one of Pindar's odes, that certainly do commemorate victories in which the owners drove, establish the owner's participation explicitly;[6] moreover, Hieron would have had to have been an exceptional charioteer to be driving at his age. He was at least in his early fifties, and perhaps older, and, although charioteers could race throughout their forties and into their fifties (to judge by the charioteers of the late empire), this was surely true only of the fittest and most talented.[7] Further, there is evidence that Hieron was far from healthy around the time of this victory, the mid-to late 470s.[8] *Pythian* 1, composed in 470, compares his military exploits with those of Philoctetes, who succeeded in sacking Troy despite being sick, and a scholiast adds the information that during the campaign he was carried in a litter because he was suffering from bladder stones.[9] Hieron may thus have been in no state to race even if he was sufficiently talented to do so at his age; the driving, we must presume, was done by someone else whose contribution has been ignored. It is only an attachment to modern ideals of athletics that leads us to accept Pindar's idealized portrait of the victor preparing his own chariot and driving it to victory.[10]

Pythian 2 offers perhaps the most sustained and aggressive erasure of the charioteer's role of any memorial from this period, but, in intent, it is not especially unusual. Memorials for chariot (and mule-cart) victories generally give no credit to the driver and often hide his participation entirely.[11] This cannot be seen as a simple case of forgetting people who were beneath notice; rather, the victory memorials display a systematic and conscious refusal to recognize the drivers. In fact, although largely absent from the memorials, the charioteer is such an important presence that he shapes the description of the victory.

The bare statistics reveal the extent of the charioteer's exclusion. The job of a memorial is to name, but of the twenty-eight memorials for chariot or mule-cart victories from before 450 that name the victor and survive largely intact, only four name the charioteer or driver.[12] Further, there is no evidence from any of the numerous fragments of additional memorials that any other charioteer was named by any other victory memorial. Two possible namings should be rejected.[13] We cannot, of course, be sure that the charioteers were not named elsewhere in the various fragments, but the consistent silence of what does remain supports the contention that it was extremely rare for charioteers to be named.

Not being named is one thing, but it was even unusual for charioteers to be mentioned or represented. The fame of the Delphic charioteer, and the fact that the charioteer is the only element of Polyzalus' dedication to survive in any quantity, may give the impression that charioteers were often included in memorials, but a majority of the intact memorials, including the sculptural groups, avoids any reference to the charioteer.[14] This silence, as a survey of these memorials demonstrates, is not the relatively benign silence of neglect, but a purposive exclusion of the charioteer from the victory record. He is missing from depictions of the racing chariot itself, which, of course, he drove, and charioteers more generally are missing from other representations of chariots where we might expect them to be included. Despite the Delphic charioteer, therefore, the conclusion cannot be avoided that most memorials made a sustained and conscious effort to exclude the charioteer.

A number of memorials that include a representation of the racing chariot also include the charioteer. These are Pindar's *Pythian* 5, the three coin issues that commemorate equestrian victories, two memorials at Olympia, for Cleosthenes and Hieron, and the one dedicated at Delphi by Hieron's brother Polyzalus from which the famous Delphic charioteer survives.[15] In addition, the overwhelming majority of those vases that were not specially commissioned, but nevertheless seem to have been intended for purchase mostly by those wishing to celebrate chariot victories, perhaps following the lead of the Panathenaic vases, include the charioteer when they include the chariot.[16] The quiet inclusion of the charioteer should not be especially surprising; he did, after all, drive the horses and, like the horses themselves, was instrumental in the winning of the victory which the memorial celebrates. What is surprising is that there are some monuments that represent the racing chariot, but omit the charioteer. Pindar's *Pythian* 2, which simply misrepresents the race by setting the victor in the charioteer's place, has already been examined. No other of Pindar's odes is so bold, but there is a parallel from the visual arts. On the front of a black-figure neck amphora that no longer survives was a four-horse chariot being greeted by Athena, and above the charioteer appeared the slightly damaged name of Alcmaeon (Figure 1).[17] J. D. Beazley rightly concluded that the vase depicted the victory that Alcmaeon won at Olympia in 592 and that Herodotus so memorably describes as the direct result of Alcmaeon taking advantage of the king of Lydia's generosity (and good humor) by stuffing his pockets full of the king's gold.[18] Beazley did not note, however, how surprising the vase's representation of a chariot victory was: Alcmaeon was represented as driving his own chariot. This probably misrepresented the race; certainly, it would be rash to assume that Alcmaeon did drive his own team. Although he was probably younger than Hieron at the time of his victory, he most likely used a specialist charioteer, as his son, Alcmaeonides, did for a victory in the Panathenaea about forty years later.[19]

It is, however, impossible to establish whether Alcmaeon did drive his own chariot, or, if he did not, whether he hired a driver or instead used a slave, tenant, bondsman, or friend. Yet this is of little consequence, because the vase itself was produced much later than the victory, at a date when it was the norm to hire drivers, and when it was probably assumed that Alcmaeon had hired a driver, particularly since his victory was associated with a huge increase in his portable wealth (rather than, say, a family tradition of horse racing). On the grounds of style, Beazley dated the vase much later than the victory it commemorated, to around 480, and T. B. L. Webster accordingly suggested that it was commissioned as part of the celebrations of a later Alcmaeonid victory, the Pythian victory of Alcmaeon's great-grandson Megacles in 486, which Pindar celebrated in *Pythian* 7.[20] This is an attractive hypothesis, but whether the vase can be so closely attached to a specific victory celebration or not, it certainly expressed the anxieties that attended the charioteer in this later period.[21]

1. Alcmaeon as the charioteer in his chariot victory. Black-figure neck amphora from South Italy, obverse, ca. 480. Courtesy of the Staatliche Antikensammlungen und Glyptothek, Munich.

A rather earlier Panathenaic prize amphora may also be intended to suggest that the victor drove his own team in the chariot competition.[22] Because it is a prize amphora, the vase cannot have been specially commissioned by the victor, but the designer evidently sought to represent the chariot victory in a way that served his interests; he may have had greater latitude in the representation of the event, since at the time of

2. Four-horse chariot with charioteer. Panathenaic prize amphora from Orvieto, reverse, ca. 550. Courtesy of the Soprintendenza per i Beni Archeologici della Toscana, Florence.

the production of this vase, the middle of the sixth century, the design of prize Panathenaics was not fully formalized. On the back appears the picture of the event that became canonical: the charioteer in the traditional white tunic directs his four horses, seen from the side, with the reins and a goad (Figure 2). Two aspects of the vase are unusual, however. First, the prize inscription appears on the back, above the chariot, while, on the front, the Figure of Athena Polias is displaced from the central position and appears facing a naked, bearded man, holding a

3. Athena with victor in the chariot race. Panathenaic prize amphora from Orvieto, obverse, ca. 550. Courtesy of the Soprintendenza per i Beni Archeologici della Toscana, Florence.

fillet in his left hand (Figure 3). Beazley infers that this is the victor, who is not usually represented on prize amphorae, and this is surely correct.[23] His nakedness, the mark of an athlete, is surprising, however (an equestrian victor on a second prize amphora appears clothed).[24] The implication of the design seems to be that the victor won his chariot race much as, say, a wrestler wins his victories – by doing the physical work himself. This unusual design cannot be explained as the memorial of a race in which the victor did actually drive; because this was not a special commission, the designer's assumption must have been that the victor would not have been the driver. Rather, this vase offers a third memorial where the driver has been replaced with the victor.

There are, however, few memorials where the charioteer is so obviously missing. It is much more common to find general chariot scenes, in which a charioteer might or should be expected, represented without that charioteer. The practice is particularly common in victory odes, the complex structure of which allows for mythical detours. By looking back to a mythical past, odes are able to picture a world where the nobles drive themselves and do not employ specialized charioteers. This picture is then easily projected onto the present: audience members will assume, if they do not think too hard about it, that their world works much as the world depicted in the myths, and that the aristocratic victors, like the princely heroes of the mythical past, drive their own chariots. Mythical portrayals of chariot driving thus provide a simple, but highly effective, mystification of archaic competitive racing for the original audiences of these odes; modern readers, however, should note when and how the charioteers are missing.

Throughout Pindar's myths, heroes do their own driving, but the most telling cases involve those myths where charioteers known from other versions of the myths are not included. In *Nemean* 9, an ode celebrating the chariot victory at Sicyon of Chromius, one of Hieron's supporters, the seven heroes who attacked Thebes are pictured hurtling to destruction with chariots (ἱππείοις τε σὺν ἔντεσιν, "with horse equipment," 22), and no mention is made of charioteers.[25] Pindar adds that Amphiaraus himself was swallowed up by the ground "together with his horses" (ἅμ' ἵπποις, 25), but again there is no sign of a charioteer. This is particularly surprising, given that in vase paintings Amphiaraus is almost always accompanied by a charioteer, even when he is swallowed by the ground. The charioteer was well known: on vases he is named as Baton, although in an alternative tradition he was called Schoenichus.[26] The two odes have thus taken a well-attested myth and stripped out the charioteer.

A similar transformation of tradition occurs in *Pythian* 6, an ode for a chariot victory of Xenocrates in the Pythian games of 490.[27] The myth in this ode describes how Nestor was nearly killed by Memnon when one of the horses leading his chariot brought the chariot to a halt after being struck by an arrow shot by Paris (Νεστόρειον γὰρ ἵππος ἄρμ' ἐπέδα / Πάριος ἐκ βελέων δαϊχθείς, 32–3). His son Antilochus came to his defense, however, and bought his father's life at the cost of his own. This story was told in the lost *Aethiopis*, but a very similar episode is told in the *Iliad*: Nestor is again fleeing in a chariot, when his chariot is brought to a halt by the arrows of Paris after one of the horses is shot. In this case, however, it is Hector who threatens his life and Diomedes who comes to his aid, without cost to himself.[28] The Iliadic version of the story makes explicit what is hidden in the Pindaric version: that Nestor had a charioteer (which is what allowed him to fight from the chariot). Diomedes persuades Nestor to mount his own chariot by noting that his horses are slow and "his henchman weak" (ἠπεδανὸς δέ νύ τοι θεράπων, 8.104) and then leaves Nestor's chariot to this henchman and his own. Both henchmen are named: Diomedes' is called Sthenelus and Nestor's Eurymedon. The narrative in *Pythian* 6 is certainly more compressed, and we should expect details to be left out, but that does not mean that the details that are left out have no significance. As in his retelling of the saga of the Seven against Thebes, Pindar has managed to avoid mentioning the presence of a charioteer assumed by other sources.

Perhaps most striking is *Olympian* 1. Although this celebrates Hieron's victory in the Olympic horse race of 476, it puts considerable effort into promoting an ideology of chariot racing and so can be considered alongside odes for chariot victors. Hieron was, after all, probably already competing in chariot races, and his family had certainly competed in the grander event before.[29] The myth describes how, in response to his request, Poseidon lends to Pelops his chariot and horses so that he may defeat Oenomaus in the race for his daughter Hippodameia's hand. This race offers an obvious prototype for the Olympic chariot race, but in this race the owners do the driving.[30] Alternative traditions involve various charioteers, however: in one, Pelops' victory is owed to a charioteer, Cillas, who died suddenly but was honored lavishly; in another his victory is owed to the treachery of Oenomaus' charioteer Myrtilus; a third tradition names Pelops' charioteer as Sphaerus.[31] Pindar's choice of myth is certainly motivated by a number of considerations, including preserving Pelops' good character,[32] but there was at least one version that represented Pelops as noble, but also spoke of a charioteer. The absence of charioteers in *Olympian* 1 should be seen within the wider pattern of exclusion traced here. Once again Pindar depicts a world in which the nobility drive themselves and there seems to be no such thing as a specialist charioteer.[33]

Charioteers are also missing from the contemporary scenes involving chariots that the memorials draw on. Processions were certainly a feature of victory celebrations, and some of these were surely equestrian.[34] One type of wedding procession may provide a basic model here: just as the groom often brought his bride from her house to his in a mule cart driven by a muleteer, so the victor must often have been conveyed to his house in a mule cart as he brought his victory home.[35] The one procession of this type that is recorded occurred only late in the fifth century, and it was conceived on a grand scale. The victor, Exaenetus of Acragas, had won the Olympic stadion race for the second time in 412 and was accompanied as he was conducted into the city in a chariot by no less than three hundred two-horse chariots.[36] Such parades were almost certainly held earlier in the century; indeed it seems likely that this particular one was modeled on the parades of the earlier tyrants of Sicily.[37] Not all parades needed to be so lavish, however, and so it is possible that smaller parades, on the scale of wedding processions, were relatively common.

It seems most likely that in such parades, as in the wedding processions, the victor's chariot (a larger ceremonial chariot, rather than a racing chariot) was driven by a driver, not by the victor himself.[38] Yet when these parades are represented in the odes, a driver is once again nowhere to be found. At the opening of Pindar's *Nemean* 9, the victor Chromius of Syracuse is pictured mounting a chariot and ushering in the celebration:

Κωμάσομεν παρ᾽ Ἀπόλλωνος Σικυωνόθε, Μοῖσαι,
τὰν νεοκτίσταν ἐς Αἴτναν, ἔνθ᾽ ἀναπεπταμέναι
  ξείνων νενίκανται θύραι,
ὄλβιον ἐς Χρομίου
  δῶμ᾽. ἀλλ᾽ ἐπέων γλυκὺν ὕμνον πράσσετε.
τὸ κρατήσιππον γὰρ ἐς ἅρμ᾽ ἀναβαίνων
  ματέρι καὶ διδύμοις παίδεσσιν αὐδὰν μανύει
Πυθῶνος αἰπεινᾶς ὁμοκλάροις ἐπόπταις.

We will revel from Apollo at Sicyon, Muses, to the newly founded city of Etna, where the open gates are overwhelmed by guests, to the fortunate house of Chromius. But make a sweet song of words. For he, mounting the chariot, victorious with its horses, signals a song for the mother and her twin children who keep joint watch over steep Pytho.

(*Ne.* 9.1–5)

The image here is certainly one of a victory parade, rather than of a race. Like Exaenetus, the victor is pictured returning from the games and about to enter the city (here Etna, to which Chromius presumably moved after its foundation by Hieron), and his mounting of the chariot is a signal for the celebration to start. Yet the victory parade has been altered in a significant respect: there seems to be no muleteer or charioteer in the car. The ode thus creates the presumption that Chromius will do the driving.

The parade has been altered in a second way also. Pindar suggests that the chariot that Chromius mounts was the actual racing chariot, the one that "won with the horses" (κρατήσιππον). This was certainly not so,[39] but the suggestion serves to lay the image of the parade over the image of the race. We are led to think not only that Chromius normally drives his own chariots, but also that he drove the chariot in his recent victory.[40]

A similar representation of a victory parade may be offered by *Olympian* 4, an ode for another Sicilian, Psaumis of Camarina, but some difficult, and possibly corrupt, lines make a conclusive interpretation of the passage impossible. These lines may have pictured Psaumis riding in a car back from Olympia to Camarina, crowned with the victor's olive wreath (*Ol.* 4.6–12):

ἀλλὰ Κρόνου παῖ, ὃς Αἴτναν ἔχεις
ἶπον ἀνεμόεσσαν ἑκατογκεφάλα
   Τυφῶνος ὀβρίμου,
Οὐλυμπιονίκαν
δέξαι Χαρίτων θ᾽ ἕκατι τόνδε κῶμον,
χρονιώτατον φάος εὐρυσθενέων ἀρετᾶν.
   Ψαύμιος γὰρ ἵκει
ὀχέων, ὃς ἐλαίᾳ στεφανωθεὶς Πισάτιδι κῦδος ὄρσαι
σπεύδει Καμαρίνᾳ.

The difficulty comes with Ψαύμιος γάρ ἵκει / ὀχέων. The best understanding of these lines takes the subject as the victory procession from the previous line and understands both nouns as genitives, with ὀχέων indicating the object of the celebration[41]:

But son of Cronus, you who hold windy Etna, the trap of mighty hundred-headed Typhon, for the Graces' sake, receive an Olympic victor and this procession, a light for strong virtues to last through the ages. For here comes the procession of the car of Psaumis, who, garlanded with the olive of Pisa, hurries to stir up glory for Camarina.

As *Nemean* 9 shows, even though Psaumis is not actually placed in the parade, the most obvious understanding of this passage is that Psaumis is riding in the car as the procession enters the city or makes its way to his house. The passage may have been clearer on this point. This reading of the passage is so awkward that it is hard to accept: the two consecutive genitives are clumsy, and ὀχέων is properly plural. It is surely preferable to take ὀχέων as a participle and Ψαύμιος as a corrupted nominative form; Psaumis' name was unfamiliar, as the variant nominative forms that are attested in the scholia and Oxyrhynchus victory lists attest.[42] The lines would then read "For Psaumis comes on his chariot" and would explicitly set the victor in the car in his victory procession. It is certainly feasible that Psaumis held such a victory procession himself. At any rate, if a victory parade is depicted here, the victor is pictured in a chariot without a driver.

Victory parades were also represented by dedications at Olympia. In the first half of the fifth century, the Cyrenean Cratisthenes dedicated a bronze chariot group in which was placed a statue of himself. That this should be thought of as a representation of a parade is suggested by the size of the chariot: Cratisthenes was joined in the car by a charioteer, the goddess Nike.[43] Unlike the odes considered earlier, therefore, the monument indicated that there was a role for a charioteer to play, but, like them, it still denied any recognition to the actual charioteer who drove in the parade: whereas the rest of the parade chariot is depicted realistically, the charioteer is replaced by a metaphor. This metaphor became more common in fourth-century monuments for chariot victories, where Nike replaces the driver of the racing chariot itself, but it seems to have been rare before that.[44] There is an example of the image in an ode of Simonides, but it cannot be determined whether the victor being celebrated by the ode won a chariot race.[45] More promising but from the late fifth century is a red-figure column-krater, which may use the image to celebrate a Pythian chariot victory: on the obverse, Apollo appears with Nike who is driving a chariot.[46] The vase is not a special commission, however, and the reverse offers a scene with little relevance to chariot racing – a youth leaving home.

In the examples offered here, the absence of the charioteer is pointed: he is missing from the races in which he drove, missing from the victory parades held to celebrate these races, and missing from myths in which, in other versions, he plays an important role. Elsewhere drivers are not nearly so anonymous: they appear on the prize Panathenaics commissioned by the city of Athens, on vases that depict wedding processions, and in narratives of wars or races. It is clear that their absence from most victory memorials is the result of a conscious exclusion, not a casual forgetting.

The driver's absence is not always so pointed, however. The remainder of this chapter examines the other strategies through which victory is represented that avoid reference to the charioteer. In these examples, the charioteer is not the only component of the race missing – sometimes the horses are also missing, sometimes the chariot, and sometimes the event itself fades almost completely out of view – but, given the silences traced earlier, it is safe to conclude that the primary locus of anxiety shaping these representations is the charioteer.

Several dedications at Olympia seem only to have included a bronze statue of the racing chariot, but not the horses or charioteer. Gelon dedicated bronze statues of himself and his chariot to commemorate his victory in 488,[47] whereas Polypeithes of Sparta, victor in perhaps 484, dedicated an undersized chariot. On the same base stood a statue of his father, Calliteles, who was an Olympic wrestling victor.[48] The combination of the car with the wrestler was perhaps intended to elide the differences between equestrian and gymnastic competition and open the possibility that Polypeithes drove the chariot.[49]

More eloquent was the monument of the elder Cimon who won the chariot race at three Olympics, perhaps 536 to 528 but allowed Pisistratus to be announced victor at the second in return for his recall from exile.[50] Herodotus tells us that the three victories were all won by the same team of mares and that these mares were buried opposite Cimon on the Sunk Road outside of Athens after his murder by the sons of Pisistratus soon after the third victory.[51] Aelian adds the information that exact likenesses made in bronze of the horses were set up in Athens.[52] If Aelian's description is taken literally, these statues cannot have been set up at the burial site, but it is probably better to understand the location more generally, connect the statues with the ostentatious burial of the horses, and understand them as funeral monuments. Aelian offers the information to reproach the Athenians for setting up such undignified statues; by memorializing horses, they compare with those Greeks who set up a gold statue of the courtesan Phryne on a tall pillar in Delphi. But the statue is, in fact, a way of protecting aristocratic dignity. By focusing on the horses, through the burial and the statues, Cimon's family represents them as the primary element of the racing team. One wonders if the same charioteer drove in all three victories; the information is certainly not preserved.[53]

A much larger group of memorials pushes the event itself into the background so that the particular mechanics of the victory, and, more specifically, the role the charioteer played in winning it, do not receive attention. Victory is seen from the point of view of a family's status, not from that of the race itself, and it becomes a possession owned by a family, rather than a crown won through a demanding competition. In fact, the event in which the victory was won is often so unimportant to the design of the memorial that one might easily pass over or forget it.

One such memorial is Pindar's *Pythian* 7, which celebrates the Megacles who won a Pythian victory in 486 and may have commissioned the vase celebrating Alcmaeon's Olympic victory of 592.[54] The ode is the shortest of Pindar's odes for equestrian victors, and its center is taken up with a catalogue of Alcmaeonid victories, including

Megacles' recent Pythian win:

> ἄγοντι δέ με πέντε μὲν Ἰσθμοῖ νῖκαι, μία δ' ἐκπρεπὴς
> Διὸς Ὀλυμπιάς,
> δύο δ' ἀπὸ Κίρρας,
> ὦ Μεγάκλεες,
> ὑμαί τε καὶ προγόνων.

Five victories at the Isthmus lead me on, and one shining one at Zeus' Olympia, and two from Cirrha, the victories of you and your ancestors, Megacles.

(*Py.* 7.13–17)

The event in which these victories were won is not identified, and it is only Pindar's brief statement at the beginning of the ode that he is "laying a foundation of songs for chariot races" (κρηπῖδ' ἀοιδᾶν/ ἵπποισι βαλέσθαι, 3/4) that indicates that all these Alcmaeonid victories were won in the most prestigious event.[55] The lack of reference to the event in the catalog focuses attention on the simple fact that the family has won a number of victories; how the family won, and even what specific events the family won, are made to be of secondary importance.

Comparable to *Pythian* 7 is a sixth-century dedication found in Tegea. An inscribed marble pillar supported a dedication, but only part of the pillar, and part of the inscription, survive.[56] The victor's identity is lost, but enough of the second line survives to reveal that the victor won six victories and that he won them in chariot races, although the location of the victories is unclear.[57] The inscription thus gave all the relevant information about the victories, how many there were, and where and how they had been won, but the dedication itself had a different focus. Evidence suggests that small horses, in bronze or marble, were dedicated to gods, but not small chariot groups; a bowl or statue of a god probably sat on top of this column.[58] The race itself was thus not represented by the dedication, and its effect was to deflect attention away from the awkward mechanics of the victory to the good fortune of the dedicant.[59]

A couple of dedications at Olympia from perhaps the third quarter of the fifth century suggest the variety of options open to memorials that sought to deflect attention from the race itself. The monument commemorating the Spartan Anaxander's chariot victory represented only the victor praying to Zeus,[60] whereas that of another Spartan, Polycles, represented him standing with two children. Polycles held a fillet in his right hand, while one child held a hoop and the other asked for the fillet.[61] The event that both won was presumably identified by inscriptions on the bases of the statues, but, like the Tegean dedication, the overall effect of these statues was to focus attention on the person of the victor, and his good fortune in winning and being able to make the dedication. Of the Olympic race little is left: not only the charioteer but also the horses and the chariot have gone.

In his treatise on horsemanship, Xenophon makes it clear that to make a realistic attempt at winning a major equestrian contest an owner would have required not only a charioteer, but also grooms, horse breakers, and trainers.[62] A whole crew was thus involved in winning these victories, but for the most part all go unnoticed when the victory is commemorated. Yet all silences are not equal. As I have demonstrated in this chapter, the silence that surrounds the charioteer is of a different quality to those that surround the grooms and horse breakers. The memorials did not simply pass over the charioteers. Victory was mostly represented in ways that avoided reference to the charioteer; and, more tellingly, although their contribution was recognized by other representations of chariot driving, in victory memorials charioteers were missing from the events and narratives in which they played a part.

Why was the charioteer such a problematic figure? The obvious answer is simply that the charioteer did work that many thought the owner should have done, and several considerations do indeed suggest that this is what caused the anxiety: first, when a victor did drive his own chariot, this fact is clearly noted in the victory memorial;[63] second, there were some equestrian events that required the owners to compete themselves, the *apobates* and the various events for "warriors" at the Panathenaea;[64] and, lastly, in the early fourth century, Agesilaus attempted to criticize chariot racing on the grounds that it demonstrated only wealth by encouraging his sister Cynisca to enter.[65]

Yet these last two examples also suggest that, although praise was certainly due to an owner who drove his own chariot, the bare fact that someone else usually did the driving was not especially important. As the prize list demonstrates, the *apobates* and warrior events at the Panathenaea never attained the prestige of the open competitions in which competitors did not have to perform themselves,[66] and that Cynisca, a woman, was allowed to enter the chariot race indicates that the driving was mostly not seen as the proper preserve of the victor.[67] Moreover, although some of the memorials examined in this chapter set the victor in the place of the charioteer, many do not. Some are content to take the driving out of the victory altogether, and others replace the charioteer with Nike or give the credit instead to the horses. This suggests that the central problem is not that the victor does not do the driving, but that the charioteer does; that is, what is crucial is that the charioteer be removed from the picture, not that the victor be credited with the equestrian skills necessary to win the victory. In the following chapter, I argue that this is indeed the case. By examining two memorials in which the charioteer is praised rather than excluded, I argue that the problem did indeed lie with the charioteer and, more specifically, with charioteers who had no prior relationship with the owners for whom they drove.

2

CARRHOTUS AND CNOPIADAS

τῶ σε μὴ λαθέτω,
Κυράνᾳ γλυκὺν ἀμφὶ κᾶ-
πον Ἀφροδίτας ἀειδόμενον,
παντὶ μὲν θεὸν αἴτιον ὑπερτιθέμεν,
φιλεῖν δὲ Κάρρωτον ἔξοχ᾽ἑταίρων·
ὃς οὐ τὰν Ἐπιμαθέος ἄγων
ὀψινόου θυγατέρα Πρόφασιν Βαττιδᾶν
ἀφίκετο δόμους θεμισκρεόντων·
ἀλλ᾽ἀρισθάρματον
ὕδατι Κασταλίας ξενω-
θεὶς γέρας ἀμφέβαλε τεαῖσιν κόμαις
ἀκηράτοις ἁνίαις
ποδαρκέων δώδεκ᾽ἂν δρόμων τέμενος.
κατέκλασε γὰρ ἐντέων σθένος οὐδέν· ἀλλὰ κρέμαται
ὁπόσα χεριαρᾶν
τεκτόνων δαίδαλ᾽ἄγων
Κρισαῖον λόφον
ἄμειψεν ἐν κοιλόπεδον νάπος
θεοῦ· τό σφ᾽ἔχει κυπαρίσσινον
μέλαθρον ἀμφ᾽ἀνδριάντι σχεδόν,
Κρῆτες ὃν τοξοφόροι τέγεϊ Παρνασσίῳ
καθέσσαντο, τὸ μονόδροπον φυτόν.
ἑκόντι τοίνυν πρέπει
νόῳ τὸν εὐεργέταν ὑπαντιάσαι.
Ἀλεξιβιάδα, σὲ δ᾽ἠύκομοι φλέγοντι Χάριτες.
μακάριος, ὃς ἔχεις
καὶ πεδὰ μέγαν κάματον
λόγων φερτάτων
μναμήϊ᾽· ἐν τεσσαράκοντα γάρ

πετόντεσσιν ἀνιόχοις ὅλον
δίφρον κομίξαις ἀταρβεῖ φρενί,
ἦλθες ἤδη Λιβύας πεδίον ἐξ ἀγλαῶν
ἀέθλων καὶ πατρωίαν πόλιν.

Wherefore, [Arcesilas], let you not forget, as you are hymned in the sweet garden of Aphrodite in Cyrene, to set up as cause of everything a god, and to love Carrhotus beyond your other companions. He came to the palace of the Battiads who rule by right not bringing Excuse, the daughter of late-thinking Epimetheus, but, entertained by the water of Castalia, he crowned your hair with the prize for the best chariot, with reins unsullied in the precinct of the twelve swift-run courses. For he broke no part of his strong equipment, but it hangs there, all the close-wrought work of skilled craftsmen which he brought when he went past the Crisaean hill to the hollow field of the god. The hall of cypress wood holds it close beside the image which Cretan bowmen set up in the Parnassian chamber, the plant plucked from a single trunk. Truly it is right with willing mind to meet one's benefactor. Alexibiades, the fair-tressed Graces make you gleam. Blessed one, who also have after great toil a memorial of highest words. For among forty charioteers who fell, with fearless mind you brought your car through in one piece, and now you have come from the glorious games to the plain of Libya and your ancestral city.

(*Py.* 5.23–53)

Given the usual representation of the charioteer in archaic victory memorials, Pindar's *Pythian* 5 is an anomaly. The ode celebrates the victory of Arcesilas IV, king of Cyrene, in the chariot race at the Pythian games of 462, but almost a quarter of the ode is devoted to the person who guided Arcesilas' team to victory, Carrhotus. He is named by both his own name (27) and his patronymic, Alexibiades (45), and his achievement is described in detail. He is praised for bringing his chariot home undamaged (34), while every other charioteer, among the forty-one competitors, crashed (49–51); this emphasizes not only his skill, but also his bravery (ἀταρβεῖ φρενί, 51) in a genuinely dangerous competition. Further, Pindar's observation that his reins were "unsullied" (ἀκηράτοις, 32) may be intended to suggest that the reins were not dirtied by dust kicked up by teams in front of him, that is, that Carrhotus led from start to finish.[1]

Through this lengthy treatment, the charioteer also becomes, as Mark Golden notes, "a kind of surrogate" of the victor.[2] Arcesilas

(5–9, 20–2) and Carrhotus (45–53) are the only two mortals to be addressed in the vocative case, and both are pronounced "blessed" (μάκαρ, 20, and μακάριος, 46). Like Arcesilas, Carrhotus is identified with Battus, the founder and first king of Cyrene: both received great rewards for great toils (46–9), and both made the journey from Delphi to Cyrene (52–3).[3] Lastly, the image of Carrhotus not bringing home Excuse (27–9) fits the charioteer into a role more commonly associated in epinician with the victor, that of a bridegroom. As noted in Chapter 1, Greek weddings often involved a procession in which the groom brought the bride in a cart from her house to his own, and it is this procession that is alluded to here: the charioteer is pictured bringing to the Battiads' palace not Excuse, the daughter of Epimetheus, but, presumably, Victory or Glory.[4] It is, however, the victor who is usually represented by Pindar as the bridegroom.[5]

The extraordinary attention accorded the charioteer in *Pythian* 5 requires an explanation. Such an explanation cannot appeal to Pindar's idiosyncrasies because, in paying such attention to the charioteer, Pindar's ode seems to mirror a dedication made at Delphi in memory of the victory. According to *Pythian* 5, the undamaged chariot was itself dedicated in Apollo's temple at Delphi, "close beside" the actual statue of Apollo (ἀμφ' ἀνδριάντι σχεδόν, 40), which the Cretans set up when they founded the sanctuary.[6] Although Pindar presumably exaggerates when he says that the chariot was hung near Apollo's statue,[7] the dedication must still have been a striking one: to judge from Pausanias' descriptions of dedications at Olympia, it was most unusual, first, for a victory dedication to be made anywhere in the temple at all and, second, for the actual chariot used in the race to be dedicated.[8] The effect of such a dedication must have been, as Pindar suggests in *Pythian* 5, to highlight the action of the race itself, and the victorious charioteer's skill in bringing the chariot, and all its rigging, to the finishing line unscathed. The emphasis on Carrhotus was thus not peculiar to Pindar's ode.

The only explanation offered in recent criticism for the emphasis on the charioteer is that of Mary Lefkowitz, who argues that the manner of the victory was so impressive that some mention of the driver had to be made.[9] This idea is, however, insufficiently tied into the discourse governing the representation of charioteers in archaic victory memorials. As established in the previous chapter, in the late archaic period, victory memorials were organized around the exclusion of charioteers; their absence was not a simple case of forgetfulness, but a purposeful and consistent erasure.[10] Given this, it is unclear why a particularly impressive performance would be given the credit Carrhotus' driving receives here; indeed, a charioteer who was seen as particularly crucial would seem to be even more problematic for the victory memorial and thus even more likely to be passed over in silence. There is certainly no other indication that impressive performances by charioteers were recorded; the other memorials that name a driver do not describe the manner of the victory as especially outstanding.[11]

One might also question whether what Carrhotus did was all that extraordinary, compared with other victorious charioteers. It cannot have been that odd for the winner to be the only chariot left in the race: although several chariots were probably expected to finish (at the Panathenaea in the first part of the fourth century, prizes were awarded for coming second),[12] crashes were frequent, and the large numbers of competitors must have made multiple wrecks common.[13] Sophocles describes a fictional Pythian race in which all but one of the chariots did not finish,[14] and it may be that the Delphic course was especially dangerous. Given the frequency of accidents, the winners must often have hung back, as Orestes in Sophocles' race, or led from the start, as Carrhotus may have done.[15]

It seems, therefore, unlikely that the manner of the victory explains the extraordinary emphasis on the charioteer. The explanation should be sought instead not in how the charioteer won the race, but in who the charioteer was and, more specifically, how he was related to the victor. I argue that a distinction should be made between two groups of charioteers, those who had an enduring connection with the owner, either as members of his household or as his friends, and those who had no enduring connection, and that it was only the latter type of charioteer who posed problems for the aristocratic hippotrophs. The majority of charioteers in the late archaic period were, however, professional and so were seen to have no enduring connection with their patrons, being neither members of their estates nor their aristocratic friends, but the revelation that hired charioteers were crucial to victory made equestrian competition very awkward for aristocrats. It undermined the idea that victory was dependent on qualities that were the aristocrats' exclusive possessions and, moreover, validated a mode of exchange that threatened the aristocrats' control of society.

Carrhotus, however, did have an enduring connection with the man for whom he drove; he was his friend and brother-in-law, and so his success affirmed the aristocratic model of society. Unlike most victors who relied on outsiders for their victories, Arcesilas relied only on the favor of a friend but had nevertheless proved that such connections were quite sufficient to win the toughest competitions. Far from constituting a threat, therefore, the lengthy praise of Carrhotus both redounded to Arcesilas' glory and constituted an implicit critique of those aristocratic clans that were unable to win without compromising their aristocratic principles.

That Carrhotus was a close relation of Arcesilas is stated by the scholia, one saying that he was the father of Arcesilas' wife, another that he was her brother.[16] The latter claim is the more persuasive of the two because the source from which it is taken, the first book of the historian Theotimus' work on Cyrene, is quoted:

> Realizing that the affair was going wrong, and wishing to settle the Hesperidae himself, Arcesilas sent Euphemus to the games with horses to be entered into the competitions, and, when he had won the Pythian contest, he crowned his fatherland and gathered settlers for the Hesperidae. Euphemus died, but Carrhotus, the brother of Arcesilas' wife, took over leadership of the settlers.[17]

In recording this small piece of Theotimus, the scholia have preserved some interesting information: as well as stating that Carrhotus was Arcesilas' brother-in-law, Theotimus reveals that the team had a manager, Euphemus, as well as a charioteer[18] and claims that Arcesilas' prime motive in competing at Delphi was to strengthen his rule at home.[19] Mary Lefkowitz doubts this evidence, however; the scholia certainly have a habit of inventing historical details to explain things they cannot understand, and, as she points out, much of the rest of this scholion is incoherent.[20] It was Didymus who quoted Theotimus, and either his argument was already incoherent, or it was rendered so by the critic or critics who summarized it.[21] Two ideas seem to have been confused: that Carrhotus took over the job of raising the settlers from Euphemus after his death and that, although, Euphemus was responsible for the chariot victory, the ode gives Carrhotus the credit. Didymus introduced the quotation from Theotimus to support the contention that Carrhotus was gathering an army for Arcesilas,[22] but either Didymus or a scholiast used it to conclude that Pindar wrongly attributed Euphemus' work in raising the army to Carrhotus.[23] Pindar does not, however, mention anything about Carrhotus raising an army, although he does make him key to the Pythian victory, without ever mentioning Euphemus.[24]

The scholiast's commentary on this part of *Pythian* 5 is thus considerably jumbled, but this provides no reason to reject the evidence that Theotimus offers. The account offered by the quotation is plausible, given the political troubles that confronted Arcesilas early in his reign; it is also internally coherent and consistent with Pindar's account.[25] That Carrhotus is not specifically said to be Arcesilas' kinsman in the ode is no impediment; this would have been well known to the audience.[26] Theotimus' evidence should be trusted.

Carrhotus was, then, an important political and military leader for Arcesilas, as well as a good charioteer, but what was most important for his representation in Pindar's *Pythian* 5, and in the dedication in Apollo's temple, was the fact that he had a permanent connection with the victor. Why this was so becomes clear if we hypothesize that the problems of chariot racing were created by the commodification of chariot driving, not by the simple fact that someone else could, and often did, drive the victor's chariot.

Commodity exchange in archaic Greece was not just an alternative way for the same people to exchange the same objects or services. Rather, it was a type of exchange that was fundamentally suited to, and so also indicative of, parties to an exchange that had no connection with each other. Central to commodity exchange was the minimization of personal costs: no trust was required of the parties to the exchange, because the objects were exchanged immediately and were of equivalent value to the parties. There was thus no need for future contact between the parties. Between parties who did have an enduring connection, the appropriate form of exchange was gift exchange. What was important here was less the relationship between objects themselves than the relationship between the parties to the exchange. Precisely because there was an expectation that the parties would continue to be connected, the exchanges could be more fluid: objects did not have to be exactly equivalent in value or exchanged at the same time. Indeed, in gift exchange, the very fact of an exchange becomes hidden by the passage of time between a service and its reciprocation and the frequent lack of equivalence between any two given services. The exchanges certainly balanced out over time, but the focus in the exchange was on the continuing relationship between the parties.[27]

That his charioteer was not bound to him in a continuing relationship presented a significant problem to an aristocrat competing in the games in the late archaic period. Athletics offered the aristocrats an arena in which they could attempt to demonstrate that they possessed certain superior qualities by virtue of their birth (qualities that made them better rulers as well as better athletes).[28] A given victory could demonstrate not only that the victor possessed these qualities, but also, because in most cases it continued a tradition of family victories, that these qualities were inherited and not freely available. In equestrian competition these qualities included not skill but the favor of the gods, determination, character, and the intelligence needed to spend wealth wisely, but the idea that these really determined the course of the competition was fatally threatened by the use of unrelated charioteers. Bringing in a charioteer from outside the victor's circle threw the spotlight on an outsider, making him central to the victory and deflecting attention away from any particular virtues the victor might have possessed. It suggested that the victor's supposedly inherited qualities – divine favor, intelligence, and character – were less important than some driver who might work for anyone. The commodification of the charioteer thus threatened one of the fundamental reasons for an aristocrat to compete in athletics; indeed, it actually altered the perception of what was key to equestrian victory.

Moreover, hiring a charioteer validated a mode of exchange that threatened both the power and identity of the aristocrats. The aristocrats defined their community, their estate, their clan, and the wider international community of aristocrats by gift exchange;[29] by contrast, the desire to trade was seen not as a desire for a convenient and undemanding exchange, but as an effort to swindle and deceive.[30] This suspicion was, in fact, well founded: the spread of commodity exchange did threaten the aristocrats' position because it enabled individuals to bypass the traditional networks of reciprocity and redistribution that the aristocrats largely controlled, and so weakened their control of society and of the movement of goods and services within it.[31]

As is often the case with ancient history, there is no explicit evidence for this reconstruction. There are, however, pieces of circumstantial evidence, and one of these is that the reconstruction explains why Carrhotus, the charioteer in Arcesilas' Pythian victory, is celebrated at such length in Pindar's *Pythian* 5 (as well as in the dedication of the racing chariot in Apollo's temple) and not hidden away like the charioteers in the majority of memorials from the same period. As Arcesilas' brother-in-law, Carrhotus is part of his inner circle, not an outsider who might drive for anybody who paid his wage. The lengthy praise may still raise the profile of the charioteer's work, but not at the expense of the praise of aristocratic excellence, because the qualities being praised belong to a kinsman of the victor. Moreover, aristocratic modes of exchange are revealed as central to the victory: the chariot driving appears as just one more gift in a long series of exchanges between the owner and the charioteer (a series that included the gift of Carrhotus' sister to the king) and is revealed as an expression of an enduring relationship, not the sole moment of contact between the two. Carrhotus is marked both as an aristocrat and as a close friend of Arcesilas.

It is certainly in these terms that *Pythian* 5 represents Carrhotus and his work: he appears as a friend of Arcesilas, bound to him by aristocratic networks of gift giving. Pindar refers to Carrhotus first as one of the king's companions (ἑταίρων, 26) and then as his benefactor (εὐεργέταν, 44), binding his hair with the "prize of the best chariot" (ἀρισθάρματον . . . / . . . γέρας ἀμφέβαλε τεαῖσιν κόμαις, 30–1). In return for this gift, the king owes him love (φιλεῖν, 26) and remembrance (λόγων φερτάτων / μναμήι', 48–9).[32] The idea that he is Arcesilas' benefactor is particularly significant because it turns the usual relationship between charioteer and owner on its head: rather than earning a wage from the owner, Carrhotus gives him a gift, for which the owner now owes him. Carrhotus is thus distinguished from professional charioteers: he is part of the victor's circle, and his relationship with the victor is organized not around a brief commodity exchange, but around an enduring friendship and the giving of gifts.

The exchange of gifts between Carrhotus and Arcesilas is, in fact, just part of a network of gift giving that binds Carrhotus not only to the king, but also to Pythian Apollo and to the Cyrenean leaders of the past. Although Carrhotus' success at Delphi is later described as an expenditure of effort (47), it is initially described by two metaphors; first, his marriage to a bride, whom he now leads home to the Battiads' house from Delphi (27–9), and second his "entertainment by the water of Castalia," presumably by Apollo or his servants (ὕδατι Κασταλίας ξενωθεὶς, 31).[33] Both images thus represent the victory as a gift from Apollo himself, which Carrhotus in turn gives to Arcesilas. The chariot that Carrhotus dedicated at Delphi perhaps represents a gift from the Battiads to Apollo; as Kurke notes, the description of the chariot as χεριαρᾶν/τεκτόνων δαίδαλ', "the close-wrought work of skilled craftsmen," represents the chariot as a precious object.[34] At any rate, the passing of gifts between Carrhotus, Arcesilas, and Apollo binds the two Cyreneans to the founder of the colony, Battus, whose success was the gift of Apollo (ἔδωκ', 60) and who repaid the god by instituting processions and sacrifices (90–3) in which he was still honored at the time of the ode's performance (77–81). The specific relationship of Arcesilas and Carrhotus is perhaps also foreshadowed by that of Battus' men and the sons of Antenor, "a horse-driving people" (ἐλάσιππον ἔθνος, 85): the sons of Antenor are described as ξένοι (82), "friends" or perhaps "guests," whom Battus' men welcomed "coming forward with sacrifices and bearing gifts" (θυσίαισιν ἄνδρες οἰχνέοντές σφε δωροφόροι, 86).[35]

The charioteer is thus firmly incorporated into the world of the aristocracy by the metaphorical weave of *Pythian* 5: he is bound by the exchange of gifts into a community that embraces not only the aristocratic figures of contemporary Cyrene, but also Apollo, and the aristocrats present at the very foundation of the city. In being dominated by the discourse of gift exchange, *Pythian* 5 is little different to Pindar's other odes; what is different is that this discourse extends to the charioteer, a figure whom most other memorials leave unmentioned, and the reason for this is simply that the discourse could be extended to include the charioteer. Carrhotus was an aristocrat and friend of the victor, not a hired hand.

We may also note here that Carrhotus serves as something of a model for the poet in his dealings with the victor. On one hand, the poet presents himself as enjoying Apollo's feast and honoring Cyrene through, presumably, the ode (Ἄπολλον, τεᾷ,/Καρνήϊ', ἐν δαιτὶ σεβίζομεν/Κυράνας ἀγακτιμέναν πόλιν, "in your feast, Apollo Carneius, we honor the well-founded city of Cyrene," 79–81), just as Carrhotus had been entertained at Castalia and then brought Arcesilas the gift of victory. On the other hand, Pindar claims mutual ancestors with the Cyrenean aristocracy, the Aegidae, who brought the Carneia from Sparta to Cyrene,[36] so that, like Carrhotus, he is bound to the king and his city not just by a network of gift exchange, but also by kinship. In Pindar's case, however, the production of the ode is not, in fact, part of series of exchanges in an enduring relationship, but an isolated exchange of words for payment, so that the parallel with Carrhotus serves to hide his real relation with the king. Like most charioteers, he is a wage earner, but he makes use of this unusual charioteer to suggest that he is an unusual poet, that he too enjoys a long-standing relationship with the king.[37]

The hypothesis that the commodification of chariot driving was the central problem for the representation and conception of chariot victories in the late archaic period has considerable explanatory power. It explains both why most memorials consigned the charioteer to silence and why Pindar's *Pythian* 5 (and the dedication that commemorated the same victory in Delphi) celebrated the charioteer involved in Arcesilas' victory so loudly. The treatment of the charioteer, although anomalous, should not, in fact, be unexpected: far from presenting the victor with a potential hindrance to his own glory, the charioteer serves the ideological ends of the victory memorial. Arcesilas is shown to be free from the taint of commodity exchange, and gift exchange, the aristocratic mode of organizing people and resources, is shown to be quite able to win the greatest victories.[38]

Arcesilas' equestrian endeavors, and their consequent celebration, were clearly intended to publicize the king's membership in the Greek aristocracy. Because of its expense, chariot racing was a particular mark of that aristocracy,[39] but the way that Arcesilas celebrates his victory made his aristocratic credentials even clearer. The location of the actual chariot in Apollo's temple indicates a special relationship between Arcesilas and the god, and *Pythian* 5 fills this in: Apollo guided Arcesilas' ancestor Battus in his foundation of Cyrene. The description of the foundation also serves to root Arcesilas' heritage on the mainland, in the Dorian tribes, specifically in the Aegidae, a family that Pindar claims transferred the cult of Apollo Carneius to Cyrene.[40] A second dedication at Delphi, which should probably also be ascribed to Arcesilas, also focused on Cyrene's links to the Greek world: in the sanctuary of Apollo at Delphi, close to the end of the Sacred Way near the east end of the temple, stood a chariot carrying three figures, Battus, Cyrene, and Libya; Cyrene drives the chariot, while Libya crowns Battus.[41]

Arcesilas' racing should, however, be understood not merely as a claim to membership of the aristocracy, but as a claim to superiority over other aristocratic competitors. The loud trumpeting of the charioteer should be read against the background of contemporary equestrian practice, according to which it was normal for competitors at the great games to hire charioteers. Carrhotus' presence serves as a critique of those other competitors, a boast that Arcesilas does not use hired charioteers and has no need to; his aristocratic friends can match up to the best. The critique may be directed toward a local aristocrat, Cratisthenes, who may have won the Olympic chariot race only two years earlier,[42] but it may also be directed toward the great chariot-racing lords of Sicily from the previous fifteen years, Hieron and Theron; as they did, Arcesilas has won a great victory, but he has done so without resorting to commodity exchange. One wonders if Carrhotus was still driving two years later when Arcesilas won the Olympic chariot race; the victory was certainly not accompanied by the same publicity.[43]

I have made commodification the central problem in the representation of the charioteer and argued that it was the relations of exchange between owner and charioteer that separated out those charioteers that were acceptable to the aristocracy from those that were not. It might be objected, however, that, although it was acceptable for certain other people to drive an owner's chariot, the boundary between who was or was not acceptable was made according to a different criterion. An obvious suggestion is that those within the owner's household were acceptable, and those outside were not. Victory was represented in memorials as a possession of the house, rather than of the individual victor: previous victories by family members are remembered in victory memorials,[44] a single victory memorial may be used to celebrate more than one family victory,[45] and there are even two examples in which a single racehorse victory was won by two members of the same family.[46] As Leslie Kurke argues, the house was "in some sense the unit of integrity" for the aristocracy and the individuals who constituted it "only its appendages or members."[47] If the house provided the boundary, a smaller pool of drivers would be acceptable, but nevertheless immediate family, slaves, serfs, tenants, and other members of the owner's estate would be allowed.[48]

This conclusion would be a mistake, however. There is no particular reason to expect the same boundaries to govern the ownership of a victory as its winning, and, as we have seen in *Pythian* 5, what Pindar stresses is not that Carrhotus is a member of Arcesilas' household, but that he is bound to him by ties of friendship and gift giving. Indeed, Carrhotus, as the brother of the king's wife, probably did not belong to the king's household, but to another household joined to the king's by marriage.[49] Moreover, a second memorial that is similar in many ways to *Pythian* 5 makes it clear that it was gift exchange that was crucial: as in *Pythian* 5, the charioteer is given a position of prominence, but it is clear that this charioteer is not from the victor's household; what makes him an acceptable charioteer is simply that he enjoys close ties with the victor.

What remains of the memorial is an inscription found at the Ptoion, a sanctuary of Apollo in Boeotia. It dates from the middle of the sixth century and records the chariot victory in the Panathenaea of Alcmaeonides, the son of Alcmaeon.[50] This was the Alcmaeon who was victor in the Olympic chariot race of 592 and so Alcmaeonides belonged to one of the greatest chariot-racing families in Athens. The text is damaged, but most of the holes can be easily restored:

> [Φοί]βο μέν εἰμ' ἄγαλ̣[μα Λ]ατ̣[ο]ί̣δ̣α̣ καλ[ό]ν·
> [*h*ο δ' Ἀ]λ̣κμέονος *h*ῦϊς Ἀλκμεονίδες
> *h*̣ίποισι νικέ̣[σας ἔ]θεκέ μ̣'[ὀκέαις],
> *h*̣ὰς Κνοπ̣ι[ ]ς̣ ἔλαυν' *h*ο [ ]
> *h*̣ότ' ἐ͂ν Ἀθάναις Παλάδος πανέ̣[γυρις].[51]

I am a beautiful statue of Phoebus, the son of Leto. The son of Alcmaeon, Alcmaeonides, dedicated me when victorious with the swift mares which Cnopi[ ], the [ ], drove, when it was the festival of Pallas in Athens.

The inscription appeared on a column that, presumably, supported a statue of Apollo.[52] It was carved around three sides of the column's capitol, the first two lines on the front, the third and fourth on the right, and the fifth on the left; the victor and Apollo thus appear on the front, the driver and the event on the right side, and the contest on the left.

The dedication offers two surprises. First, it was not made either at the site of victory or in the victor's hometown, which is all but unparalleled;[53] second, it is one of only four memorials that certainly name a charioteer or driver. The naming is particularly surprising because in other respects the inscription follows the usual pattern for dedications: first, a reference to the dedicated object; second, the name of the dedicant; third, the event (*h*̣ίποισι νικέ̣[σας is the usual formula for describing a chariot victory without mentioning the charioteer); and, last, the place of victory. The line naming the charioteer is simply inserted between the third and fourth elements of the victory memorial. These two surprises are, in fact, closely connected, but let us begin with the charioteer.

The presence of the charioteer cannot be explained by his being a member of Alcmaeonides' household. His name, probably Cnopiadas but perhaps Cnopis,[54] has clear Boeotian connections: there was a Boeotian town called Cnopia or Cnopos, set on a river also called Cnopos somewhere between Thebes and the Ptoion, and so it seems safe to conclude that he lived close to the site of the dedication, rather than in Athens.[55]

What makes Cnopiadas an acceptable charioteer is, instead, that his connection with the victor does not involve commodity exchange. First, it seems likely from the dedication that Cnopiadas was a person of some status in the local community, an aristocrat of similar status to Alcmaeonides, not a wage laborer. As the victor, Alcmaeonides appears on the front of the capitol, but in other respects he is not elevated above the driver. Both he and Cnopiadas fill the second line of the couplets on the side of the capitol on which they appear, and both are named by two names, their own name and a second name. In Alcmaeonides' case, this name is his patronym, while in the charioteer's case, a lacuna makes it uncertain whether his patronym or the name of his town was given.[56] Second, Cnopiadas' driving appears from the dedication as part of an aristocratic network of giving, not a service done for a wage. The dedication itself is not only a gift to Apollo, but also a gift to the driver because it serves to honor him in a prestigious sanctuary near his home; it is thus with honor that Cnopiadas is repaid, not wages. The description of the dedication as an ἄγαλμα καλόν, "a beautiful statue," underlines this relationship; the word ἄγαλμα is used particularly of precious gifts passed between aristocrats.[57]

The network of gift exchange implied by the dedication includes the gods as well, as it did in *Pythian* 5. As noted earlier, Apollo is the recipient of a gift from the victor, but this is also something of a surprise: the usual recipient of such a dedication would be Athena if it was made at the site of the games, or a god with whom the victor had special connections if made in his hometown.[58] Alcmaeonides had no special connections with Apollo, but, because this dedication was made not in his hometown but close to the charioteer's, it is with him that we should look for the special connection: as a neighbor of the Ptoion, Apollo is presumably Cnopiadas' special benefactor. A triangular relation of giving is thus mapped out: Apollo favors Cnopiadas' driving, Cnopiadas wins a victory for Alcmaeonides, and Alcmaeonides makes a dedication to Apollo, Cnopiadas' patron deity. That a god is represented as a party to the exchange of gifts between aristocrats is typical of archaic notions of both exchange and aristocracy: as Louis Gernet argues, prestigious gifts were thought to possess a magical power that linked them to the world of the gods.[59]

The connection between victor and charioteer that allows the charioteer to be named is thus conceived by this monument in terms not of family or household, but of gift exchange. It can therefore be easily understood why the connection between Arcesilas and Carrhotus was expressed primarily in these terms, even though they were closely connected by marriage; for it was gift exchange that separated appropriate and inappropriate charioteers within the aristocratic ideology of equestrian athletics. An owner could use any charioteer as long as he had an enduring connection with him, but such connections were both defined and constituted by the exchange of gifts.

The close connection between Alcmaeonides and Cnopiadas is also of interest for the second surprise offered by the Ptoion dedication: its location. The location should not be explained by the simple fact that the charioteer lived close by; this was, rather, a bonus that the Alcmaeonids exploited in the service of a larger political project, a project that must be seen against the background of the shifting balance of power between Boeotian sacred sites in the sixth century.[60]

By the middle of the sixth century, the Alcmaeonids had already won considerable influence at Delphi through their benefactions there, but at this point the standing of Delphi temporarily waned, while that of the Ptoion temporarily waxed. Albert Schachter argues convincingly that Alcmaeonides' expensive dedication should be seen as part of an Alcmaeonid effort to win the same kind of influence with the priests of the Ptoion that they already enjoyed at Delphi.[61] The particular choice of vehicle for the benefaction, a thank offering for a Panathenaic chariot victory, should not be ignored, however. No special reason was needed to make a dedication at a sacred site,[62] so that this particular dedication should be seen as the result of a calculated decision that this dedication was superior to others. This is where Alcmaeonides' relationship with the charioteer is important. It is precisely because Cnopiadas, a local man from a prominent aristocratic family, was a friend, bound by gift exchange, that the dedication was especially suited to Alcmaeonid aims: by indicating that they had old ties to a family in the area, the Alcmaeonids were able to represent their patronage of the Ptoion as an effort not to create a new connection, but to widen an old one. The dedication is thus extremely complex: it represents a generous benefaction to the sanctuary but makes use of the particular circumstances of Alcmaeonides' victory to claim a preexisting connection to the area.

Before concluding, we should look at two memorials for chariot victories that make use not of the silences traced in Chapter 1, but of the rules governing what was acceptable in the representation of a hired charioteer. Both suggest that the charioteer was closely bound to the victor, the first, Pindar's *Pythian* 6, hinting that he was the victor's son, and the second, a black-figure vase, depicting him as the friend or henchman of the victor (rather than a wage laborer). Both memorials provide indirect evidence of the argument advanced in this chapter, for if charioteers closely connected to the victor were not acceptable, these representational strategies would make no sense.

Pythian 6 celebrates the victory of Xenocrates of Acragas at Delphi in 490,[63] and it hints in a number of ways that the charioteer was the victor's son, Thrasybulus. First, Thrasybulus occupies a position of prominence that is unique in extant epinician. *Pythian* 6 is one of only two odes addressed to the victor's son. The other ode, Pindar's *Isthmian* 2, also celebrates a victory of Xenocrates, but it is clear in this ode that Xenocrates has actually died since the victory,[64] which cannot be the case for *Pythian* 6. This unique prominence, combined with the usual erasure of the actual charioteer, may have been intended, if only in part, to suggest that the son was the one who drove the chariot.[65]

Second, to illustrate Thrasybulus' filial piety, the mythical portion of the ode describes Antilochus' service to his father in saving his life by sacrificing his own life to Memnon's charge. Antilochus is a perfect example of filial piety and is thus an apposite choice, but in the context of the celebration of a chariot victory, the mention of Antilochus may also recall his most memorable feat in the *Iliad*: he entered the chariot race in Patroclus' funeral games, and after listening to the advice of his father Nestor, himself too old to compete in athletics, succeeded in forcing his way past Menelaus and coming home second (a result overturned on appeal).[66] The choice of Antilochus may thus have been motivated not simply to illustrate Thrasybulus' filial piety, but also to intimate that he drove his aging father's chariot.[67]

Third, the difficult lines σύ τοι σχεθών νιν ἐπὶ δεξιὰ χειρός, ὀρθὰν/ ἄγεις ἐφημοσύναν, "You, holding her at your right hand, lead upright Precept" (*Py.* 6.19–20), present Thrasybulus, just as Carrhotus in *Pythian* 5, as a groom leading home his bride, in this case Precept rather than Victory or Glory.[68] This particular bride confirms Thrasybulus' filial piety rather than his glory or victory (the precept he shepherds is that one should honor Zeus among the gods and honor one's parents likewise), but it also represents Thrasybulus, as a bridegroom, in a chariot or mule cart: the marriage procession is presumably to be imagined as an equestrian one.[69]

Pythian 6 thus gives the impression that the victor's son drove his chariot, and a number of commentators have accepted that Thrasybulus was the charioteer.[70] But it is surely clear that this was not the case. The owner is known to have used an unrelated driver for a lesser competition, a Panathenaic victory;[71] moreover, if the son had driven the chariot, Pindar would not just have hinted at this, but would have noted it as clearly as he noted that Carrhotus drove Arcesilas' chariot in *Pythian* 5. What *Pythian* 6 suggests, therefore, is not that Xenocrates used his son to drive his chariot, but that some charioteers other than the victor were perfectly acceptable to aristocratic ideology: in place of a victory organized around a professional, *Pythian* 6 offers its aristocratic patron a victory organized around the victor's son.

The second memorial is a black-figure amphora from the mid-sixth century, found in Vulci and now in Copenhagen.[72] The vase was not a special commission, but its unique and thoughtful design suggests that the painter was confronting the problematic status of the charioteer. The back of the vase depicts a victor lifting a large tripod and flanked by four naked athletes, two on each side, which suggests that the vase was intended to commemorate a victory; at the very least, athletic victory is its subject (Figure 4).[73] An identical scene is found on the reverse of another amphora from Vulci (probably from the same workshop),[74] but their obverses, although both depicting chariots, diverge in striking ways. The second amphora shows a chariot wheeling round, a not uncommon design on prize Panathenaic vases,[75] although not as common as a simple linear movement from left to right. Copenhagen 109 depicts a much more crowded scene, however (Figure 5). A chariot moves from left to right; it is driven by a bearded

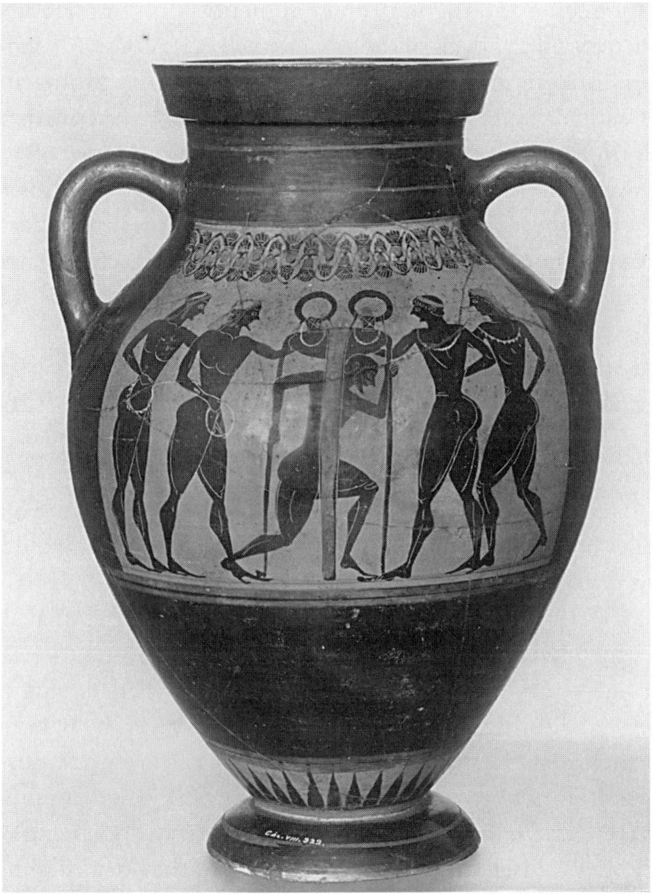

4. Victor with tripod. Black-figure amphora from Vulci, reverse, ca. 550. Courtesy of the Department of Classical and Near Eastern Antiquities, National Museum of Denmark, Copenhagen.

charioteer wearing the white tunic that is characteristic of, although not restricted to, charioteers of racing chariots,[76] but in contrast to the obverse of the second amphora, two further figures intrude on this scene. A helmeted warrior brandishing a spear joins the charioteer in his chariot, while a second warrior with a shield is being trampled by the four horses as they proceed in their course.

What seems to have happened here is that two sorts of chariot action have been superimposed on one another. The charioteer's white tunic suggests a racing scene, and the idea of a competition is reinforced by the scene of victory on the back of the vase, as well as by comparison to the second amphora. Yet imposed on this racing chariot is a Homeric-style battle in which a warrior mounted in a chariot attacks a warrior who proceeds on foot. The chariot itself belongs to both types of action, because war chariots and racing chariots were depicted in an identical manner, one more suited to a racing chariot; the warriors conveyed in the war chariots were usually wedged between the chariot and the horses, much as the warrior who brandishes the spear on this vase.[77]

Racing and war are joined on the front in the single figure of the fallen warrior. Although he primarily belongs to the war scene, the device on his shield, a tripod, alludes to the tripod on the reverse and serves to link together the two sides of the vase. The victory being claimed on the reverse would appear to be the result of the full action, the war and the racing, on the obverse.

A Homeric war chariot is thus superimposed on a racing chariot, and the transformation of the chariot in turn transforms the charioteer. It locates the charioteer in a world, the world of Homeric epic, where his service is not a commodity but a gift provided as part of some enduring relationship. In the *Iliad*, chariots are driven by friends, relatives, or henchmen;[78] what they all share is an enduring relationship with the warriors they drive. Indeed, some henchmen, such as Diomedes' driver Sthenelus or Achilles' driver Automedon, seem to be bound extremely closely to the people for whom they drive. Thus, the imposition of the war scene on the racing scene seems to represent an effort to transform the charioteer from a laborer performing a service for a wage to an old friend or relative of the aristocratic victor. The isolated exchange between owner and charioteer is replaced by the enduring relationship of a hero with his friends, family, or henchmen. In effect, this vase makes the claim for the patron who purchased it that in his equestrian exploits he did not have to hire a driver but could draw on the help either of a trusted member of his estate or of an old, and talented, friend such as Cnopiadas.

What makes it likely that Copenhagen 109 misrepresents the charioteer's relationship to the victor is that the vase is not a special

5. Four-horse chariot with charioteer and two warriors. Black-figure amphora from Vulci, obverse, ca. 550. Courtesy of the Department of Classical and Near Eastern Antiquities, National Museum of Denmark, Copenhagen.

commission. Special commissions are marked out by the presence of inscribed names on the vases; because names have to be added prior to a vase being fired, their absence strongly suggests that the vase was not made in response to a particular request. The vase must rather have been made with a more general market in mind, victors in the chariot races at athletic festivals, and because it was rare for victors not to hire their charioteers, the painter's assumption must have been that the charioteer would be working for a [79]wage.

In Chapter 1, I argue that the majority of memorials for chariot victories in the late archaic period aggressively denied the presence of the charioteer. In this chapter, I argue that what generated this denial was not that someone other than the victor was doing the driving, but that the drivers were hired. Certain drivers were perfectly acceptable to aristocratic ideology: friends (like Cnopiadas), family (like Carrhotus), and other members of the owner's household, such as slaves, serfs, or tenants (like Neleus' charioteer described in the *Iliad*);[80] all these were bound to the owner in a permanent relationship of gifts and services. What was not acceptable was that there be no such permanent relationship between owner and charioteer and that the owner and his victory be, therefore, implicated in commodity exchange. This both undermined the aristocratic owner's sense of what defined the aristocracy and challenged the success and efficiency of an economy controlled by the aristocrats' preferred mode of exchange, gift exchange.

It makes little sense to believe that the charioteer posed a problem from the inception of equestrian competition, and so a theory is needed that explains how and why the charioteer developed into a problem. Unlike a theory that focuses on the simple fact that someone other than the owner drove, a theory that focuses on the relations of exchange between charioteer and owner can explain this change. For a considerable period, perhaps more than two centuries,[81] charioteers had posed no problems because, in an age of tight aristocratic control over the movement of labor, the vast majority of charioteers were either members of the owner's estate or his friends. As this aristocratic control over labor loosened in the sixth century, the circulation of charioteers, particularly the successful ones, increased, however, and the relations between them and the owners became correspondingly attenuated.[82] It was through this process that charioteers were formulated as a problem for aristocratic ideology: ambitious owners often had no choice but to pass over their friends and slaves and hire the best that was available.

The date of this development is indicated by the memorials themselves. The earliest memorials, from the middle of the sixth century, evidence anxiety concerning the charioteer through their persistent exclusion of this figure and were presumably responding to the new challenges that hired charioteers posed. A sharp increase in the volume of memorials in the last quarter of the century suggests, however, that professional charioteers only became common at this time. This was the time when, under Simonides, epinician began to flourish, and when, according to Pausanias, a portrait statue of the victor was included for the first time in a chariot group at Olympia.[83] Both these developments should be read, in part, as efforts to reaffirm the value of a chariot victory in the face of its new and unwelcome dependence on commodity exchange.

The last quarter of the sixth century was also the time when praise poetry became a source of anxiety to the aristocracy because of its commodification.[84] Many of the factors that encouraged the commodification of this poetry also encouraged the commodification of chariot driving, but that the two products became commodified around the same time was not predictable. Commodification does not spread evenly; indeed, even within equestrian athletics, its encroachment was partial: it was only late in the fifth century that the horses used in the competitions ceased to be the product of an owner's stable and were instead bought and sold.[85] The fact that poetry and chariot driving did become commodified at the same time did, however, serve to link the two professions, and, as we shall see in the next two chapters, this was a source of some concern to Pindar.

3

NICOMACHUS

οὐκ ἄγνωτ᾽ ἀείδω
Ἰσθμίαν ἵπποισι νίκαν,
τὰν Ξενοκράτει Ποσειδάων ὀπάσαις,
Δωρίων αὐτῷ στεφάνωμα κόμᾳ
πέμπεν ἀναδεῖσθαι σελίνων,
εὐάρματον ἄνδρα γεραίρων,
Ἀκραγαντίνων φάος.
ἐν Κρίσᾳ δ᾽ εὐρυσθενὴς
εἶδ᾽ Ἀπόλλων νιν πόρε τ᾽ ἀγλαΐαν
καὶ τόθι κλειναῖς[1] Ἐρεχθειδᾶν χαρίτεσσιν ἀραρώς
ταῖς λιπαραῖς ἐν Ἀθάναις, οὐκ ἐμέμφθη
ῥυσίδιφρον χεῖρα πλαξίπποιο φωτός,
τὰν Νικόμαχος κατὰ καιρὸν
νεῖμ᾽ ἁπάσαις ἀνίαις·
ὅν τε καὶ κάρυκες ὡ-
ρᾶν ἀνέγνον, σπονδοφόροι Κρονίδα
Ζηνὸς Ἀλεῖοι, παθόντες πού τι φιλόξενον ἔργον·
ἁδυπνόῳ τέ νιν ἀσπάζοντο φωνᾷ
χρυσέας ἐν γούνασιν πίτνοντα Νίκας
γαῖαν ἀνὰ σφετέραν,
τὰν δὴ καλέοισιν Ὀλυμπίου Διός
ἄλσος· ἵν᾽ ἀθανάτοις Αἰνησιδάμου
παῖδες ἐν τιμαῖς ἔμιχθεν.

I sing of a victory not unknown, an Isthmian victory in the chariot race that Poseidon gave to Xenocrates when he sent a crown of Dorian parsley to him to bind on his hair, honoring a man victorious with his chariot, a light of the Acragantines. In Crisa, wide-mighted Apollo saw him and gave him glory, and there, fitted to the glorious graces of the sons of Erechtheus in shining Athens, he did not blame the chariot-preserving hand of the man who whipped the horses, the hand which Nicomachus wielded on all the reins in due measure. His name did the heralds of the seasons read aloud, the Eleans who keep the truces of Zeus the son of Cronus, after receiving some service of hospitality, I think. And they welcomed him with sweet-breathing voice as he fell in the lap of Golden Victory in their land, which they call the grove of Olympian Zeus. And there the sons of Aenesidamus were mixed with immortal honors.

(*Is.* 2.12–29)

Apart from Carrhotus, only one other driver is treated at length in Pindar's odes, and that is Nicomachus, the charioteer in *Isthmian* 2.[2] The inclusion of Nicomachus in this ode is especially strange because he was not actually the charioteer who drove in the victory that occasioned it. That victory was the Isthmian victory that is mentioned first and that determines the placement of the ode in the manuscripts. The driver in that Isthmian victory is not named, and there is no suggestion that it was Nicomachus; Nicomachus drove only in the Panathenaic and Olympic victories mentioned in the catalogue.[3] It is unusual enough to name a charioteer, but to name the charioteer from a different victory is exceptional.[4] Why does Nicomachus receive such prominence?

The prominence of Carrhotus in *Pythian* 5 was motivated by the fact that he was an aristocrat who gave his driving to the owner, and not a hired charioteer who drove for wages. The prominence of Nicomachus cannot, however, be easily explained in this way, because there is no evidence that he was an aristocrat. Pindar's description of Nicomachus as a guest-friend of the Elean officials, being welcomed to Olympia in return for some deed of hospitality (24–5), has led a number of scholars to think that he was a man of considerable status, perhaps a *proxenos* of the Eleans, but this is to confuse representation with reality.[5] Pindar regularly represents victories as the result of guest friendships, usually between the victor and the presiding authorities of the games, divine or human, so that the language of gift exchange in this passage reveals nothing more than that Nicomachus drove a victorious chariot at Olympia.[6]

Furthermore, there are three pieces of evidence that together argue strongly that Nicomachus was not an aristocrat. First, the lack of a patronym or other additional identifying name in *Isthmian* 2 suggests that Nicomachus was of a lower status; in contrast, Carrhotus' patronym, Alexibiades, and either Cnopiadas' patronym or his hometown were also given in their memorials. Second, the scholia to *Isthmian* 2, which as we have seen with *Pythian* 5 had access to information no longer available (and on occasion accurate), do not indicate, let alone provide compelling evidence of, such a relationship. Third, and most important, the Olympic victory in which Nicomachus drove, and at which he was, according to Pindar, welcomed by the Elean officials, was a victory that Pindar celebrated in two odes, *Olympians* 2 and 3, but Nicomachus is not named in either. Yet if it was his aristocratic status that motivated his inclusion in *Isthmian* 2, an ode that is occasioned by a victory in which he had no part, he would surely have been included at some point in either *Olympian* 2 or 3, odes that are occasioned by a victory in which he actually drove, Theron's Olympic victory.

Nicomachus cannot thus be thought of as an aristocrat. The presumption must be instead that, like the majority of charioteers in this period, he was hired, but this presumption offers the key to understanding his role in the ode. As its opening image declares, this ode has as its primary concern commodification, and the prominence of Nicomachus must be set in the context of the ode's treatment of commodity exchange more generally.

Isthmian 2 begins with Pindar's famous contrast between professional and amateur poets:

Οἱ μὲν πάλαι, ὦ Θρασύβουλε,
    φῶτες, οἳ χρυσαμπύκων
ἐς δίφρον Μοισᾶν ἔβαι-
    νον κλυτᾷ φόρμιγγι συναντόμενοι,
ῥίμφα παιδείους ἐτόξευον μελιγάρυας ὕμνους,
ὅστις ἐὼν καλὸς εἶχεν Ἀφροδίτας
εὐθρόνου μνάστειραν ἁδίσταν ὀπώραν.
ἁ Μοῖσα γὰρ οὐ φιλοκερδής
    πω τότ᾽ ἦν οὐδ᾽ ἐργάτις·
οὐδ᾽ ἐπέρναντο γλυκεῖ-
    αι μελιφθόγγου ποτὶ Τερψιχόρας
ἀργυρωθεῖσαι πρόσωπα μαλθακόφωνοι ἀοιδαί.
νῦν δ᾽ ἐφίητι <τὸ> τὤργείου φυλάξαι

ῥῆμ' ἀλαθείας < > ἄγχιστα βαῖνον,
"χρήματα χρήματ' ἀνήρ"
ὃς φᾶ κτεάνων θ' ἅμα λειφθεὶς καὶ φίλων.

Men of old, Thrasybulus, who mounted the chariot of the gold-filleted Muses, touching a glorifying lyre, quickly shot out honey-voiced songs to boys, at whoever was beautiful and had the sweetest late bloom that woos fair-throned Aphrodite. For the Muse was not yet then a lover of gain, nor did she work for hire. Nor, with their faces silvered, did the sweet soft-sounding songs of honey-voiced Terpsichore sell themselves. But now she bids us keep safe the word of the Argive that comes closest to the truth: "Money, money is the man," he said, deprived at once of possessions and friends.

(*Is.* 2.1–11)

The older poets are pictured in chariots, firing off odes at beautiful youths, while the modern, mercenary (φιλοκερδής, 6) Muse and her poems are depicted as prostitutes who silver their faces with makeup in an attempt to attract clients.[7] The portrayal of the modern poet is clearly unfavorable: with their silvered faces (ἀργυρωθεῖσαι πρόσωπα, 8), his prostituted poems represent a decline from the poems of the old poets who rode in the chariots of the gold-filleted (χρυσαμπύκων, 1) Muses; and while the old poets chose their targets and fired off their poems like hunters, the modern poems wait for a buyer to choose them.[8]

A number of explanations have been offered for the contrast between the old and new poets, but only that of Leslie Kurke is fully convincing.[9] She argues that the unfavorable presentation of the modern poet must be understood in terms of the changes in the production of poetry in the late archaic period and the aristocratic perception of commodity exchange. Praise poetry had become increasingly commodified in the latter part of the sixth century as the relation between poet and patron had been gradually pared down until the poets were remunerated for individual works and often worked for several patrons concurrently.[10] Patrons now had to step outside of traditional aristocratic channels to secure their praise, and when that praise was produced, it was no longer validated by the knowledge and trust that a lengthy relation between poet and patron provided. To Pindar's aristocratic patrons, a relationship with a poet seemed like a relationship with a prostitute.

The new mode of production of poetry was viewed extremely negatively, as Pindar's image attests, but *Isthmian* 2 does not simply lament the estrangement of the praise poet and the encroachment of commodification. Instead, it sets about making the relationships of the new economy fit into the traditional aristocratic code. It does this, as Kurke demonstrates, by fitting the patronage of praise poets into a sequence of practices that are framed as exchanges of gifts and expressions of friendship: sacrifices to the gods, entertaining friends, and equestrian competition itself. What had appeared as a commodity provided by a stranger now becomes, in Pindar's ideological vision, the generous gift of an old friend.[11]

Kurke's reading of *Isthmian* 2 is particularly powerful in that it makes the ode not about the hiring of praise poets (the poet's main concern), but about the perception of commodity exchange more generally. What needs more attention, however, is how equestrian competition is wrapped in the security blanket of gift exchange. Kurke pays little attention to the role of Nicomachus in this ode; yet, as I argued earlier, Nicomachus is a surprising and awkward inclusion, and almost certainly a hired charioteer, so that his unexpected presence raises the question of the role of commodity exchange in chariot racing. This was an awkward question, so awkward that the image of the hired charioteer, unlike the image of the hired poet, is never directly spoken; but although it is not spoken, the silent image does structure the ode, appearing through various screens, such as the prostitute poet, the representation of Nicomachus in the catalogue, and Pindar's poetic helper, Nicasippus.[12] The hired charioteer may, in fact, be the central problem that the ode addresses, and its solution to this problem turns out to be quite opposed to its solution of the problem of the hired poet.

The opening lines of *Isthmian* 2, as we have seen, raise the issue of commodification in the shocking image of the epinician poet as a prostitute. Although this opening may encourage the audience to examine more generally the role of commodity exchange in athletics, nothing is initially said about charioteers. In fact, when we turn to Xenocrates and his victory, he seems untouched by the commodification that swirled around the opening lines. He is described in terms that set him firmly among the older poets, as a man "victorious with his chariot" or "having a fine chariot" (εὐάρματον ἄνδρα, 17).[13] The positioning of this phrase at the opening of the second triad emphasizes the parallel between Xenocrates and the older poets, because the latter open the first triad riding the chariot of the Muses. The epithet "light of the Acragantines" (Ἀκραγαντίνων φάος, 17) perhaps reinforces the parallel by echoing φῶτες (1). Moreover, Xenocrates' chariot victories are represented as gifts from the gods, not commodities purchased from strangers: Poseidon gave (ὀπάσαις, 14) the Isthmian victory to him as a γέρας or gift of honor (γεραίρων, 17), and Apollo gave him brilliance (πόρε τ' ἀγλαΐαν, 18) at Delphi.[14]

After the Pythian victory, Pindar turns to Xenocrates' Panathenaic victory and the service of the charioteer Nicomachus. Although Nicomachus was almost certainly a professional, his mention does not prove to be a segue into the theme of commodification that dominated the second strophe of the first triad; like Xenocrates, Nicomachus is kept well away from the taint of commodity exchange. He, too, is described in terms that ally him with the older poets: he is pictured with a chariot, and ῥυσίδιφρον (21) and φωτός (21) pick up the specific vocabulary used to describe the older poets in the proem (φῶτες, 1, and δίφρον, 2). Furthermore, the charioteer's deeds at Olympia are represented as part of a gift-exchange network, not as the work of an alienated professional. Nicomachus receives praise, not wages, from his patron for the victory at Athens (οὐκ ἐμέμφθη, 20), and the victory he won at Olympia is represented, as was noted earlier in this chapter, as the welcome (ἀσπάζοντο, 25) of the Elean heralds given in return for some deed of hospitality (τι φιλόξενον ἔργον, 24).[15] This last phrase underlines Nicomachus' difference from the modern poets: where the mercenary Muse loves gain (φιλοκερδής, 6) and works for hire (ἐργάτις, 6), Nicomachus' work (ἔργον) is done out of love for his guest-friends (φιλόξενον).

The particular victories described in the catalogue reinforce the notion that Nicomachus enjoys a particular connection to Xenocrates' family. The Olympic victory in which he drove was not, in fact, won by Xenocrates, but by his brother Theron. This is not explicitly stated, but was well known to the audience and is tacitly admitted in the ascription of the victory to the sons of Aenesidamus, rather than just Xenocrates (28–9).[16] That Nicomachus drove for two brothers makes it seem that his driving for Xenocrates was part of a broader preexisting connection with the Emmenids, just as Carrhotus' was an expression of a prior relationship with Arcesilas.

The victory catalogue thus obscures the real circumstances of the production of this victory by representing Nicomachus as an old friend of the victor and his family. Yet, in contrast to *Pythian* 5, the overall effect of this representation is far from comforting because rather than enhancing the glory of the victors, the charioteer is made to take their place. This challenge is clearest in the structure of the catalogue, as a comparison with the victory catalogue of *Olympian* 2 reveals. This catalogue is almost the mirror image of that in *Isthmian* 2; the victory it primarily celebrates is Theron's Olympic victory, but it also lists the Isthmian and Pythian victories of his brother.[17]

Ὀλυμπίᾳ μὲν γὰρ αὐτός
γέρας ἔδεκτο, Πυθῶνι δ' ὁμόκλαρον ἐς ἀδελφεόν
Ἰσθμοῖ τε κοιναὶ Χάριτες ἄνθεα τε-
    θρίππων δυωδεκαδρόμων
ἄγαγον·

For at Olympia [Theron] himself received the honor, but at Pytho and the Isthmus, shared joys brought the flowers of the chariots that run twelve times round to his brother of equal lot.

(*Ol.* 2.48–51)

This catalogue is typical of Pindar's victory catalogues in that it clearly, even somewhat clumsily, promotes the central principle of aristocratic ideology that excellence runs in the family.[18] To say, as Frank Nisetich does, that the catalogue of *Isthmian* 2 illustrates the same principle is to ignore the particular structure of the two catalogues.[19] What links the victories in *Olympian* 2 is the fact that they are won by brothers, but in *Isthmian* 2, this blood link is relegated to the background and overshadowed by the fact that the same charioteer drove in the brothers' victories. This is especially clear on the grammatical level, where it is through Nicomachus, through a relative pronoun referring to him, that Pindar moves from Xenocrates' victory in Athens to Theron's victory at Olympia.[20] The catalogue of Emmenid victories in *Isthmian* 2 is thus more like a catalogue of Nicomachus' wins.

The suggestion that Nicomachus is the real victor is reinforced by the description of the Olympic win. As noted earlier, this victory is vaguely ascribed to the sons of Aenesidamus, rather than to the actual victor, Xenocrates' brother Theron. This serves to suggest that the victory is at least partly Xenocrates', but it also allows the less welcome suggestion that Nicomachus was the victor, and, in fact, this is a suggestion that Pindar plays up.[21] At the games, heralds announced each victor in turn, along with his city, the event he had won, and perhaps his father, and victory odes often imitated this announcement;[22] but in the catalogue of *Isthmian* 2, it is the charioteer whom the Elean heralds are said to have proclaimed victor (22–3). This was, of course, simply false (although no more false than the suggestion that the sons of Aenesidamus were victorious).[23] Theron was proclaimed victor at Olympia, but Nicomachus has taken his place in Pindar's retelling of this event.[24]

Nicomachus may have seemed even more like the victor being celebrated by the catalogue given the particular circumstances of this ode's performance. Xenocrates was certainly dead at the time,[25] and most commentators date the ode after Theron's death as well.[26] As the only remaining human component of the Emmenid victories in Athens and Olympia (apart from the grooms and trainers), Nicomachus may have seemed to some more properly the heir to the victories than Xenocrates' son, Thrasybulus, the patron of this ode.[27]

The representation of the charioteer in the central triad of *Isthmian* 2 thus has mixed results. On one hand, it certainly insulates Xenocrates and Theron from contact with commodity exchange, but on the other hand, the newly ennobled charioteer, unlike Carrhotus, threatens to deprive them, and Thrasybulus, of the victories. An appropriate way to represent the hired charioteer, and so protect the meaning of the victory, is thus still wanting. In the third and final triad Pindar offers a second representation of the chariot victory that proves less troubling, while still avoiding the specter of commodity exchange. The charioteer continues to be bound to the victors in an enduring relationship but ceases to be their equal, becoming instead their trusted servant.

As Kurke argues, the final triad of *Isthmian* 2 gives a positive value to the praise poetry it earlier scorned as commodified, as well as to the victor's chariot racing, which was susceptible to the same criticism.[28] Pindar figures his own praise as an outstanding discus or javelin throw (35), an image that places his work outside of the reach of commodity exchange. Praise poets more generally are connected to the poets of old by being fitted into the chariot imagery that organized the description of those older poets, as well as of Xenocrates and Nicomachus: οὐ γὰρ πάγος οὐδὲ προσάντης ἁ κέλευθος γίνεται, / εἴ τις εὐδόξων ἐς ἀνδρῶν ἄγοι τιμὰς Ἑλικωνιάδων, "It is neither a rocky hill nor a steep road if someone brings to the houses of glorious men the honors of the daughters of Helicon" (33–4). The connection with the image of the chariot is made by κέλευθος, which, as Kurke notes, refers particularly to carriage roads. Meanwhile, Xenocrates' chariot racing is seen as maintaining social relations, not breaking them up; it is represented as respectful both of the townspeople and of Panhellenic custom, and made parallel to sacrifices to the gods and generous hospitality (37–42).

The closing lines focus only on the praise poet, just as the opening lines had done:

ἐπεί τοι
οὐκ ἐλινύσοντας αὐτοὺς ἐργασάμαν.
ταῦτα, Νικάσιππ', ἀπόνειμον, ὅταν
ξεῖνον ἐμὸν ἠθαῖον ἔλθῃς.

For, I did not make [these songs] to stand idle. Nicasippus, deal them out when you come to my trusted friend.

(*Is.* 2.45–8)

Pindar's poetry has been completely separated from the degraded poetry of the ode's opening triad. His poem is not traded for money, as the prostitutes traded their bodies, but constitutes an expression of a friendship. Pindar has become a friend of his patron, Thrasybulus, and thus of the victor Xenocrates and his brother. Further, ἐργασάμαν reformulates the earlier idea of a poem generated by the image of the poet as a "working girl" (ἐργάτις, 6) by dissociating the poet's work from commodity exchange. Work may be exchanged as a commodity, but it may also be a gift from one friend to another, and the poet's work falls in this latter category.

This representation of the poet caps the ode's project of redefining the boundary between gift and commodity exchange, and so it should be no surprise that the lines also return specifically to the problem of the hired charioteer. Nicasippus, who is here assigned the role of performing Pindar's ode,[29] is the final screen through which the hired charioteer is addressed. He is an obvious double of Nicomachus, both because their names share the same first syllable and because Nicasippus means "Conquers with horses,"[30] but he constitutes a very different articulation of the charioteer's work to that of the central triad. Where before Nicomachus was represented as an aristocrat, the close friend of the Emmenids, and the host of the Elean officials (τι φιλόξενον ἔργον, 24), here the deeds of friendship (ἐργασάμαν, 46) and the close relationship with the Emmenids (ξεῖνον ἐμὸν ἠθαῖον, 48) belong to Pindar. Meanwhile, Nicomachus' double occupies a lower rank where he can be given orders by the poet. The particular order (ἀπόνειμον, 47) picks up and refigures the earlier description of Nicomachus' chariot driving: his "dealing" of his hands to the reins (νεῖμ', 22) now stands revealed as an action ordered by the owner of the chariot.

His lower status does not mean that Nicasippus has no relationship with the poet. He is clearly trusted and important enough to be assigned the safe keeping and proper performance of a gift for an old friend in a distant city. In consequence, his work, like the poet's and unlike the prostitute's, does not appear to be commodified, and he seems instead most like a servant in an aristocratic household.[31] Further, in so far as he transfers the gift from Pindar to Thrasybulus, Nicasippus has a part in the gift exchange between poet and patron. Again, however, this part refigures the part played earlier by Nicomachus: where Nicomachus linked the Emmenids and the Elean officials by actually exchanging gifts with both, Nicasippus provides the link between Pindar and Thrasybulus only by ensuring the passage of a gift between the two.

Nicasippus thus offers a second way of thinking about Nicomachus that avoids representing his chariot driving as a commodity. Rather than the aristocratic friend of the second triad, Nicomachus becomes at the end of the ode a trusted and senior servant. This picture does not necessarily deny that Nicomachus was paid wages for his service; instead, it suggests that any such remuneration should not be taken as indicating that the victor stepped outside the usual aristocratic channels of exchange to secure his victory. Nicomachus may have been paid for this specific victory, as for the victory of Theron at Olympia, but such payments are, according to this ode, part of a more permanent connection.[32] The fact that Nicomachus drove for Theron is thus a boon for Xenocrates, since it reinforces the idea that Nicomachus was connected to the Emmenids, but in reality this connection was almost certainly tenuous and interrupted. Nicomachus was a professional driver who drove several times for this family, but in between those jobs also drove for other patrons.

A second feature of this formulation is that, unlike *Pythian* 5 and many of the memorials considered in Chapter 1, as well as the central triad of this ode, it plays down the importance of equestrian skills in winning a chariot victory. The relationship between owner and charioteer is figured as the relationship between the composer and the performer of an ode: the charioteer performs, as it were, the script that the owner has composed, and his role in the production of the victory, like the performer's role in the production of the ode, is negligible. This strategy of downplaying rather than ignoring the role of the charioteer is paralleled by those odes and dedications that emphasize the victor's stables, by focusing either on multiple victories or multiple entries.[33]

Isthmian 2 thus has something of a chiastic structure. At the start of the ode, Pindar is likened to a prostitute, whereas Nicomachus is represented as an aristocratic friend of the Emmenids, but at the end of the ode, through the mediation of Nicasippus, the charioteer becomes a servant, while the poet becomes the guest-friend. *Isthmian* 2, it turns out, does not treat all wage laborers alike. The wages that both receive are covered by the construction of permanent relationships between them and their patrons, but these relationships cast the poet as a man of status and the charioteer as a servant.

The final representation of the charioteer, although unusual, is far from shocking; the aristocrats cannot have viewed the charioteers that they hired as their equals. It is rather the central stanza that represents a daring assault on the epinician status quo. Why does Pindar, even if only temporarily, represent a hired charioteer as an aristocrat?

The answer to this question lies partly in the structure of sympotic poetry. There is a growing appreciation of the extent to which sympotic poetry does not simply confirm and maintain the aristocracy's sense of who it is and what it stands for, but also, temporarily, displaces and disorients this self-definition, before once again affirming it.[34]

The central triad can be seen as fulfilling this sympotic function. By describing the charioteer as the victor's equal, and even replacing the victor with the charioteer, Pindar is able to undermine, temporarily, his aristocratic audience's understanding of what defined the aristocracy and who the εὐάρματοι ἄνδρες, the chariot-racing class, included. The uncertainty is only temporary, however; by the end of the ode, the familiar hierarchical order is restored, and Nicomachus is reduced to the status of a servant.[35]

Such an explanation is only partially satisfying, however, because it does not account for the particular way in which Pindar chooses to unsettle the Emmenids. Why use a charioteer to unsettle the Emmenids, when most memorials are able to pass over this figure in silence? And why use Nicomachus, who did not even drive in the Isthmian victory that occasioned this ode? Because of the nature of the evidence available, any answer must be tentative, but one possible reason that Nicomachus was selected was that he had gained considerable prominence through his services as a first-class racing charioteer and had reduced the traditional gulf in status between owner and charioteer.

Most charioteers surely remained insignificant, but some must have attained a higher profile. According to the Pindaric scholia, Chromius, the victor celebrated in Pindar's *Nemeans* 1 and 9 and an important figure in the regimes of both Gelon and Hieron, "served as Hieron's charioteer from a young age, and, through his association with Hieron and excellence in horsemanship, became rich and, separating himself from Hieron, began to race chariots on his own."[36] The story is certainly fiction, but the idea that some charioteers became wealthy through their office is surely credible, even for the fifth century. Commodification must have provided the most talented charioteers with great opportunities to enrich themselves as different owners competed for their services; the increased availability of coinage allowed wealth to be amassed in more fluid forms, and the athletic festivals themselves provided an efficient marketplace, joining buyers and sellers, owners and charioteers, together in one place. Other trades certainly enriched their most successful practitioners without the benefits of such an arena: Herodotus tells of both a poet, Arion, and a doctor, Democedes of Croton, who became extremely wealthy through remuneration by their aristocratic patrons.[37] The small fortune that

Alcibiades reportedly paid for the Argive chariot that won the Olympic race under his banner in 416 indicates the resources that patrons were prepared to commit to securing a chariot victory in a major contest, and, having paid so much for a chariot team, such patrons would surely have paid handsomely for a charioteer with a proven track record to protect their investments.[38] Such charioteers must have gained at least some wealth and fame, particularly if they were employed, like Arion, by the tyrants of Sicily and Italy. They may even have become so prominent that in certain circumstances they could be easily mistaken for the victors.

Nicomachus looks like such a charioteer: he worked for one of the great chariot-racing families of the West, and seems to have had a strong curriculum vitae, including a Panathenaic victory and an Olympic win at what was an especially prestigious Olympic festival,[39] and these were only the victories he had won with the Emmenids. Particularly after the Olympic win in 476, Nicomachus may have become famous, and he was thus perhaps included in *Isthmian* 2 because Xenocrates wanted the Olympic victory won by his brother to be mentioned but felt that the Emmenids could not be convincingly praised for the victory without some credit being given to the famous charioteer who secured it. Victory memorials that entirely excluded famous charioteers were becoming, I would suggest, increasingly unconvincing, and so Pindar perhaps experimented with a new solution to the problem of representing the charioteer. A solution that obscured the commodification of chariot driving was required, as the initial equation between trading skills and prostitution makes very clear, and the solution that Pindar fixed on was to represent the charioteer as a senior household servant. Yet he also flirts with a second solution, to represent the charioteer as an aristocrat and friend of the victor, and the reason behind this representation is, I would suggest, that it more nearly reflected reality. Nicomachus' wealth and fame made him more like an aristocrat than an aristocrat's servant.[40]

The new standing that some charioteers enjoyed can perhaps be inferred from a source other than *Isthmian* 2. A beautiful statue discovered on Motya, a Punic island facing Sicily, may represent a dedication from the 470s set up by a charioteer to commemorate his achievements in driving chariots to victory. The statue is made of marble, perhaps slightly over life-size, and of high quality, but at some point the face and genitals were damaged. The figure stands upright, with a slightly curving posture culminating in the head being turned to the left. The most striking attribute of the statue is the sleeveless ankle-length tunic: the folds of the cloth are represented in considerable detail, and the whole clings to the figure's body so that the outline of the genitals is clear. A chest band running just beneath the statue's armpits binds the tunic to the body. Both arms are broken just beyond the shoulders, but the remains of the left hand can be seen resting on the figure's left hip. Four bronze nails were placed around the statue's head.

The identification of the statue is disputed, but, as Malcolm Bell argues, it is most probably the statue of a charioteer.[41] The long sleeveless tunic was a usual article of dress for a charioteer, and, although the chest band was unusual, it is found in depictions of charioteers on coins, and on the statue of the Delphic charioteer.[42] The lightness of the fabric and the eroticism produced by the close contouring of the genitals may surprise, but the tunic seems usually to have been made of a fine material, and the Greek appreciation of the male athlete's body is well known.[43]

The statue certainly belongs to the fifth century (or before) because it was buried by the Syracusan capture of Motya in 397, but a date in the 470s is suggested by stylistic criteria. The particular hairstyle, with the hair gathered into a ring of beads encircling the head, has parallels around 500, but the careful representation of the diaphonous drapery suggests a slightly later date. Bell also argues that the style of the face, the hairstyle, and the drapery indicate that the statue was produced in Athens.[44]

What makes this statue different from the Delphic charioteer is that it appears to have been freestanding, not part of a chariot group. The statue, being made of marble rather than the bronze of the Delphic charioteer and the groups described by Pausanias, seems designed to be seen in the round. Moreover, the charioteer was not pictured driving a chariot. A charioteer's hands are usually depicted holding the reins, but in this statue, the charioteer leans his left hand on his left hip. Further, Bell argues persuasively that the missing right hand was not holding any reins either, but instead touching a crown, which was secured to the charioteer's head by the four bronze nails.[45] The charioteer was therefore depicted without his chariot and wearing a victory crown.

The Motya statue thus seems to be a remarkable departure from the usual representations of charioteers: no longer part of a group including the chariot, the horses, and perhaps even the victor, the charioteer appears alone. This can only be explained by the circumstances of its commission; it must have been, as Bell concludes, a charioteer who commissioned this statue.[46] The charioteer must certainly have been wealthy to be able to afford such a dedication, but we should question Bell's assumption that he was an aristocrat, not least because most charioteers were not. If this was indeed the dedication of a charioteer, it more likely illustrates the new wealth and yearning for status of a successful professional charioteer such as Nicomachus in the early fifth century.[47]

Caution must be exercised here, however. The intentional damage done to the face and genitals is hard to explain if the statue was a charioteer. Bell notes that the statue that had been set up in Croton of the runner Astylus of Croton was pulled down when he defected to Syracuse,[48] and it is possible that the more famous charioteers were seen as credits to their home cities also, but the damage may also suggest that someone more important, perhaps Hamilcar of Carthage, was represented here.[49]

Vases offered a cheaper vehicle to charioteers who wished to be remembered, but no examples of vases commissioned by charioteers to commemorate themselves can be identified with certainty. Two specially commissioned pseudo-Panathenaic vases seem to refer to a specific race and may have been commissioned by a victorious charioteer. The first depicts a four-horse chariot and beside it offers the inscription "Nikon is beautiful" (Νίκων καλός); the second depicts two chariots racing side by side, and bears the names Nikon and Mynnon beside the horses (Figure 6); one is perhaps the victorious charioteer, and the other might be a distinguished competitor that he defeated.[50] But this can only be speculation; it cannot be determined whether Nikon and Mynnon are charioteers, owners, fans, or people entirely unconnected to racing.[51] Even greater doubts attend those vases that seem to name charioteers but do not depict racing scenes.[52]

6. Two four-horse chariots and charioteers, with names Nikon and Mynnon. Panathenaic amphora, reverse, ca. 525. Courtesy of the Réunion des Musées Nationaux, Paris.

A more promising parallel to the Motya statue is a dedication made by a horse trainer and recorded by Xenophon. Horse trainers received no credit for their work with racehorses and chariot teams, but they, too, were presumably paid a wage for their services, and good wages if their charges were repeatedly successful. Some time before Xenophon writes, one horse trainer, Simon, dedicated a bronze statue of a horse with an inscription recording his own deeds in the

Eleusinium at Athens. It is possible that Simon trained horses for equestrian competition, because the Eleusinium was an important marker for the course of the *apobates* race of the Panathenaic games,[53] but it is more likely that he trained horses for the Panathenaic processions. These passed by the Eleusinium, and Xenophon mentions Simon particularly in connection with his advice on training horses for parades.[54] The dedication implies that Simon had considerable wealth, but, more than that, it implies a desire for recognition for an important and difficult job that was mostly ignored. Perhaps Simon was an aristocrat whose talents lay in an unusual field, but perhaps both he and the dedicant of the Motya statue made their wealth through the wages they commanded for their outstanding services, and, finding themselves robbed of recognition in traditional memorials, proclaimed their achievements through dedications of their own.[55]

Dedications such as the Motya charioteer or Simon's bronze horse in the Eleusinium can help us better understand the ideological struggles in which *Isthmian* 2 was engaged. Pindar's general goal in the ode was to move the boundary between gift exchange and commodity exchange so as to include beneath the umbrella of gift exchange a number of activities characteristic of the economy of the polis. One special object of concern was equestrian competition. For some time memorials had hidden the fact that victors in the chariot races were implicated in commodity exchange by erasing the presence of the charioteers they hired, but this strategy had lately become less effective due to the fame and wealth that the most successful charioteers were beginning to achieve through their trade. This is the background against which *Isthmian* 2's different representations of the charioteer should be mapped: the hired charioteer was the central ideological problem of the ode, particularly the hired charioteer who, like Nicomachus, had a curriculum vitae to attract the attention of many owners.

Those commemorations of chariot victories that can be securely identified today were dedicated by the victors and promoted a representation of the victory favorable to their interests, but it is not fanciful to imagine that chariot victories were commemorated by other people, from other perspectives. At the very least, the insistent exclusion of hired charioteers from the memorials commissioned by the aristocratic victors suggests that some of the charioteers, with Nicomachus perhaps at the forefront, found much greater recognition elsewhere.

4

PHINTIS

The only ode to name a poetic helper other than *Isthmian* 2 is *Olympian* 6, and it is surely no coincidence that this ode also names a driver. Although both drove in Olympic victories, Phintis, the driver who is named by *Olympian* 6, is different from Nicomachus in at least one important respect: the event in which he drove was the mule-cart race, not the chariot race. Phintis is thus particularly interesting: one of only four drivers to be named in memorials, he was the only one to drive mule carts.

Although introduced to Olympia only around the beginning of the fifth century, mule-cart races were discontinued little more than half a century later and may never have been fully accepted as a proper event.[1] Victors in the event were not recorded in the Oxyrhynchus victory list, and Aristotle relates the telling, although certainly fictional, story that Simonides initially felt that celebrating the mule-cart victory of Anaxilas of Rhegium was beneath his dignity.[2] The event was seen as a poor relation of the horse races; a recurrent motif among the memorials that survive is the suggestion that the victory was won with horses rather than mules. Simonides opened his ode for Anaxilas by addressing the mules as the "daughters of storm-footed mares" (ἀελλοπόδων θύγατρες ἵππων), although, as Aristotle points out, they were the daughters of asses also.[3] Similarly *Olympian* 5, for Psaumis' victory in the Olympic mule-cart race, probably in 456, stresses the victor's competition in the horse and chariot races, as well as the mule cart, and ends by praying that he may enjoy his horses in his old age.[4]

Victories in the mule cart were certainly considered worth celebrating, however.[5] In fact, it may have been precisely its second-class status that made the mule cart an attractive competition for its entrants.[6] The victor celebrated by *Olympian* 6, Hagesias, was an important figure at Olympia, a descendant of a family famous throughout Greece for its prophetic abilities, but in Syracuse, his hometown, he was second in importance to Hieron, praise of whose tyranny is carefully included in Hagesias' victory ode.[7] Hagesias' entry into the mule-cart race seems designed to demonstrate an easy acceptance of this hierarchy. The victory took place either in 472 or 468, and at both festivals Hieron entered (and won) one of the more prestigious equestrian events, the horse race in 472 and the chariot in 468.[8] Hagesias' entry into the mule-cart race was a public declaration that, although he sought glory in the games, he was happy to play, as it were, the mule to Hieron's horse.

The use of the mule cart to articulate political relations among the West Greek elites had already been established by Anaxilas of Rhegium, who minted coins depicting his mule-cart victory to signal his acceptance of Gelon's overlordship (Figure 7). Although the previous coin issues of Rhegium and Messana had been weighted according to the Euboeic standard and had depicted a lion's head on its obverse, these issues adopted both the Attic standard and the equestrian design of Syracusan coins, which had depicted a four-horse racing chariot since the beginning of the century.[9] Anaxilas' coins showed mules, rather than horses, and this signaled his subordination to Gelon. Indeed, the reference to his Olympic victory is especially pointed, because the four-horse chariot on the Syracusan issues also referred to an Olympic victory, but this one a victory in the chariot race. Around 485, Gelon had tied the design to his chariot victory in 488 by adding a flying Nike carrying a crown above the chariot on the obverse, and introducing Arethusa, the river that joined Syracuse and Olympia, to the reverse, or at least making her more prominent.[10] Anaxilas' coins thus used not only their weights, but also the metaphor of equestrian athletics to proclaim his recognition of Gelon's authority: just as his victory was less prestigious than Gelon's, so, too, was his power less great.[11]

Whether they were introduced for this reason or not, mule-cart races provided an arena for the second rank of the elite to demonstrate their aristocratic credentials without competing against their superiors.[12] Yet these credentials were also potentially undermined by the manner of the competition; for we cannot doubt that, like chariot driving, mule-cart driving had for the most part become a commodity and that mule-cart drivers had few permanent connections to their patrons, but drove for a variety of owners.[13] The mule-cart driver was thus rather more problematic than the mules, and so there must have been some reason for his inclusion in *Olympian* 6. Nicomachus was included in *Isthmian* 2 because he was an especially successful professional driver, but, although this ode should be interpreted against the same background of the increasing commodification of driving, it seems unlikely that Phintis' presence can be explained in the same way as Nicomachus'. Rather, the explanation should be sought in the political hierarchy of Syracuse, the victor's hometown.[14]

The ode oscillates between two inconsistent strategies in its representation of the mule-cart driver: on one hand, it projects a world where drivers are not used by obscuring Phintis' participation in the race and the use of drivers more generally, but, on the other hand, it presents Phintis as a trusted servant, performing an important job that will bring both him and his master credit. The ode begins by following the more usual path of excluding the driver from mention of the race. Explaining why Hagesias can expect praise, Pindar reflects,

ἀκίνδυνοι δ' ἀρεταί
οὔτε παρ' ἀνδράσιν οὔτ' ἐν ναυσὶ κοίλαις
τίμιαι· πολλοὶ δὲ μέμναν-
ται, καλὸν εἴ τι ποναθῇ.

Excellences that involve no danger are not honored among men or in hollow ships, but many remember when something fine has been achieved through toil.

(*Ol.* 6.9–11)

Although Hagesias' military exploits may have involved considerable toil and danger,[15] the toil and danger of this mule-cart race were the

7. Mule cart and driver. Coin issued by mint at Messana, after 480. Photograph © Copyright The British Museum, London.

driver's, not the victor's. The suggestion that Hagesias deserves praise for these reasons thus serves to make us think of him as the driver.

This suggestion is reinforced by the comparison of Hagesias to Amphiaraus that follows:

> Ἁγησία, τὶν δ᾽ αἶνος ἑτοῖμος, ὃν ἐν δίκᾳ
> ἀπὸ γλώσσας Ἄδραστος μάντιν Οἰκλεΐ-
>   δαν ποτ᾽ ἐς Ἀμφιάρηον
> φθέγξατ᾽, ἐπεὶ κατὰ γαῖ᾽ αὐ-
>   τόν τέ νιν καὶ φαιδίμας ἵππους ἔμαρψεν.
> ἑπτὰ δ᾽ ἔπειτα πυρᾶν νε-
>   κρῶν τελεσθέντων Ταλαϊονίδας
> εἶπεν ἐν Θήβαισι τοιοῦτόν τι ἔπος·
>   "Ποθέω στρατιᾶς ὀφθαλμὸν ἐμᾶς
> ἀμφότερον μάντιν τ᾽ ἀγαθὸν καὶ
>   δουρὶ μάρνασθαι."

Hagesias, the praise readily fits you which Adrastus once rightly uttered from his tongue over the prophet son of Oecles, Amphiaraus, when the earth caught him and his shining horses. Then, when seven pyres of dead bodies had been finished, the son of Talaos spoke such a word in Thebes, "I miss the eye of my army, both a good prophet and a man good at fighting with the spear."

(*Ol.* 6.12–17)

Pindar compares Hagesias to Amphiaraus because both combined skills in prophecy with skills in war, but the representation of Amphiaraus also serves to create a false picture of equestrian racing. As described in Chapter 1, other representations of Amphiaraus being swallowed by the earth and of his part in the expedition against Thebes almost invariably set a charioteer, often named Baton, in the chariot with him. In this passage in *Olympian* 6, however, Amphiaraus alone is mentioned with his horses.

With the second triad comes recognition of the driver, but that recognition is brief, as he soon yields ground to the poet and the mules:

ὦ Φίντις, ἀλλὰ ζεῦξον ἤ-
  δη μοι σθένος ἡμιόνων,
ᾇ τάχος, ὄφρα κελεύθῳ τ' ἐν καθαρᾷ
βάσομεν ὄκχον, ἵκωμαί τε πρὸς ἀνδρῶν
καὶ γένος· κεῖναι γὰρ ἐξ ἀλ-
  λᾶν ὁδὸν ἁγεμονεῦσαι
ταύταν ἐπίστανται, στεφάνους ἐν Ὀλυμπίᾳ
ἐπεὶ δέξαντο· χρὴ τοίνυν πύλας ὕ-
  μνων ἀναπιτνάμεν αὐταῖς·
πρὸς Πιτάναν δὲ παρ' Εὐρώ-
  τα πόρον δεῖ σάμερον ἐλθεῖν ἐν ὥρᾳ·

Phintis, yoke for me now the strength of mules as swiftly as possible, so that on a clear road we may mount the car and I may come also to a race of men. For above all others, those [mules] know how to lead this way, since they have received garlands at Olympia. Indeed the gates of song must be opened for them, and I must come in good time today to Pitana beside the ford of Eurotas.

(*Ol.* 6.22–8)

The driver's skill in yoking the mules is indicated, and poet and driver are presented as equally responsible for the celebration underway, riding the mule cart of song together.[16] Yet the mule-cart driver quickly fades in importance. First, the shared celebration (βάσομεν) becomes Pindar's solitary journey to Hagesias' Spartan ancestors (ἵκωμαί), and then the focus passes to the mules themselves. It is for the mules that the ode is said to be sung, and it is the mules that are said to have received the garlands of victory. Further, that they "know how to lead" Pindar on his way (ἁγεμονεῦσαι . . . ἐπίστανται) suggests that they can follow a course without Phintis' guiding hand.[17]

There is little mention of chariots or carts in the central myth of Iamus, but what little there is promotes the idea that the elite does its own driving: Aepytus, Iamus' adopted grandfather, is said to have driven back from Delphi after consulting the oracle (ἐλαύνων, 48). More striking is the transition from the mythical ancestors of the Iamidae to their present success:

> ἐξ οὗ πολύκλειτον καθ' Ἕλ-
>   λανας γένος Ἰαμιδᾶν·
> ὄλβος ἅμ' ἕσπετο· τιμῶντες δ' ἀρετάς
> ἐς φανερὰν ὁδὸν ἔρχονται· τεκμαίρει
> χρῆμ' ἕκαστον· μῶμος ἐξ ἄλ-
>   λων κρέμαται φθονεόντων
> τοῖς, οἷς ποτε πρώτοις περὶ δωδέκατον δρόμον
> ἐλαυνόντεσσιν αἰδοία ποτιστά-
>   ξῃ Χάρις εὐκλέα μορφάν.

Since then the clan of the Iamidae has had great fame among the Greeks. Prosperity followed with them. Honoring virtues, they have come to a road clear to all. Each event bears witness. Blame from envious others hangs over those on whom, as they drive first around the twelfth lap, reverend Grace drips glorious beauty.

(*Ol.* 6.71–6)

The progress of the Iamidae along the road of fortune merges into the final lap of their victorious chariots, and the conflation of these two images of forward progress allows Pindar to suggest, despite earlier mentioning the driver in Hagesias' victory, that the Iamidae, like other victors, actually "drive first around the twelfth lap." It hardly needs adding that it was their drivers that drove around the laps in the equestrian competitions.

These various references to driving serve not only to hide the drivers, but also to transform the mules into horses, in much the same way as Simonides' address to Anaxilas' mules as the "daughters of storm-footed horses" hides the fact that they also had asses for parents. Amphiaraus is actually seen with horses, and the reference to twelve laps means that the Iamidae are envisaged winning four-horse chariot races. Although the number of laps in the mule race is not recorded, twelve laps was the distance of the four-horse chariot race, and it is certain that two mules would not have been required to do the same distance as four horses. When they were introduced later, the colts' four-horse chariot race and the full-grown pair only did eight, and the colts' pair only three.[18] Thus, through this seemingly innocent phrase, Pindar not only makes Hagesias (and every other victor) the driver in his victory, but the driver of a four-horse chariot as well. We may also note that this passage suggests that the Iamidae had won a number of chariot victories at Olympia, but there is no evidence that they had won anything apart from Hagesias' mule-cart victory; the only other evidence of their competition is of a failed effort to win the pentathlon in the early fifth century.[19]

It is, however, the representation of the mule driver that is our primary focus here. In the final triad, the ode in fact turns back to its earlier limited recognition of the driver. The triad initially continues with the general erasure of drivers with a brief mention of "horse-driving Theba" (πλάξιππον . . . Θήβαν, 85), but then, through the description of Pindar's poetic helper Aeneas, proceeds to recognize and elaborate on the driver's role in the victory:

    ὄτρυνον νῦν ἑταίρους,
Αἰνέα, πρῶτον μὲν Ἥραν
    Παρθενίαν κελαδῆσαι,
γνῶναί τ᾽ ἔπειτ᾽, ἀρχαῖον ὄνειδος ἀλαθέσιν
λόγοις εἰ φεύγομεν, Βοιωτίαν ὗν.
    ἐσσὶ γὰρ ἄγγελος ὀρθός,
ἠυκόμων σκυτάλα Μοι-
    σᾶν, γλυκὺς κρατὴρ ἀγαφθέγκτων ἀοιδᾶν·
εἶπον δὲ μεμνᾶσθαι Συρα-
    κοσσᾶν τε καὶ Ὀρτυγίας·
τὰν Ἱέρων καθαρῷ σκάπτῳ διέπων,

ἄρτια μηδόμενος, φοινικόπεζαν
ἀμφέπει Δάματρα λευκίπ-
  που τε θυγατρὸς ἑορτάν
καὶ Ζηνὸς Αἰτναίου κράτος.

Goad up your companions now, Aeneas, first to proclaim Hera Parthenia, and then to learn whether we escape with true words the ancient reproach of the Boeotian sow. For you are a straight messenger, a cipher-stick of the fair-tressed Muses, a sweet mixing-bowl of loud-sounding songs. And I told you to remember Syracuse and Ortygia, which Hieron orders with a pure scepter, counseling aright, while he tends crimson-footed Demeter, the feast of her daughter of the white horses and the power of Etnaean Zeus.

(*Ol.* 6.87–96)

The parallel between Aeneas and Phintis is immediately clear. First, like Phintis, Aeneas receives a command from the poet (ζεῦξον, 22, ὄτρυνον, 87), and this command specifically links Aeneas' actions to those of a driver: although often used of encouraging people, ὀτρύνω is also used of goading horses and mules.[20] Second, Aeneas is asked to perform a similar task to Phintis, because, when he appeared earlier, Phintis was asked to yoke the mules not for a race, but to serve Pindar's mule cart of song. Third, the reference to the sow also joins Aeneas to Phintis, in that he, too, was associated with a comic animal, the mule.[21]

The figure of Aeneas serves to elaborate the role of Phintis. Aeneas, like the driver, is a subordinate, subject to the orders of those above him, but it is also clear that he has a certain seniority and produces work of great importance. Although given orders himself, he is in the position to give orders to others: where Nicasippus was figured as the actual performer of the ode in *Isthmian* 2, Aeneas, as the scholia note, is pictured as a chorus master training others to perform this ode.[22] Aeneas' work is also presented as important to his patron's fortunes: Pindar says that Aeneas' work will determine whether they both escape reproach. Aeneas thus maps out a positive role for Phintis, and, through the mediation of this chorus master, Phintis is represented as a senior and trusted servant whose work is important to the victor's fortunes.

Thus, although it often ignores the work of the mule-cart driver, *Olympian* 6 ends by giving him a positive role in procuring the victory.

The image of the driver as the equestrian equivalent of Aeneas should be understood, just as the image of Nicomachus as Nicasippus in *Isthmian* 2, in terms of the problems of commodification affecting equestrian athletics. The image avoids all suggestion that Phintis' driving was a commodity bought by the victor from someone with whom he had had no previous contact. Rather, it suggests that the relationship between Hagesias and Phintis was a close and continuing one, and that Phintis served Hagesias in this race as part of an ongoing relationship of service to his master. Indeed, Aeneas' motivation is expressed specifically in the terms of gift exchange: his hope is that he can remove from himself and the poet the "ancient reproach of the Boeotian sow" (ἀρχαῖον ὄνειδος . . . Βοιωτίαν ὗν, 89–90), not earn his wages. The relationship between Phintis and Hagesias seems like that between Xenocrates and Nicomachus in *Isthmian* 2: there the patron was represented not as paying the charioteer, but as praising him (οὐκ ἐμέμφθη, 20). Thus, the ode maintains the basic requirement of aristocratic equestrian ideology that the victor be protected from contact with commodity exchange.

Yet although the ode is shaped by the same concern with commodity exchange, the representation of the charioteer is still unusual and requires an explanation. Chapter 3 argued that Nicomachus was included in *Isthmian* 2 because he had won particular prominence through his successes in chariot racing, but it seems unlikely that Phintis was equally prominent. First, although he drove in an Olympic victory, there is no evidence that Phintis drove in any other wins. Nicomachus, by contrast, certainly drove in victories at both the Olympics and the Panathenaea and was well known enough to be named in an ode that celebrated a victory in which someone else drove. Second, there is no evidence that Phintis drove anything but mule carts, and, as a mule-cart driver, he simply did not have the same opportunity to win wealth and fame. The mule-cart race did not attract the attention that the chariot races did and was left to lesser tyrants and second-rank aristocrats. Less money must have been spent on the competition, including the drivers' wages; Hagesias' resources were certainly more limited than those of Theron and his brother.

Third, *Olympian* 6 itself does not display the anxiety concerning Phintis that *Isthmian* 2 does concerning Nicomachus. On one hand, the ode does not raise Phintis as high as Nicomachus is raised in the central triad, while, on the other hand, it seems happy to grant him a more significant role in the victory. Nicasippus is simply shown as the performer of the ode, but Aeneas, Phintis' double, is described as a chorus master, in charge of the performers. Further, although the description of Aeneas as "a cipher-stick of the fair-tressed Muses" and "a sweet mixing-bowl of loud-sounding songs" (ἠυκόμων σκυτάλα Μοισᾶν, γλυκὺς κρατὴρ ἀγαφθέγκτων ἀοιδᾶν, 91) does mark him as the passive intermediary between poet and victor, it is still flattering;[23] and, like Phintis earlier, Aeneas is represented, at least to some extent, as engaged in a shared journey with his patron. *Olympian* 6 thus seems less concerned than *Isthmian* 2 to deny its driver a significant role in the victory, and this suggests that there was less concern that Phintis might be mistaken for the victor.

The inclusion of the driver in *Isthmian* 2 also served the poet's interests, and this is true of *Olympian* 6. Pindar is able to represent himself as an aristocrat, and his ode as gift and not a commodity, through joining the two servants in the ode. Just as Hagesias has a servant, Phintis the mule-cart driver, so Pindar has Aeneas the chorus master, and, by linking Aeneas to Phintis as fellow servants, Pindar is able to imply that he and Hagesias, the two servants' masters, share the same status. Two commodity exchanges are thus clothed in gift exchange by *Olympian* 6: Hagesias' hiring of Phintis becomes the service of a senior household member, while his hiring of Pindar becomes the gift of a fellow aristocrat.

But the poet's concerns about the commodification of his own product are surely not sufficient to motivate Phintis' inclusion. The reason for this should be sought instead with the victor. Just as the relation between mule and horse was used by Hagesias to articulate his relations with Hieron, so, I suggest, the relation between driver and victor was also used to articulate his place in the Deinomenid hierarchy. Hagesias was not just the mule to Hieron's horse, he was also the driver to Hieron's victor.

It is noticeable that the introduction of Aeneas coincides with a change in the way the relationship between Hieron and Hagesias is represented. Hieron's supremacy is, in fact, asserted in the orders that Pindar gives Aeneas, as the poet asks Aeneas to sing of Hieron's rule of

Ortygia.[24] But Hieron's superiority is not evident early on. When the ode opens, Hagesias is praised, among other things, for being "the fellow founder of famous Syracuse" (συνοικιστήρ τε τᾶν κλεινᾶν Συρακοσσᾶν, 6). This is surprising. Hagesias was certainly not involved in the foundation of Syracuse, which was attributed to Archias in the eighth century. The scholia suggest that it is an ancestral title, earned by the participation of one of the Iamidae in the foundation; but, as Irad Malkin carefully notes, there is no parallel for such a title, and the scholia are clearly guessing.[25] Rather, the title should be understood in the contemporary Syracusan context. It is well known that both Gelon and Hieron had aspirations to be remembered and worshipped as founders, and, although there is no other evidence connecting Hieron with the title of Syracuse's founder, Malkin argues that this reference makes it likely. Hagesias was certainly closely associated with Hieron (according to a somewhat confused scholion, he was murdered soon after Hieron's fall), and it seems likely that he assisted him, as a prophet, in his project of refoundation.[26] This is a persuasive reconstruction, but that Hagesias bore the title of cofounder with Hieron seems unlikely; rather, Pindar has stretched the truth here to enhance Hagesias' status.

Hagesias thus shifts during the ode from being Hieron's equal, his "fellow founder," to being his subject, and the fact that this shift is articulated at the moment that Aeneas is introduced suggests that Aeneas' relationship to the poet, and so also the driver's relationship to the victor, constitute models for Hagesias' relationship to Hieron. The use of chariot metaphors to illustrate political relations may have been common enough. The fact that Carrhotus actually drove for Arcesilas may have helped to articulate his status in a turbulent time in Cyrene, and Pisistratus' reduction of the elder Cimon from victor to manager of his second victorious Olympic team demonstrated his control of Athenian politics.[27]

One curious coincidence supports the idea that Hagesias is to be identified, at least in part, with the subordinates, Aeneas and Phintis. Aeneas, although a fine name for a cipher-stick of the Muses, is also a name attested in Hagesias' family.[28] It seems extremely unlikely that the chorus leader is actually being pictured as a relative. No relation between Aeneas and the victor is mentioned; and, although Pindar does on occasion speak of the poetic talents of members of the victor's family, he speaks of these members as poets, not chorus leaders and does not place them in a position subordinate to himself.[29] It is safer to conclude that Aeneas was not actually a relative of the victor but that the name serves to associate the victor with the poet's chorus master.

It may seem odd that a victory ode should expend such effort articulating the victor's junior position to Hieron, but it cannot be assumed that such plotting out of hierarchies was unwelcome. As we have seen, by entering mules when Hieron was entering horses, Hagesias himself was publicly proclaiming not only his aristocratic credentials, but also his inferior status to Hieron. Further, Aeneas, as we have also noted, is, in contrast to Nicasippus in *Isthmian* 2, in a position of some authority himself, set over a chorus of companions whom he teaches to sing the ode. Similarly, being second in rank to Hieron did not mean Hagesias was powerless or unimportant. The position presumably conferred considerable status and power and was not necessarily something Hagesias chafed at.

Phintis is thus different from the other drivers that are named by victory memorials, and not only because he drove mule carts. The inclusion of the other drivers was motivated by some special quality of the drivers: either they were aristocratic friends of the victor, like Carrhotus and Cnopiadas, or hired charioteers who had won great prominence through their driving, like Nicomachus. In contrast, Phintis was neither an aristocrat nor well known, and, while his inclusion in *Olympian* 6 should certainly be related to the increased pressure to recognize the work of charioteers in victory memorials, the immediate reason for it does not lie with Phintis, but with the victor, Hagesias.[30] Just as Phintis served Hagesias in the race at Olympia, so he again serves his patron in the ode as part of a series of comparisons (horse and mule, poet and chorus master, owner and driver) that articulate Hagesias' relation to the leader of his city.

There may, however, have been a twist to the representation of Hagesias as a driver. Although the identification of Hagesias with a mule or a chorus leader seems straightforward, that with a charioteer or driver is surely rather more complex. As the last chapter argued, the status of drivers was probably disputed. While the memorials commissioned by the aristocratic victors gave them little or no recognition, some charioteers, particularly in the Greek West, gained wealth and fame, and, in some quarters, may have come to look much like the aristocratic victors. In an ode composed for performance in Syracuse, therefore, the comparison of Hagesias to Hieron's driver may thus have served less to clarify the relationship between the tyrant and his lieutenant than to problematize it. After all, Hieron may have been the leader of Syracuse, but his aristocratic credentials were not as good as Hagesias': Hagesias' family, the Iamidae, were a prominent Panhellenic clan that claimed descent from Poseidon and Apollo, while Hieron's ancestors were priests of Demeter and Persephone whose origins were not recorded and who came to prominence only in Sicily.[31] As argued in Chapter 3, sympotic poetry often also disturbed the aristocratic hierarchy it affirmed, and in this case, the target seems to be less the poet's patron than the victor's patron, Hieron, who welcomes Hagesias' victory revel.[32] To some, Hieron may have seemed closer in status to his "driver" than he cared to admit.

5

PHERENICUS AND LYCUS

Pausanias records a story told by the Corinthians about the victory of one of their fellow citizens, Pheidolas, in a horse race at Olympia in the latter part of the sixth century. His racehorse was a mare named Aura, and, according to the story,

> she happened to throw her rider just as the race was beginning, and ran off in exactly the way she was supposed to. She turned round the post and, when she heard the trumpet, speeded up her pace, reached the Hellanodicae first, realized that she had won, and stopped running. The Eleans proclaimed Pheidolas to be the winner of the victory and allowed him to dedicate [a statue of] this mare.
>
> (6.13.9)

This is a rather absurd story, for two reasons. First, it presupposes that victory was still awarded to the owner of the horse that finished first, even if it had lost its jockey, which was surely not the case;[1] second, it presents Aura's continued participation and eventual victory in the race as something of a miracle. Yet in ancient racing, as in modern flat racing, riderless horses must have occasionally come in ahead of those with jockeys because of the simple fact that they had much less weight to carry.

The story of Aura thus fails to measure up to the canons of reality, but it is fully comprehensible when measured against a different set of canons, those of the aristocratic ideology of the jockey. Just as most charioteers and mule-cart drivers in the late archaic period raised awkward questions about the nature of an owner's participation in equestrian contests, so also did most jockeys. Those memorials that survive for victories in the horse race, like those for chariot victories, are organized around the exclusion or denigration of the horseman and his work in winning the race. The race is represented as a race between horses, and only horses; the horses are seen as fully determining the result, as knowing where to run and when to speed up, while either the jockey or the jockey's role in the races is erased. Within the aristocratic discourse of victory commemoration, the Corinthian story of Aura thus makes perfect sense.

Although there is no evidence for who served as jockeys or how they were remunerated, the shape of their representation in surviving memorials for horse races strongly implies that what made them problematic was the nature of their relationship with the owners whose horses they rode, not the fact that they rode and the owners did not. Like most charioteers, many jockeys must have been hired and have had no preexisting relationship with the person who hired them, and no expectation of one to follow. By contrast, the relationship between the owner and his horse seems to have been genuinely untainted by commodity exchange; in the late archaic and early classical period owners typically seem to have bred their horses in their own stables. Certainly, the relationship is represented as one that is close, respectful, and enduring. What is, therefore, at stake in these memorials is thus not the participation of the jockey but the buying and selling of his services; the high profile that the racehorse enjoys serves to deny the centrality of commodity exchange to the victory by hiding the isolated purchase of the jockey's services behind the enduring relationship of owner and horse.

Fewer memorials for horse races than for chariot races survive intact or are sufficiently well recorded, but two specific groups of victories are well represented: Hieron's victories, at Delphi in 482 and 478 and Olympia in 476 and 472, are commemorated by three odes and one large dedication made at Olympia by his son for all his Olympic victories,[2] and more than half of the Olympic victories from the last quarter of the sixth century and the first quarter of the fifth have left memorials. Excavations at Olympia have yielded a dedication by Pantares of Gela, the father of the Cleander and Hippocrates, who established the tyranny that would later belong to the Deinomenids; this belongs to the end of the sixth century or the beginning of the fifth.[3] Damage to the inscription has rendered the event unclear, but the victory was surely in an equestrian event, given both Pantares' age and the name he gave to Hippocrates. Moretti favors the chariot race, but Ebert argues convincingly that the dedication consisted of a bronze horse and thus that the event was the horse race.[4] Around the same time two victories, one in 508, according to the Elean records, were won by the sons of the Corinthian Pheidolas, whose mare, Aura, was said to have thrown her rider but nevertheless come in first. Both victories were won by the same horse and so were probably won at consecutive Olympic festivals.[5] There was some dispute in Pausanias' time over these victories; the Elean records spoke only of one victory. Various emendations can be made to the inscription that Pausanias records, but, given that his transcriptions are consistently reliable, it is better to discount the Elean records, which must have been imperfect for the sixth century.[6] Pheidolas himself also dedicated a memorial of his horse victory, although Pausanias gives no details about the dedication, concentrating instead on the Corinthians' story about the manner of victory.[7] Finally, also around this time, an Eretrian, Crocon, dedicated a small bronze horse. Given that Eretria was destroyed in 490, a late archaic date for the dedication is certain, and one around the end of the sixth century or the beginning of the fifth most likely.[8]

There are certainly gaps in this record – most regrettably, perhaps, there is no memorial for the victory of the Argive people in 480, presumably won, like their chariot victory in 472, over Hieron[9] – but more significant is the absence of memorials for contests other than Olympia. Apart from one of the odes for Hieron and a mention in one of the Olympic memorials for an Isthmian win,[10] victories in other competitions are celebrated by only one other memorial, a victory vase for Dysniketos, commissioned from the Swing Painter.[11] The style of the vase indicates a date in the third quarter of the sixth century, and the precise games at which the victory was won are not known; the tripod that appears behind the racehorse is a generic marker of victory, not an indication that the prize won in the contest was actually a tripod.[12]

Thus, nine memorials for racehorse victories either survive sufficiently intact or are recorded in sufficient detail for analysis: three odes, five dedications, and one vase.[13] In addition, fragments survive of three odes that seem to celebrate victories in the horse race, two by Simonides[14] and one by Ibycus,[15] as well as of a dedication in Delphi that may celebrate Hieron's two victories in the horse race there, as well as his chariot victory.[16] These fragments are, however, too brief to indicate whether their treatment of the horse race victories reflected the practice of the other memorials (or often even whether they celebrate a victory in the horse race). The sample of memorials is thus small and further compromised by the fact that the three victory odes celebrate only victories won by the same horse, Hieron's horse Pherenicus. At the same time, however, the various types of memorial prove to be remarkably consistent in their representation of racehorse victories, and, when read together, they yield patterns that can safely be considered part of the discourse governing horse races in victory memorials.

The memorials make it clear that jockeys were excluded from the victory record. The jockey that rode the racehorse is not named by any of the memorials; this is particularly striking because the memorials often name the racehorse. Of the nine memorials listed earlier, seven are preserved in sufficient detail to know whether they did or did not name the racehorse, and four of these do so. Hieron's racehorse Pherenicus is named in the three odes that celebrate the victories he raced in, twice in the ode by Bacchylides,[17] and the horse of the sons of Pheidolas, Lycus, who raced in two Olympic victories, is named by their dedication:

> Ὠκυδρόμας Λύκος Ἴσθμι' ἅπαξ, δύο δ' ἐνθάδε νίκαις
> Φειδόλα παίδων ἐστεφάνωσε δόμους.[18]

Swift-footed Lycus, by winning once at the Isthmia and twice here, crowned the house of the sons of Pheidolas.

The naming of Lycus is emphasized not only by its position at the beginning of the inscription, but also by the fact that it is only their father and not the sons who are named.[19]

It might be suggested that these examples are exceptions, that Pherenicus and Lycus are only named because their feats were extraordinary, but there are two reasons to think that these four memorials were not unusual in naming the victorious racehorse. First, it is not at all clear that Pherenicus was much more distinguished than the average Olympic victor. He had certainly won at Delphi also, but only once, in 478; it is likely that Hieron used a different horse for his Pythian victory of 482.[20] Although this brace of victories constitutes an impressive record, it cannot have been especially impressive for an Olympic victor; it is certainly less impressive than Lycus' two Olympic wins, and both of these victory hauls pale beside the feats of the chariot teams of Cimon and Evagoras, both of which had won three consecutive Olympic chariot races within the previous eighty years.[21] Furthermore, that the dedication made by Hieron's son at Olympia did not elevate Pherenicus above the racehorse that brought Hieron victory in 472 suggests that he was not considered unique.[22] What has made Pherenicus the most famous racehorse in antiquity is that Pindar and Bacchylides named him; they did not name him because he was already the most famous.

A second reason not to believe that the namings of Lycus and Pherenicus are exceptional is provided by the anecdote about Pheidolas' mare. This anecdote names the horse as Aura, or "Breeze," which shows that at least in some celebratory tradition, that horse's name was preserved.[23] Pausanias does not make it clear whether this name appeared on the Olympic monument, however. It has been argued that Aura's name, like Lycus', was included in the inscription: the Palatine Anthology preserves a couplet that purports to be the inscription on the dedication of Pheidolas, and Ebert suggests that this couplet is a corruption of an original inscription that named the horse as Οὖρος, also "Breeze."[24] There is, however, a crucial inconsistency between the couplet and the monument described by Pausanias, so that it cannot be considered contemporary: the couplet speaks of a stallion, whereas Pausanias, who saw the statue of the horse that was dedicated at Olympia, speaks of a mare. In addition to appearing in the main inscription, it is also possible that Aura's name appeared somewhere else on the base of the statue, as was the case with the names of chariot team of Cleosthenes, which appeared on a memorial around the time of Pheidolas' victory.[25]

It seems probable, therefore, that there was a tendency in memorials to name the racehorse through which the victory was won, and not just to name especially distinguished racehorses. It is certain, however, that jockeys are never named, whether they are especially distinguished or not: we do not know whether Pherenicus had the same jockey at Delphi in 478 as at Olympia in 476, or whether Lycus had the same jockey for two or more of his Olympic and Isthmian victories. The jockey is simply not included when names are entered into the victory record.

It is not only by being named that the racehorses are given precedence over the jockeys; when they represent the horses, the memorials often omit the jockeys altogether. Although the jockeys were included with the racehorses in the memorial of Hieron's multiple victories at Olympia, it seems to have been common in memorials of only racehorse victories to dedicate a statue of the racehorse without its jockey. The dedications of Pheidolas, Pheidolas' sons, and Crocon of Eretria all consisted of statues of horses, and none of the three included a jockey.[26] Here we must believe that if Pausanias does not mention a jockey in his descriptions, then a jockey was not present, but this is not a dangerous assumption: as with the memorial of Hieron's victories, Pausanias carefully notes when boys are seated on racehorses, as well as when charioteers are included in chariot groups.[27] Further, the anecdote about Pheidolas' mare Aura provides some confirmation that no jockey was represented riding her: the presence of a jockey on the mare would surely have prevented the circulation of the legend at Olympia, at the least.

The dedication of Pantares of Gela also seems to have avoided all reference to a jockey. What survives of the inscription mentions only the victor, his father, his place of residence, and the contest itself; in the lacuna the event must have been specified, but there is hardly room for mention of a jockey.[28] Furthermore, it is likely that the bronze plate that remains supported a small bronze horse and, if this is so, we must assume that it, too, did not carry a jockey.[29]

The tendency to derogate the jockey is perhaps best illustrated by the victory odes. In general, epinician odes also seem to have avoided any mention of the jockey; if he is included, it is only to minimize the contribution he made to the race and actually represent him as a burden on the horse, rather than a necessary part in the victory. Both Pindar's *Olympian* 1, for Hieron's victory in 476, and *Pythian* 3, for the victory in 478, speak of Pherenicus, but neither ode pictures him carrying a jockey. *Olympian* 1 does, however, tacitly recognize his presence, but only to suggest that he served no useful function, when it describes Pherenicus as "speeding its body ungoaded alongside the Alpheus" (παρ' Ἀλφεῷ σύτο δέμας / ἀκέντητον, 20–1). It was the jockey's job to quicken the horse's pace at the right time through use of a whip (κέντρον), and the timely use of the whip was crucial to any victory; Panathenaic vases often depict the jockey using the whip.[30] The idea that one might win without one is laughable: when Apollo strikes the whip from Diomedes' hand in the chariot race at the funeral games of Patroclus, his opponent pulls further ahead and his eyes fill with tears of rage.[31] Yet according to the picture Pindar provides, Pherenicus, like Pheidolas' horse Aura, had no need of the whip, but was able to up his pace at the appropriate moment without any help from the jockey (whom, unlike Aura, he still had to carry to the finishing line).

In his ode for the same victory, Bacchylides' treatment of the jockey is less harsh, but its overall direction is the same. After swearing that no dust has ever been kicked back onto Pherenicus by a horse in front of him as he sped (ὀρνύμενον, 45) towards his goal, Bacchylides continues,

ῥιπᾶι γὰρ ἶσος βορέα
ὃν κυβερνήταν φυλάσσων
ἵεται νεόκροτον
νίκαν Ἱέρωνι φιλοξείνωι τιτύσκων.

For, like to the blast of the North Wind, guarding his helmsman, he speeds, aiming at a freshly-applauded victory for Hieron, fond of entertaining.
(5.46–9)

The jockey is described as a helmsman, and this metaphor was certainly a positive one (Pindar uses it of a ruler and a wrestling trainer),[32] but the structure of the sentence accords him little influence. The racehorse is the subject of two active (φυλάσσων, τιτύσκων) and two middle verbs (ὀρνύμενον, ἵεται), whereas the jockey is only the object of an action. That action is also telling: while φυλάσσων, "guarding," may suggest that the horse obeyed his jockey,[33] it more naturally suggests that he kept him safe and that the jockey is a burden that the horse has to protect. Two subtexts contributed to this glorification of Pherenicus and reinforced the idea that of the racehorse and his jockey, the racehorse was the important actor. First, the horse's treatment seems to allude to a description of Pegasus in Ibycus' work, and Pegasus, of course, was an immortal (and winged) horse that, although temporarily mastered by the mortal Bellerophon, had the power to throw its master when he attempted to attack Olympus.[34] Second, as Mary Lefkowitz notes, the image of the eagle that appears earlier in the ode is linked to that of Pherenicus by the description of the eagle's feathers as a mane (ἔθειραν, 29),[35] but this image emphasizes the eagle's untrammeled agency: while the eagle is the messenger of Zeus, Bacchylides describes it as "trusting in its mighty strength" (κρατερᾶι πίσυνος / ἰσχύϊ, 21–2) and "guiding" (νω-/μᾶι, 26–7) its own wings through the sky, a word used elsewhere of both helmsmen and charioteers.[36]

The racehorse's profile is further raised in several memorials by the fact that it, and not the victor, is described as winning the contest. Bacchylides describes Pherenicus as "victorious alongside the wide-eddying Alpheus," (Ἀλφεὸν παρ' εὐρυδίναν / . . . νικάσαντα, 38–40), and "victorious in the running" (νικάσας δρόμωι, 183), while the dedication of the sons of Pheidolas describes Lycus as "victorious once in the Isthmian games and twice [at Olympia]" (Ἴσθμι' ἅπαξ, δύο δ' ἐνθάδε νίκαις). In *Pythian* 3, although Pindar does not use the verb νικάω of Pherenicus, he does describe the horse as "excelling" (ἀριστεύων, 74), a verb he uses elsewhere in the odes as a synonym for victory.[37] In these memorials, this language is not used of the victor.

Moreover, in using such language, these memorials depart from the practice of memorials for chariot victories. In these memorials, such language is almost never used of chariots and chariot teams, but, as in the victory announcements at the games themselves, it is the actual victor, the owner, who is described as the victor, and if mentioned, the chariot team is rendered an instrument through which the victory is won.[38] Alcmeonides' dedication at the Ptoion on behalf of his Panathenaic chariot victory is illustrative: it describes him as "victorious with the swift mares" (*ḥ*ίπποισι νικ̣έ[σας ἔ]θεκέ μ̣' [ὀκέαις]). The Olympic memorial of Hieron's equestrian victories follows this practice: it describes Hieron as "victorious . . . once with a four-horse chariot and twice with a single racehorse" (νικήσας . . . / τεθρίππῳ μὲν ἅπαξ, μουνοκέλητι δὲ δίς).[39] Some memorials for racehorse victories alone may also have followed this construction; the inscription on the dedication of Pantares of Gela for his victory in the horse race seems to have marked Pantares as "victorious with a horse" ([hίπ(π)οι νικάσας]), but the relevant section of the inscription has to be reconstructed.[40] This context makes the departures in Bacchylides' and Pindar's odes and the dedication of the sons of Pheidolas even more striking: the shift of the horse from the instrumental dative typical for chariot teams (and perhaps some racehorses) to the subject of the sentence represents an obvious elevation in the horse's status.

In the victory odes, the racehorse even seems to be assimilated to a victor in a gymnastic event through an emphasis put on its supreme physical efforts. Just as Pindar describes how a victorious wrestler "fell from on high on four bodies, with intent to do them harm" at the Pythian games (τέτρασι δ' ἔμπετες ὑψόθεν / σωμάτεσσι κακὰ φρονέων, *Py.* 8.81–2), so he tells how Pherenicus "sped his ungoaded body along the Alpheus, giving his all in the race" (παρ' Ἀλφεῷ σύτο δέμας / ἀκέντητον ἐν δρόμοισι παρέχων, *Ol.* 1.20–1). Bacchylides describes the feat in even more glowing terms, swearing that the racehorse has not been soiled by dust kicked up from horses in front of him in this, or any other, contest (γᾶι δ' ἐπισκήπτων πιφαύσκω· / οὔπω νιν ὑπὸ προτέ[ρω]ν / ἵππων ἐν ἀγῶνι κατέχρανεν κόνις / πρὸς τέλος ὀρνύμενον, "leaning on the earth I make my declaration: not yet has dust from horses in front dirtied him as he speeds to the finishing line in a contest," 5.42–5). Such grandiose claims to a special quality of victory find their closest parallel in the praise of wrestlers and pancratiasts: Pindar and Bacchylides both tell of wrestlers who won titles without conceding a fall, Pindar's at Marathon (ἀπτωτὶ, *Ol.* 9.92) and Bacchylides' at Delphi (οὐκ ε[ἶ]δέ νιν ἀέλιος / κείνωι γε σὺν ἄματι πρὸς γαίαι πεσόντα, "the sun did not see him falling to the ground on that day at least," 11.22–3).[41] An even more impressive feat in the combat sports was to win "without dust" (ἀκονιτί), that is, without having to face a challenger, as a Spartan, Acmatidas, did in the wrestling section of the pentathlon at the end of the sixth century or as Dromeus of Mantinea was said to have done in the pancration because Theagenes of Thasos was exhausted by his efforts in winning the boxing.[42] By saying that no dust (κόνις, 5.44) soiled the body of Hieron's racehorse, as Mark Golden notes, Bacchylides alludes to a "victory without dust" in the combat sports and so likens Pherenicus to the best wrestlers and pancratiasts.[43]

The general tendency of memorials for victories in the horse race to raise the profile of the racehorse at the expense of the jockey is well illustrated by the earliest extant memorial for a horse race, the victory vase of Dysniketos.[44] This vase, from the third quarter of the sixth century, is modeled on Panathenaic amphoras, and so its representation of victory should be seen within this framework. On the reverse appears a large racehorse ridden by a young jockey with bare feet and wearing an embroidered tunic (Figure 8). It walks left to right, while behind walks a naked young man, carrying a tripod, and in front a bearded man in an ankle-length robe; this man is presumably a herald, because to his right appears an inscription that seemingly comes out of his mouth.

The jockey is, therefore, pictured by the vase, but his role is minimized in two ways. First, the choice to depict a static scene from after the victory seems designed to downplay his role. Typically prize amphoras depict the horse race in action; the focus tends to be on both the physical strength of the horses and the skill of the jockey, who may be shown using his whip.[45] In contrast, in the scene on Dysniketos' vase, the jockey sits clothed and upright on the back of the horse, quietly holding its bridle. Second, an inscription on the vase makes it clear which component of the victory really matters. The inscription, somewhat badly spelled, announces the horse as the victor, making this vase the fourth memorial from our sample to do so: ΔΥΝΕΙΚΕΤΥ : ΗΙΓΟΣ : ΝΙΚΑΙ, "The horse of Dysniketos wins."[46] The emphasis on the horse is not spoiled by the inclusion of the actual victor in this scene; he is instead pictured on the front, in a variation on the typical Panathenaic pattern (Figure 9). Athena Polias appears in the middle, Hermes appears to her left, perhaps the divine counterpart to the human herald announcing the victory, and a well-dressed and bearded man, presumably Dysniketos, appears to her right.[47]

A second vase, painted by the Mastos painter and roughly contemporary with Dysniketos' vase, also minimizes the role played by

8. Racehorse, with jockey, herald and man carrying tripod. Panathenaic amphora from Vulci, reverse, ca. 550–525. Photograph © Copyright The British Museum, London.

the jockey, but it does so by focusing on the victor, not the horse (Figure 10).[48] Although a genuine Panathenaic prize amphora and so not a special commission, its departures from the usual Panathenaic design mean that it, like the Panathenaic vase now in Florence that commemorates a chariot victory, should be understood as a conscious effort on the part of the painter to promote a particular ideology of racing. Like Dysniketos' vase, this Panathenaic vase avoids depicting

9. Hermes, Athena, and victor. Panathenaic amphora from Vulci, obverse, ca. 550–525. Photograph © Copyright The British Museum, London.

the race in action, choosing instead the moment just after the race has been won. The horse again appears in the center, with a jockey riding it, this time naked, and there are figures in front of and behind it, although this time these figures are both clothed and both reach out victory sprays toward the horse. In contrast to Dysniketos' vase, however, both the jockey and the horse are partially obscured by the victor, who appears in an embroidered knee-length gown, holding the horse's halter. The obverse of the vase is canonical. This vase thus shifts

10. Racehorse, with jockey, victor, and two men with sprays. Panathenaic prize amphora, reverse, ca. 550–525. Courtesy of the Office of Prehistoric and Classical Antiquities, Nauplion.

the focus from the horse and jockey to the victor, from the physical effort needed to finish first in the race to the ownership of the horse and the celebration of victory. It represents the relationship between horse and victor more in the terms in which the memorials for chariot victories represent the relationship between the victor and his team: the horse is deprived of the subject position and becomes the tool with which the victor gains his victory.

These two vases perhaps indicate that in the third quarter of the sixth century, two strategies for erasing or minimizing the jockey's role in a racehorse victory were available to memorials, that of Dysniketos' special commission, in which the horse is represented as the crucial component of victory, and that of the genuine Panathenaic, in which the victor is given precedence, as he is in most memorials for chariot victories. To judge by the memorials that remain from the last quarter of the sixth century and the first quarter of the fifth, however, one of these strategies soon came to dominate, generating a significant cleavage among memorials for equestrian victories.[49] Of the eight remaining intact memorials for victories in the horse race from that period, six, and perhaps seven, marginalize the jockey by privileging the racehorse.[50]

The erasure of the jockey, like the erasure of the charioteer, should be traced not to the fact that he did work that some thought the victor should have done, but to the fact that the jockey's work was traded as a commodity. Certainly it is clear that no anxiety was attached to the fact that the owner was not involved in the actual running of the race; by representing the racehorse as the crucial component of victory, the memorials emphasize that the owner expended no physical effort in winning his victory. Indeed, one of the most interesting things about these memorials is that they evidence no incompatibility between the owner's status as victor and the claim made by several of the memorials that the horse did the winning: the horse may have won, but somehow the owner was still the victor. The source of the anxiety lies elsewhere, in the jockey's relationship with the victor.

There is little agreement among scholars as to who performed the role of jockey in the late archaic period. Gardiner and Beazley suggest that most jockeys were professionals, although Beazley also thinks that the owner's son may often have taken the reins; Mark Golden, by contrast, suspects that most jockeys were slaves.[51] It is clear, however, that at least in major contests, the jockey was a locus of anxiety, and so the likelihood is that, as in chariot racing, professionals dominated at the major festivals, but that professional jockeys were less prominent than professional charioteers at the more local games. The rest of the field at these contests would likely have been made up first of slaves and second of bondsmen and other youths from the owner's circle of influence, some of whom would later become the professionals at the bigger races.[52] Although some owners are recorded who drove their own chariots, there is no evidence that owners sometimes used their sons as jockeys or rode themselves if young enough;[53] it may even have been considered inappropriate.[54] It is worth considering the possibility, however, that at the major festivals some slaves were used who were bought specifically for the purpose of riding horses in competition, rather than being slaves who had grown up, or at least spent a considerable portion of their lives on an owner's estate;[55] such slaves, particularly if they were intended for later resale, would have presented the same problems for aristocratic ideology as professionals.

What makes jockeys different from charioteers is their youth. Like professional charioteers, professional jockeys were, presumably, used in the most prestigious games. These attracted the wealthiest patrons, and competition there was accordingly fiercest. In such circumstances, these wealthy owners were surely more likely to seek out a successful jockey than to rely on the resources of their own estates. Because youths were used as jockeys (and not light adults as in modern flat racing), however, the window during which talent could be spotted and developed was much briefer than for a charioteer. Unlike a successful charioteer, a successful jockey at one Olympic festival will probably not be viable for the next one four years later. Talented youths must, therefore, mostly have caught the attention of owners at local festivals. These were numerous,[56] so that there were plenty of opportunities to discover a jockey for the next Panhellenic contest, but most of the jockeys discovered at these festivals were surely from the surrounding area. Whatever market there was for a jockey's services was thus more localized and less developed than the market for a charioteer's.

Local festivals provided the opportunity to review and purchase a jockey's services, but for something to become a commodity, as Arjun Appadurai argues, there needs to be not only the opportunity to buy and sell it, but also the general perception (in some context, at least) that it is the sort of thing that can be appropriately bought and sold.[57] It might accordingly be argued that the services jockeys provided were not viewed as potential commodities precisely because of the youth of the jockey. There is, however, no reason to think of this youth as a barrier: youths could be bought and sold as slaves, or employed in trades such as potting or metalworking, most likely both as apprentices and wage workers.[58] In addition, the youth of the jockey did not create any significant distinction between horse racing and those equestrian events with adult horsemen; owners who competed in the chariot races often competed in the horse races, and, while the chariot race was certainly more prestigious, victory memorials record victories in the horse race alongside victories in the chariot.[59] The jockeys' youth can surely not have inhibited the commodification of their services.

This reconstruction contains much speculation, but good evidence for it is offered by the treatment of the jockeys in the memorials themselves. As argued earlier, memorials for victories in horse races are organized around the exclusion of the jockey, and this exclusion is effected through the increased profile of the racehorses. The substitution of horse for jockey is a good indication of the source of the anxiety that shapes these memorials, and what it suggests is that it is the taint of commodity exchange that is to be avoided. The focus on the racehorse allows the memorial to place an enduring relationship at the center of the victory, and not a commodity transaction: the jockey's relationship with the owner consisted only of the simple purchase of his riding, but the horse's relationship with the victor is represented as a lasting relationship based on respect and reciprocal service.

As noted earlier, memorials for horse races, unlike those for chariot races, tend to name the horse involved: all three of the odes that survive intact and one of the dedications described in Pausanias certainly do so, and one more of Pausanias' dedications may have done so. This apparently simple act represents the horse as a highly respected member of the victor's circle; the only contemporary figures other than the victor typically named in memorials are members of the victor's family, especially his father, as in the dedications of Pantares and the sons of Pheidolas, but also other relatives who have been successful in athletic competition. Exceptions to this rule are few, and significant.[60] Moreover, in each of the memorials, the naming of the horse seems especially emphasized. Although in Bacchylides' ode Hieron's father Deinomenes is named, and his brothers addressed (5.35), Pherenicus is named both at that moment (5.36) and at the end of the ode when only Hieron is again named (5.184). Pindar names Hieron's father in both his odes on his chariot victories, and his son as well in *Pythian* 1, but no contemporary figures other than Hieron and Pherenicus are named in either *Olympian* 1 or *Pythian* 3.[61] Finally, as noted earlier, the memorial of the sons of Pheidolas names the racehorse and the victors' father, but not the victors themselves.

Although naming is usually reserved for members of the victor's family, in the case of racehorses it is probably meant to suggest that the horse is a respected member of the owner's household. In *Olympian* 1, Hieron is explicitly referred to as Pherenicus' δεσπότης (δεσπόταν, 22). This appears to be the proper term for the owner of a horse,[62] but it is also more generally the term used for the head of a household or estate. That the term is commonly used to denote a king's rule over his subjects or a master's rule over his slaves should not obscure the fact that the central organizing idea of the term is not so much a difference in power as a connection; a δεσπότης is master of everything, and everyone, in his household.[63] What Pindar's usage of the term indicates, therefore, is not so much that the horse is subordinate to the owner but that he is part of his household.

The act of naming thus creates a sharp distinction between the racehorse and the jockey, whose association with the owner is tenuous. In addition the naming gives the relationship between horse and owner a Homeric flavor, which reinforces the impression of closeness. Horses occupy a privileged position in the *Iliad*: eleven horses are named, and horses are the only animals other than humans to be named.[64] Horses are the objects of affection from their human masters and in turn show great affection for them: Andromache feeds Hector's horses before she feeds her husband, and Achilles' horses weep for Patroclus when he is killed, unable to return to the ships or go back into battle.[65]

Behind this affection lies a continuous exchange of services. In return for respect, food, and upkeep, the horse owes the owner good service in war and racing: Hector asks his team to repay him for the care they receive by helping him to take the shield of Nestor and the breastplate of Diomedes, while Antilochus reveals the savage underside of this reciprocity when he promises that his father will deny his horses their provender and have them killed if they cannot overtake Menelaus in the chariot race at the funeral games.[66] A similar reciprocity can be seen to structure the relation of owner and racehorse in the victory memorials: the respect and commemoration accorded to the racehorse is represented as earned by the great service it has done its owner. By his victory, Lycus "crowned" (ἐστεφάνωσε, Ebert 1972 no. 7.2) the house of the sons of Pheidolas, while through his running Pherenicus brought "the leaf of happiness to Hieron" (Ἱέρωνι φέρων / εὐδ]αιμονίας πέταλον, 5.185–6), according to Bacchylides, or, according to Pindar, "mixed his owner with victory" (κράτει δὲ προσέμειξε δεσπόταν, *Ol.* 1.22). In *Olympian* 1, Pindar speaks more generally of Pherenicus' service (χάρις, 18), the service that he performed in winning, and this service is seen as part of a great network of gifts and obligations:

> ὅθεν ὁ πολύφατος ὕμνος ἀμφιβάλλεται
> σοφῶν μητίεσσι, κελαδεῖν
> Κρόνου παῖδ᾽ ἐς ἀφνεὰν ἱκομένους
> μάκαιραν Ἱέρωνος ἑστίαν,
> θεμιστεῖον ὃς ἀμφέπει σκᾶπτον ἐν πολυμήλῳ
> Σικελίᾳ δρέπων μὲν κορυφὰς ἀρετᾶν ἄπο πασᾶν,
> ἀγλαΐζεται δὲ καί
> μουσικᾶς ἐν ἀώτῳ,
> οἷα παίζομεν φίλαν
> ἄνδρες ἀμφὶ θαμὰ τράπεζαν. ἀλλὰ Δω-
> ρίαν ἀπὸ φόρμιγγα πασσάλου
> λάμβαν᾽, εἴ τί τοι Πίσας τε καὶ Φερενίκου χάρις
> νόον ὑπὸ γλυκυτάταις ἔθηκε φροντίσιν,
> ὅτε παρ᾽ Ἀλφεῷσύτο δέμας
> ἀκέντητον ἐν δρόμοισι παρέχων,
> κράτει δὲ προσέμειξε δεσπόταν . . .

The famous song that rises from [Olympia] is clothed in the wits of the wise, so that they cry aloud the son of Cronus' name as they come to the rich and blessed hearth of Hieron, who wields a lawful scepter in Sicily of the many flocks, plucking the peaks of all excellences, and in turn is made glorious in the flower of music, such songs as we men often play around his friendly table. But take down from its peg the Dorian lyre, if indeed the service of Pisa and of Pherenicus has set your mind beneath most sweet thoughts, when he sped his ungoaded body along the Alpheus, giving his all in the race, and mixed his owner with victory.

(*Ol.* 1.8–23)

Included in this network is not only the service of Pherenicus in winning, but also of Pisa in organizing and sanctioning the race, of Zeus in validating Hieron's rule, of Hieron in entertaining the poets, and of the poets in singing the praises of Zeus, Hieron, Pisa, and Pherenicus. The whole apparatus of victory and its celebration is structured by the giving of gifts, and Pherenicus occupies an important place within this giving. A similar network of exchanges is mapped out more briefly by Bacchylides when he says that Pherenicus "sped, aiming at a freshly-applauded victory for Hieron, fond of entertaining" (ἵεται νεόκροτον / νίκαν Ἱέρωνι φιλοξείνωι τιτύσκων, 5.48–9).

It can cause no surprise that Pindar and Bacchylides represent the relationships in the epinician sphere as structured by the giving and returning of gifts and services,[67] but the inclusion of the racehorse as an agent in this process should be striking, as the inscription that accompanied Deinomenes' dedication on behalf of his father's victories at Olympia makes clear:

> Σόν ποτε νικήσας, Ζεῦ Ὀλύμπιε, σεμνὸν ἀγῶνα
> τεθρίππῳ μὲν ἅπαξ, μουνοκέλητι δὲ δίς,
> δῶρ' Ἱέρων τάδε σοι ἐχαρίσσατο· παῖς δ' ἀνέθηκε
> Δεινομένης πατρὸς μνῆμα Συρακοσίου.[68]

Having been victorious at your reverend contest, Olympian Zeus, once with a four-horse chariot, and twice with a single racehorse, Hieron freely gave these gifts to you. His son, Deinomenes, dedicated them as a memorial of his Syracusan father.

In this vision of victory, the agents joined by the exchange of gifts are Zeus, Hieron, and Deinomenes: Zeus granted Hieron victory, and in return Hieron prepared a large dedication to Zeus, which his son, as a favor to his father, dedicated to Zeus after Hieron's death.[69] The racehorses (and chariot team) are not, however, participants in the network of giving, but instruments with which the victory was won. The inclusion of Pherenicus in this network in the odes of Pindar and Bacchylides is thus significant, as also is the exclusion of the jockey.

The focus on the racehorse at the expense of the jockey thus represents a shift of focus from the brief connection instantiated by commodity exchange to the enduring relationships structured by reciprocal acts of service: the horse appears as a valued member of the victor's household, permanently bound to his owner in an extensive network of services and returns. Reciprocity, in fact, appears to exhaust the signification of the racehorse in victory memorials; there is, for example, no suggestion that the horses' excellence derives from their parentage or inborn natures.[70]

That the primary intention of focusing on the racehorse is to replace the brief contact between owner and jockey with some lasting relationship is confirmed by a later memorial that pursues a different strategy with the same effect, replacing the jockey with the victor's son. The memorial is a dedication at Olympia on behalf of two victories, one in the horse race by Xenombrotus of Meropian Cos and one in the boys' boxing by his son, Xenodicus; a rough date for the dedication is fixed by one of the sculptors, Pantias of Chios, who was certainly active in the last quarter of the fifth century.[71] Dedications on behalf of victories by more than one person are rare, but this dedication is made even more unusual by the fact that it represented both victors: it consisted of a statue of Xenombrotus next to a statue of a racehorse ridden by his son.[72] It is possible but unlikely, that Xenodicus, who was clearly a talented athlete, served as his father's jockey. The inscription would surely have made this clear, and Pausanias would surely then have passed on this unusual information. Rather, this memorial made use of the son's demonstrated talent to peddle the fiction that a hired jockey was not used in the victory. A more daring effort to expunge the jockey from the victory record may be represented by the dedication of Aegyptus of Elis, which was made around the first quarter of the fourth century: according to Pausanias, Aegyptus, who seems to have won the horse race when still a youth, was represented as the jockey of his racehorse.[73] For a youth to win an equestrian victory at Olympia would be unprecedented, however, and it may be that Pausanias misidentified the figures in the memorial.[74]

There actually seems to be much truth in the earlier memorials' representation of the relationship between racehorse and owner; it seems likely that racehorses were indeed part of an owner's household from birth and not purchased to race in a particular competition. The first recorded purchase of a horse for competition is that, at considerable expense, of a chariot team from Argos by Alcibiades, for the Olympic chariot race of 416;[75] to judge by the claims of other memorials, it is around this time that it became common for owners to purchase horses for competition. Two memorials, the first that of Damonon of Sparta for numerous victories in local contests and the second that of Cleogenes of Elis for an Olympic victory in the horse race, take care to trumpet the fact that their victories were won with horses reared in the victor's stables; both probably date from the early fourth century.[76] Cleogenes' memorial speaks briefly of his own stable, while Damonon's goes into more detail, stating that on twenty-three occasions, at three local festivals, he won victories in the race for full-grown mares with horses "born from his own mares and his own stallion"; the formula is repeated for each festival. That earlier memorials do not make such claims indicates not that all horses were purchased in that period, but that the claim was not worth making because no, or almost no, horses were. By contrast, late in the fifth century, to win with horses that one had bred and raised in one's own stables had become a special source of pride. Although he is concerned primarily with war horses, it is surely also significant that Xenophon, writing in this same period, gives considerable advice to owners on buying horses, both unbroken and broken, but none on breeding them.[77]

The memorials' representation of these racehorses is still profoundly ideological, however. The horses may indeed have been permanently connected to their owners and even honored by them, but the portrait given of their connection is selective. Horseracing is represented as a drama in which only two figures are involved, the horse and the owner; yet there were many people who mediated this relationship: jockeys, grooms, trainers, stable masters, and a manager. Hieron's relationship with Pherenicus was enduring, but not intimate; if the horse was still alive in 467, he did not weep at his master's death.

Memorials for victories in the horse race are thus organized around the same problem as memorials for chariot victories, commodification. These memorials, however, although often composed by the same artists, employ a different strategy from the memorials for chariot victories: they raise the profile of the racehorse, often to the extent of marking it as the victor, to emphasize its special connection to the owner. Elements of this strategy can be seen in a few memorials for other equestrian victories: Cleosthenes' memorial named the horses in his chariot team, and Hagesias' mules were said to know how to lead the way.[78] Nevertheless, there is a clear distinction to be drawn between the ways in which memorials represent chariot (and mule-cart) victories and the ways in which they represent victories in the horse race.

Why, then, did these memorials follow a different tack? The answer is surely that they could. A successful ideology is not created without reference to reality, but adapts itself to the material that is available, making use of what is to its advantage. Horse races differ from chariot races in two significant ways: first, jockeys are youths, unlike charioteers; second, only one horse is involved in each entry in a horse race. It is much more convincing to represent a single racehorse as making all the important decisions, and keeping safe its youthful jockey, than a team of four horses. Stories such as that of Aura are simply more credible than the equivalent story would be of a chariot team, and it can cause no surprise that no anecdote exists that tells how a chariot team threw its charioteer, made it round the twelve laps of the Olympic course, and came in first. Oddly enough, one such anecdote does survive about the Roman circus, a survival made even odder by the adulation normally accorded to charioteers in this rather different context: the Elder Pliny relates how a chariot team in the Secular Games of 47 C.E. threw its charioteer at the start of the race and then did everything "which they would have done with a most skillful charioteer controlling them," that is, completed the fourteen laps of the circus without hitting the turning post, crashing into another chariot, or letting another chariot win.[79] Stories such as this can, then, find enough life to circulate, but the obstacles they face are significant; the story of Aura, although not without its own absurdities, is considerably more credible.

PART II

ATHLETIC TRAINERS

6

MORE MISSING PERSONS

The victory of Glaucus of Carystus in the men's boxing in 520 was commemorated by both a victory ode and a dedication at Olympia. The ode was composed soon after the victory by Simonides, and the dedication, the work of Glaucias of Aegina, was made, presumably after Glaucus' death, by his son.[1] The dedication consisted of a statue that represented Glaucus in the act of sparring. Such a representation seems to have been extremely rare, if not unique; in this period, boxers (as well as other victors in the combat sports) were usually depicted at rest, with one hand reaching out in a prayer of thanks, as Diagoras of Rhodes, victor in 464, and with the other hand perhaps holding a boxing thong, as Diagoras' son, Acusilaos, victor in 448.[2] Glaucus' unusual statue was surely intended to highlight his technical skill as a boxer, and indeed immediately after describing the statue's posture, Pausanias notes, presumably following the comments of his guides at Olympia, that Glaucus "was by nature the most skilled of his contemporaries at sparring" (ἦν ἐπιτηδειότατος τῶν κατ' αὐτὸν χειρονομῆσαι πεφυκώς).[3]

Glaucus' statue does not, however, fit with the famous anecdote that Pausanias relates:

This Carystian was a son of Demylus, and they say that at first he worked the land. But one day, when the ploughshare fell out of the plough, he fixed it to the plough using his hand instead of a hammer. Somehow Demylus saw what his son did, and so brought him to Olympia to box. There Glaucus, because he was not experienced in combat, was wounded by his opponents, and when he was boxing with the last one left of them, he seemed to be giving up under the number of wounds. They say that his father shouted out,

"Son, the plough-shot!" Accordingly, he struck his opponent a more violent blow and immediately won the victory.

(6.10.1–2)

The same Glaucus who was represented at Olympia as the most skilled of boxers (and whom Pausanias represents as skilled "by nature") is here represented as an athlete inexperienced in boxing who won his Olympic victory simply by virtue of brute strength and his father's encouragement.

Pausanias does not seem to notice how badly the anecdote fits with the statue; all that intervenes between the anecdote and the description of the statue is the impressive list of Glaucus' victories at the other Panhellenic games, two at the Pythian, eight at the Nemean, and eight more at the Isthmian. The lack of fit is striking, however, particularly because around Pausanias' time there was in circulation a second version of the plough-shot story which fit much better with the statue. In this version of the anecdote, related by Philostratus, there is no suggestion that Glaucus was inexperienced in boxing; and, when he was at the point of conceding to his opponent, it was not his father who called on him to use the "plough-shot" but his trainer, one Tisias.[4] This version still emphasizes Glaucus' great strength, but it does not imply that he had no skill; indeed, it makes it clear that Glaucus was trained in boxing, not simply taken from a farm and dropped in the ring at Olympia. His Olympic victory becomes the result of the formidable strength of a trained boxer.

Philostratus' version of the anecdote also avoids a second problem created by the version that circulated at Olympia. The Olympic anecdote suggests that Glaucus won his victory as a boy. This is his debut in competitive boxing, and he is referred to by his father as a παῖς (ὦ παῖ, τὴν ἀπ' ἀρότρου, "Son, the plough-shot!").[5] Yet Glaucus surely won his victory in the open category. Pausanias invariably makes it clear when the victor being commemorated is a boy, and here he does not say that the victor won the boys' contest;[6] moreover, it is surely impossible that someone who only won a boys' contest at Olympia would have become such a legendary boxer.[7] The statue itself must have made it clear that Glaucus was a man, not a youth, and so the suggestion in the Olympic anecdote that Glaucus was a boy represents a second source of conflict between anecdote and statue. Philostratus' version, of course, creates no such conflict; there is no suggestion that this is Glaucus' first fight, and, because the father is replaced by the trainer, the shout of encouragement becomes merely "The plough-shot" ("τὰν ἀπ' ἀρότρου"). According to the Olympic version of the anecdote, Glaucus' only Olympic victory is his first victory on the circuit, and a victory in the boys' division; as Philostratus has it, the victory can be understood as a victory against all comers, and the pinnacle of Glaucus' fine career.

The version of the anecdote preserved in Philostratus points to the source of the problems of the Olympic version – a desire to erase the trainer's contribution to the athlete's victory. It is the Olympic version's use of the father that generates the awkward features of the anecdote – the exaggerated emphasis on Glaucus' lack of skill and the suggestion that Glaucus was competing against the boys, both of which were refuted by the statue that the guides probably stood before as they told the anecdote. That this awkwardness was tolerated, given that it would have been avoided by a second version of the anecdote circulating in this period, needs explanation, and the explanation must be that the Olympic version placed a higher value on excluding the trainer, the only significant difference between the two versions, than on maintaining the coherence of the anecdote with the monument.

At Olympia this desire to erase the work of the trainer is far from unusual, although it rarely results in such serious incoherence. The guides' anecdote imitates the practice of the dedications made there, and indeed of victory memorials generally. For, just as most charioteers were excluded from the victory record, so were most trainers, and, as with the anecdote told about Glaucus to those who viewed his statue, this exclusion was also not a casual act of forgetting, but a purposive erasure.

This may seem an absurd contention. Pindar, after all, names a number of trainers in his odes, especially in odes composed for youths who were victorious in the combat sports. In fact, so regular is his practice of naming a trainer in such odes that it has been suggested that the presence of a trainer might be used to determine whether an ode for a boxer, wrestler, or pancratiast is for a youth or an adult.[8] In this instance, however, Pindar is not representative of the majority of victory memorials, and, even with Pindar's odes, the picture is more complicated. Although Pindar does name trainers in six odes (or pairs of odes), this does not comprise all the odes he composed for victors in the youths' combat sports. Among odes for such victors, trainers are named in *Olympians* 8 and 10, and *Nemeans* 4, 5, and 6, but not in *Pythian* 8 or *Isthmian* 8, both of which undoubtedly celebrate youths.[9] The victor celebrated in *Pythian* 8 is addressed as a youth when Pindar speaks of the song he owes him for his victory (ὦ παῖ, 33),[10] and the reference to the victor's "age-mates" (ἁλικίᾳ, 1, ἁλίκων, 65b) and "youthful prime" (ἥβαν, 70) make it certain that the victor in *Isthmian* 8 is not an adult. As Pfeijffer argues, the reference to an earlier victory as a child (68) makes it clear that he is not a παῖς either, so that the ode must celebrate a victor in the ἀγένειος, or beardless, category that some festivals inserted between the categories of παῖς and adult.[11] In addition, although *Isthmian* 6, which is almost universally agreed to be for a boy,[12] does name a trainer, it does not name the real trainer. In place of the trainer's name, Pindar offers the father's. The father was certainly not Phylacidas' trainer; his older brother was trained by the trainer named in *Nemean* 5, and one cannot believe that, if the father had the ability to coach the younger son to victory, he would not have coached the older.[13] On the surface, therefore, *Isthmian* 6 would seem to belong with those odes that name the trainer but in fact belongs with *Pythian* 8 and *Isthmian* 8 in omitting him from the victory record.

Pindar, therefore, does name trainers used to gain victories in the youths' combat sports, but he does so selectively. Yet in naming any trainers at all, Pindar is clearly the exception; if we turn to other memorials for victories in the youths' combat sports, the absence of the trainer is striking.

Bacchylides' habit seems to have been not to name the trainer; he composed odes for three victories by youths in the combat sports, and only one names the trainer.[14] Moreover, it is possible that in this ode Bacchylides was directly influenced by Pindar's practice, because Pindar celebrated the same victory and named the trainer in the ode he composed for it, *Nemean* 5. The dedications made at the site of the victory named the trainers even less than Bacchylides: there is no evidence that any trainer was named in a dedicatory inscription. Pausanias speaks of at least eight dedications at Olympia from this period that commemorate boys' victories in boxing, wrestling, and pancration but gives no indication that a trainer was named on any of the monuments.[15]

Pausanias is, in general, a reliable guide to these monuments,[16] and his silence in this particular case has been vindicated by the excavations at Olympia. Remains of a number of the inscriptions that accompanied these statues have been unearthed, and the fragments confirm that the monuments did not name trainers. Thus, the dedication of Tellon of Oresthas, victor in the boys' boxing in 472, names, in addition to the victor and his hometown, only Zeus and Tellon's father;[17] that of Cyniscus of Mantinea, victor in the same event around the second quarter of the fifth century, names only his father (who shared his name);[18] and that of Charmides of Elis, also a victor in the boys' boxing, around the middle of the fifth century, names only Olympia itself.[19]

Evidence of what the dedications made at sanctuaries other than Olympia for victories in the youths' combat sports in this period looked like is poor, but what remains is consistent with the practice at Olympia. Fragments of two memorials have been discovered on the Athenian acropolis. The first commemorated a youthful victory of Callias, the son of Didymias, and the victory was most likely in pancration or wrestling; as an adult, Callias won all four Panhellenic crowns in the pancration.[20] The second fragment contains enough of the inscription to reveal that it was part of a dedication on behalf of a boy's victory in a combat sport, but the victor's name does not survive.[21] In neither inscription is there any evidence that the trainer was named, but large parts of both are missing.

Nevertheless, it is at least clear from the blanket silence maintained at Olympia that, in naming a number of trainers, Pindar's odes are exceptional. Outside of his odes, only one trainer is named in at least eleven memorials for youths that won in wrestling, boxing, or pancration. But, even including Pindar's odes, trainers of youths who were victorious in the combat events were lucky to be mentioned in their memorials: of the nineteen memorials that survive for such victories, only six name the trainer.[22]

Although mostly excluded from the victory record, those who trained youths for competition in the combat sports were, in fact, well remembered compared with trainers of other sorts; no trainer who trained youths for events other than wrestling, boxing, or pancration, is named in an extant victory memorial.

The pentathlon offers the most surprising silence here. The final event of the pentathlon was wrestling, and, just as those who competed in wrestling itself needed coaching, so did the pentathletes. Moreover, the three field events in the pentathlon, the javelin, the discus, and the long jump were all technically demanding sports, for which we would expect a competitor to be trained. The technical demands of throwing a discus or javelin are clear enough, but the long jump also required the athlete to become proficient in the use of equipment: unlike in the modern event, the jumpers carried weights, which they swung to extend the length of their jumps.[23]

Numerous vases that date from the middle of the sixth century through the middle of the fifth support the presumption that penth-athletes were trained in the field events. Trainers are usually clearly distinguished from athletes: each wears a wreath on his head and a cloak, draped over one shoulder, and each carries a stick, often forked, which on occasion is waved at an athlete. The trainer is by no means a staple in scenes depicting long jumpers, discus throwers, and javelin throwers (there are huge numbers of such scenes),[24] but he is certainly common enough: trainers appear with long jumpers, discus throwers, and javelin throwers on numerous vases from the late archaic period through to the middle of the fifth century. To pick out one example: a red-figure kylix in Boston from about 500 shows a trainer on both sides: one trainer corrects a long jumper in midflight with his stick, while the other corrects a discus thrower who seems to be getting set for a throw.[25] Care should be taken not to read these scenes as unmediated representations of reality; just as the ubiquitous scenes of hunting on vases should not be taken as evidence that aristocrats spent much of their leisure time engaged in that pursuit,[26] so these scenes should not be taken as evidence that aristocratic youths trained regularly in gymnastics. Nevertheless, the inclusion of the trainers in the scenes cannot be discounted completely. At the least, the trainer must have served as a symbol of training, indicating that the activities engaged in took place in the context of some schooling in that event, whether with an individual trainer or in some more communal context.

Although it was possible at some festivals to compete separately in the discus, long jump, or javelin, most of the vases probably represent pentathletes.[27] The major festivals did not offer separate competitions in these events, and the evidence of the vases themselves often points toward the pentathlon. Some of the athletes named on the vases can be easily identified as pentathletes: a Phayllos appears with a javelin on an early fifth century red-figure psykter in Boston,[28] but on three other vases he carries a discus.[29] This Phayllos should be identified with a known pentathlete, Phayllos of Croton, famous not only for winning three victories at Delphi, two of them in the pentathlon, but also for equipping and commanding a ship at Salamis.[30] The vases also suggest more generally that the pentathlon is their concern. Nine of the vases cited earlier depict more than one of its events, and three add to the scene a flute player, which seems to have been a sign of the pentathlon; at Olympia a flute player, and seemingly a flute player of great distinction, accompanied the event.[31]

No certain memorials for youth pentathletes remain, but there are two strong candidates. Pindar wrote an ode for a victor in the pentathlon at Nemea, Sogenes of Aegina, whom most commentators, following the scholia and the title of the ode in the manuscripts, see as a boy.[32] The scholia are, however, confused on other details, such as the date of the ode, and there is nothing in the ode that explicitly identifies Sogenes as a boy. Ilja Pfeijffer argues that without such an explicit identification, the victor must be classed as an adult; yet there are some victory odes that do not explicitly identify the victor as a youth, and although the reference to the victor's "youthful prime" (ἥβᾳ, *Ne.* 7.99) does not say that the victor is actually in this prime at the time of the victory, it certainly implies this.[33] Indeed, as Pfeijffer argues earlier,[34] a reference to the victor's prime at a festival with more than one youth category may indicate that Sogenes won the pentathlon in the "beardless" category. It seems likely, therefore, that the ode does celebrate a youth pentathlete, and certainly no trainer is named.

The fate of the trainer is more complex in a second possible memorial, however. A vase that seems to commemorate a victory in the pentathlon does represent the work of the trainer, but, although it names the victor, it does not name the trainer or trainers involved in his victory. A black-figure neck amphora now in Würzburg, the vase was produced around the end of the sixth century, and it depicts four of the events of the pentathlon on its two sides: two sprinters and a long jumper on the front, and a discus thrower and two javelin throwers on the reverse. In addition, a bearded trainer appears on both sides, with the sprinters on the front and the discus thrower on the back. Of the athletes some are beardless and some are not, and below the two sprinters, one of whom is bearded and one not, is the inscription νικᾶς Πολυμένον ("You win, Polymenon") (Figure 11).[35] The inscription mirrors that on the victory vase of Dysniketos considered in the previous chapter, and it is safe to conclude that this was a memorial specially commissioned to celebrate a victory won by Polymenon in the pentathlon. Polymenon was probably Athenian, but it cannot be determined whether he was a youth or an adult; on the side which bears the inscription, two of the athletes are bearded and one not.

In addition to *Nemean* 7, which most likely does celebrate a youth, a second memorial for a youth pentathlete may, therefore, survive. Neither memorial names the trainer, but the vase does at least explicitly represent his work.

As the Würzburg neck amphora suggests, trainers also coached youths in the running events. Although Olympia held only one running event for boys, the sprint, other festivals offered various distances.[36] As Gardiner makes clear, there were plenty of skills for runners to learn in the different events, including a good start, tight turns in the longer races, and the form appropriate to the distance being run; Panathenaic amphorae clearly distinguish the style of sprinters from that of long-distance runners.[37] Some competitors may have learned such skills by observation, but it is clear that others had a formal training. On a handful of vases from the late archaic and early classical period, trainers can be found with runners, which suggests that running, as much as discus throwing or wrestling, was an object of training.[38] Interestingly, trainers are more commonly found with those runners engaged in the race in armor,[39] an event often thought of as less specialist than the others.[40]

As we might expect, Pausanias does not name any trainers used by runners in the late archaic or early classical period, but he does imply their use in the fourth century. Record of the statue of Deinolochus

11. A trainer, a long jumper, two sprinters, and a discus. Black-figure neck amphora from Vulci, obverse, ca. 500. Photograph courtesy of K. Oehrlein.

of Elis is accompanied by the story that his mother was motivated to have her son "trained" (ἠσκήθη) when she dreamt soon after his birth that he had a wreath on his head. Deinolochus went on to win an Olympic victory in the boys category, and the event he won was the stadion.[41]

The extraordinary success of certain towns and cities in running events should also be credited in part to the availability of superior trainers. Adult athletes from Croton won eleven of the twenty-six stadion crowns between 588 and 488, taking the top seven places at one Olympiad. A key factor in such success may have been financial support for the athletes, as well as civic pride and tradition, but the presence, and maintenance, of excellent trainers must also have played a part; Croton's trainers may have been especially successful because they were versed in medicine and dietetics.[42] To judge by the confusing traditions concerning the long-distance runner Ladas, Mantinea may also have been attractive for its running trainers in a slightly later period, the second quarter of the fifth century. Ladas was famous less for his Olympic victory than for what came next: he died as he traveled away from the contest, exhausted by his efforts, and was buried where he fell. The victory was then commemorated by a striking statue commissioned from Myron that represented him in action.[43] Although buried in Sparta, he seems to have been an Argive citizen (his statue was seen by Pausanias in the temple of Apollo Lykios in Argos); at the same time, he seems to have trained in a stadium, popularly known as the "stadium of Ladas," somewhere between Mantinea and Orchomenos in Arcadia.[44] That an Argive would train in Mantinea needs explaining, and, as with Croton, the attraction of this training facility must have been in part the personnel rather than the physical plant. It is also noticeable that Mantinea, a relatively insignificant Peloponnesian town, is disproportionately successful in the youth contests at Olympia, even allowing for its proximity to the place of competition: at least three Mantinean youths won victories at Olympia in the quarter century between 484 and 460, all in boxing.[45] At any rate, if adult runners were trained in Croton and Mantinea, youths surely were also.

There is, then, good evidence that youths preparing for running contests used trainers as much as their peers in the combat sports, but no trainer is named in the memorials that survive for youths who won footraces in the late archaic or early classical period. There are at least five such memorials: four odes, two from Pindar and two, for the same victory, from Bacchylides, and one dedication mentioned by Pausanias.[46] In addition, most commentators accept that Pindar's *Pythian* 11, which also has no mention of a trainer, is for a boy victor in the Pythian sprint.[47]

The evidence suggests, therefore, that those who trained youths for events other than the combat sports consistently had their names omitted from victory memorials, including Pindar's odes. This constitutes one of the two largest silences concerning trainers in the memorials; the second concerns those trainers who trained adults. That adults used trainers is rarely considered, but it is at the least prima facie likely; all the gymnastic events were technically demanding, the pentathlon, wrestling, and pancration especially so, and these demands did not disappear when one entered the open competitions. As Pfeijffer notes, Pindar praises an adult athlete's older brother for training him for his pancration victory, and, whatever we make of the veracity of this specific claim, it is clear that the simple fact that an adult had a trainer is not unusual or embarrassing.[48] Anecdotes also support the supposition that adults used trainers. Philostratus' anecdote concerning the boxer Glaucus of Carystus has already been mentioned: according to Philostratus, Glaucus was competing in the men's competition at Olympia, when he was encouraged by his trainer, Tisias. Philostratus describes a similar incident from earlier in the sixth century when Arrichion of Phigalia won the pancration at Olympia in 564.[49] Arrichion had won the pancration twice before, but in 564, according to Philostratus, the denouement was particularly memorable: when Arrichion was on the point of conceding, his trainer, Eryxias, cried out, "What a fine winding-sheet it is not to have conceded at Olympia!" Arrichion persevered and won, but died at the very moment of victory. That Arrichion was an adult is clear: this is his third victory, and the pancration was not offered at Olympia for boys until 200. Even more significant is the anecdote's implication that the use of trainers was entirely regular, at least in the time during which this anecdote was circulated, for athletes at the top of their events, not just for those seeking to rise up the ranks.[50]

Vases from the late sixth and early fifth century also suggest that adults had trainers. As noted earlier, a number of vases depict hoplite runners with trainers, and hoplite races do not seem to have been open to youths.[51] This may make hoplite races a special case (in so far as the competitors would not have been trained in the event as youths), but bearded sprinters are also pictured with trainers on vases.[52] Further, as argued earlier, Croton and Mantinea seem to have provided trainers for adult sprinters in the late archaic and early classical periods, respectively. Bearded discus throwers and long jumpers are also pictured with trainers.[53]

There is also some suggestion from vases that adult wrestlers, boxers, and pancratiasts used trainers; bearded combatants are pictured grappling in front of trainer-like figures.[54] Such figures are often thought of as judges or umpires, however, because they appear on the reverses of prize Panathenaic vases when combat sports are depicted; in these cases, it is clear that the figure represents the adjudicant of the bout, not the trainer of one of the athletes.[55] Yet it would be wrong to conclude from this that those trainer-like figures that appear with adults on other vases represent only umpires. Outside of formal competitions, it is probably not legitimate to draw such a clear distinction between umpires and trainers; indeed, such a distinction is probably motivated by the presumption that adults did not have trainers. Trainers and umpires were surely represented in identical ways on vases because they were often indistinguishable in real life; as well as offering advice and coaching to their charges, trainers must have refereed practice bouts in wrestling schools, punishing foul play and marking falls or submissions just as an umpire would have in formal competitions. Other than the Panathenaic vases, therefore, those vases that depict adults competing in front of trainer-like figures probably represent a mix of formal combats taking place in competitions before the eyes of an umpire and informal combats refereed by a trainer who took the role of an umpire during the course of a practice bout.

Evidence suggests, therefore, that adult athletes also used trainers; some adults may have gained success without trainers, but most surely employed their services. Moreover, to be successful almost all of those who did not use trainers as adults must have used them as youths. It is, perhaps, just possible that someone without any training might win a running event in a minor contest, but the idea that someone might win one of the most technically complex events such as boxing at a major festival without any training, an idea that Pausanias peddles with Glaucus of Carystus, is absurd.

For almost all victorious athletes, therefore, training must have been part of their experience, probably both as adults and youths, but certainly as youths, yet this is not reflected in their memorials. Of at least forty-seven basically intact memorials for gymnastic victors from the second quarter of the sixth century to the middle of the fifth, none names a trainer who trained the adult; the forty-seven memorials consist of fourteen odes of Pindar and Bacchylides and thirty-three dedications made at Olympia, Athens, and elsewhere.[56] Many of the dedications have turned up in excavations, but for others we must again rely on the assumption that, if Pausanias makes no mention of a trainer, then no trainer is recorded. Again, however, a number of the inscriptions from the dedications described by Pausanias have been uncovered by excavations, and none of these names a trainer, so this is a safe assumption.[57] Furthermore, of these forty-seven memorials, only one names a trainer from the victor's youth, Pindar's *Isthmian* 4, for Melissus of Thebes, who won his Isthmian victory in the pancration. Toward the end of the ode, Pindar lists Melissus' career victories, and it is in the context of the victories that he won as a youth that the trainer is named.[58]

This survey demonstrates that trainers were, for the most part, not named in victory memorials. Some were named in odes written for youth victors in the combat sports, but trainers' names were excluded almost entirely from all other memorials – dedications for youth victories in the combat sports and memorials of all sorts both for youth victories in the running events and pentathlon and for adult victories in all gymnastic events. In addition, a trainer is represented in only one of the memorials in which he is not named, the vase that commemorates Polymenon's victory in the pentathlon. No ode describes the victor's training by his trainer, and none of the dedications seems to have included a trainer in the statue group. This is at least certain for the dedications made at Olympia: Pausanias describes one dedication, of Cratinus of Aegeira, "the most beautiful man of his time and the most technically skilled wrestler," that did in fact include a statue of the trainer, but it is from the third century, and the inclusion of the trainer required, according to Pausanias, special dispensation from the Elean officials.[59] Whether Pausanias' information is correct or not, the fact that this story was circulated at Olympia indicates that the inclusion of the trainer in a statue group at Olympia was exceptional. It is probably safe to assume that dedications at other sanctuaries followed the same form, whether because of general custom or local rules.

That the trainer was omitted from the majority of memorials does not necessarily mean that he was purposefully excluded, rather than simply passed over. There are two reasons to think that the omission is significant, however. First, the alternative accounts of victories preserved in anecdotes suggest that trainers played a prominent role in the larger discursive context in which the memorials were commissioned. Diogenes Laertius speaks of a trainer, a Pythagoras of Samos, controlling the diet of his pupil, Eurymenes,[60] and, as seen earlier, Philostratus speaks of two trainers from the archaic period, Glaucus' trainer Tisias and Arrichion of Phigalia's trainer Eryxias, who were present while their athletes competed. In the case of Tisias, Pausanias' competing account of Glaucus' victory allows us to see that the trainer was a contested element in these descriptions of victory. Indeed, these anecdotal traditions often make the trainer crucial to the actual winning of the victory, rather than, say, responsible for the fine condition and excellent skills of the victor: without their trainers' encouragement during the bout itself, both Glaucus and Arrichion would have conceded to their opponents. Similar stories are found elsewhere in Pausanias[61] and in the Pindaric scholia.[62] Whether these stories accurately describe the bouts is unimportant; what they demonstrate is that there were in circulation plausible narratives that made trainers responsible for athletes' victories. When such stories began to circulate is more difficult to determine: all the sources that include them belong to the Hellenistic and Roman periods, and it is possible that they are all late inventions. Nevertheless, it is also possible that they accurately reflect the anecdotes that surrounded archaic athletics.

The second reason to think that trainers were far from anonymous in the late archaic and early classical period is simply that trainers were prominent enough in the minds of patrons and artists to be included in some memorials. As noted earlier, seven memorials name trainers; six of them celebrate victories by youths in combat sports, and one celebrates a victory by an adult but names the trainer in the context of a catalogue of his youth victories. In addition, the victory vase of Polymenon depicts a trainer on front and back. Although some of these trainers were, as shown in subsequent chapters, well known, not all were, and so these namings cannot simply be put down to the peculiarities of the trainers named. The omission of the trainers from the other memorials thus cannot easily be read as an unconscious neglect. Moreover, as Chapter 9 argues, even when the trainers are not named, the concerns they raise shape many of the memorials that do not actually name them.

There is thus good reason to think that trainers, much as charioteers, are actually missing from the memorials. The central reason for their exclusion is the same as for the charioteers: they were mostly professionals who sold their services for a fee and did not maintain an enduring relationship with their charges or patrons. Like the use of professional charioteers, the use of professional trainers validated a mode of exchange inimical to the aristocrats' power and sense of community and challenged the idea that the qualities necessary for victory were inherited. The circulation of trainers and the fact that they were pursued by many clients suggested that the qualities that were crucial for victory in the gymnastic events came from having the right trainer, not from being born into the right family; that these qualities were learned, not inherited. Qualities such as strength and speed that had easily been seen as inherited began to be seen in a new light, as the result of training, and, at the same time, what was key to victory was reevaluated; those qualities that were more easily seen as portable, such as skill and technique, began to be seen as the real reasons for success.

The anxieties generated by these changes are clearly reflected in gnomes from Pindar's odes. In a contradictory double movement, gnomes scorn the athlete "with taught abilities" as "an obscure man, blowing here and there, and never enter[ing] the competition with sure foot" (ὃς δὲ διδάκτ' ἔχει, ψεφεννὸς ἀνὴρ ἄλλοτ' ἄλλα πνέων οὔ ποτ' ἀτρεκεῖ / κατέβα ποδί, *Ne.* 3.41–2), while also representing "the skill of worse men" (ἀνδρῶν χειρόνων . . . τέχνᾳ, *Is.* 3/4.52–3) as a real threat to the superiority of those endowed with natural ability.[63] Aristocrats certainly did not expect that that an untutored talent could come home victorious, nor did they demand that athletes compete without any technique,[64] but they did distinguish among different types of teaching and different sorts of skill, albeit with little regard for reality. In so far as teaching was seen as endowing pupils with new abilities, and in so far as skill was seen as an ability that could be taught to those without natural talent, they were derided. But when teaching was seen as a process of confirming and bringing out what was already in a pupil and skill was seen as something primarily acquired through inheritance or something that complemented but did not challenge inherited abilities, both were entirely acceptable. Indeed, it might be more accurate to say that, as training and the skills it transmitted became increasingly commodified, they were not so much seen in a new light as radically altered in the aristocratic imagination. Where training by a family member or friend appeared as a kind of mentoring or modeling, a bringing out of what was already there, training by a professional appeared as a project of construction or fabrication, the insertion from the outside of something that was not there before and did not belong there; where the technique a family member or friend passed on appeared as a natural talent or at least a minor element in success, when taught by a professional it appeared a wholly new ability, portable and key to victory.[65]

Professional trainers thus represented a significant challenge to the aristocratic account of athletic victory, and so also to the aristocrats' basic justification of their privileged political position: if quality was not inherited, there was no reason power should be either. This challenge was met in part by stories such as that of Glaucus of Carystus told at Olympia, which Philostratus suggests follows a common pattern. He names four athletes but suggests that there were many more who became strong by laboring in the countryside, "some carrying heavy weights, some competing in speed with horses and hares, some straightening and bending thick iron plate, some being yoked beside mighty wagon-pulling oxen, and some subduing bulls, some even lions."[66] Such stories of manual laborers who rise to the heights of athletic success paradoxically sustained the aristocratic ideology of victory because, although they admitted the presence of some talent outside of the aristocracy, they affirmed that natural abilities, especially strength and speed and not training and skill, were what mattered in gymnastic contests. But it was the victory memorials that offered the most sustained support of aristocratic ideology, some, like the stories of poor athletes making good, by excluding the trainer, and others by including the trainer, but disguising the fact that he was a professional and representing him as more of a mentor than a teacher.

7

MELESIAS

That Melesias is named in three of Pindar's odes does not occasion the surprise that it should. Pindar's odes tend to be read in isolation from the wider range of victory memorials, and consequently it seems normal that a trainer be named when an ode celebrates a youth that has won a victory in a combat sport.[1] Yet the survey of victory memorials in the previous chapter has shown that even the naming of a trainer in a memorial for such a victor is odd, and so we should ask why Melesias is named and what function his inclusion serves in each of the odes in which he is mentioned.

A study of the ways in which Melesias is represented will confirm the sketch offered at the close of the last chapter of why trainers generally were consigned to silence in victory memorials. In the three odes in which he is named, *Olympian* 8, *Nemean* 4, and *Nemean* 6, Melesias is represented as an insider, closely bound to the family or community in which he works; his training is presented as a kind of teaching that tests, directs, or models behavior; and the skills that he teaches and that his pupils use are either omitted from accounts of the victory or represented as inherited qualities. These representations serve as answers to, and so mark out, the problems that attended Melesias and his activities. Moreover, although Melesias was a highly successful trainer (which explains why he is one of the coaches that is named), these were problems that the vast majority of trainers in the late archaic and early classical period shared: most trainers were professionals employed by aristocrats, and, as professional trainers, they challenged the aristocrats' ideology of athletic success, by seeming to endow their pupils with ability, rather than to draw it out of them, and by raising the profile of skill and technique.

The pictures that Pindar offers of Melesias in the three odes in which he appears should be thought of as aggressive efforts to make the use of professional trainers conform with aristocratic ideology. The targets of these efforts are several: the victors who employed the trainers and whose identity was challenged by doing so; other aristocrats who opposed the use of these trainers; and those outside the aristocracy who had to be convinced that inherited qualities were still what determined athletic success. Although very different from the simple silence that most memorials deployed, the strategy of including a suitably reformed trainer served the same end: to save the use of trainers by patrons whose power and status might be threatened by it.

Probably the latest of the three odes that name Melesias, *Olympian* 8 is the most fulsome in its praise of the trainer, so much so, in fact, that ancient commentators concluded Melesias was a co-honorand of the ode.[2] The ode celebrates the Olympic victory of Alcimedon of Aegina,[3] won in the boys' wrestling contest, most likely in 460,[4] and it is after the mythical section of the ode that Pindar turns to praise Melesias:

> εἰ δ᾽ ἐγὼ Μελησίᾳ ἐξ ἀγενείων
>   κῦδος ἀνέδραμον ὕμνῳ,
> μὴ βαλέτω με λίθῳ τραχεῖ φθόνος·
> καὶ Νεμέᾳ γὰρ ὁμῶς
> ἐρέω ταύταν χάριν,
> τὰν δ᾽ ἔπειτ᾽ ἀνδρῶν μάχας[5]
> ἐκ παγκρατίου. τὸ διδάξασθαι δέ τοι
> εἰδότι ῥᾴτερον· ἄγνωμον δὲ τὸ μὴ προμαθεῖν·
> κουφότεραι γὰρ ἀπειράτων φρένες.
> κεῖνα δὲ κεῖνος ἂν εἴποι
> ἔργα περαίτερον ἄλλων, τίς τρόπος ἄνδρα προβάσει
> ἐξ ἱερῶν ἀέθλων
>   μέλλοντα ποθεινοτάταν δόξαν φέρειν.
> νῦν μὲν αὐτῷ γέρας Ἀλκιμέδων
> νίκαν τριακοστὰν ἑλών·

But if in my song I have run back to the glory of Melesias won from beardless youths, let not envy strike me with a rough stone. For I will speak of victories, both times won at Nemea, first in such a contest, and later gained from battling with men in the pancration. Teaching is indeed easier for one who knows; it is poor judgment not to learn beforehand, for more fickle are the minds of those who have not been tested. But that man, beyond others, may tell of those deeds, that way which will advance a man who intends to win from the holy games the glory that is most desired. Now Alcimedon has given him an honor, winning for him his thirtieth victory.

(*Ol.* 8.54–66)

The basic facts of Melesias' curriculum vitae threaten the meaning of any victory won by one of his charges. Although his record as an athlete – two Nemean victories, one of them in the adult division – is respectable, his record as a trainer is stunning.[6] Alcimedon's victory at Olympia is the thirtieth Panhellenic victory Melesias has presided over; that the victories were all in Panhellenic contests is made clear by the explicit reference in the preceding line to Melesias coaching athletes who sought glory "from holy games" (ἐξ ἱερῶν ἀέθλων, 64). Such a record was rarely amassed by individual athletes in this period: only one athlete, the wrestler Milo of Croton, is known to have reached thirty Panhellenic victories, winning thirty-two in total. Exceptional athletes such as Glaucus of Carystus, with nineteen victories in boxing, and Theagenes of Thasos, with twenty-four in boxing and pancration, fell well short of thirty,[7] and even those athletes dominant enough to win at all four Panhellenic festivals tended to accrue fewer than ten such victories in total.[8] The totals typically accrued by Aeginetan clans are harder to establish, but, given that Pindar takes care to mention that Alcimedon's victory is his clan's sixth (ἕκτος . . . στέφανος . . . φυλλοφόρων ἀπ' ἀγώνων, *Ol.* 8.76), the twenty-five of the Bassids and the thirty that seem to have been won by Teisias' family look especially impressive.[9]

Much cannot be known for certain about Melesias' training, but with such numbers it seems likely that he trained adults as well as youths,[10] trained several athletes concurrently, and worked as a trainer both of wrestlers and pancratiasts for many years.[11] Certainly, thirty is a large number of Panhellenic victories for Melesias to have collected, whatever the precise circumstances, and this impressive record might have seemed to contradict the meaning traditionally attached by the aristocracy to athletic victory. Melesias' success might well have suggested an alternative explanation for Alcimedon's victory, that it was primarily the result of the training he received from Melesias, not of the qualities he inherited from his family.

That Melesias was his trainer thus represented a potential challenge to the victor and his victory, and it is this challenge that *Olympian* 8 confronts. To sustain the idea that inherited qualities were central to Alcimedon's victory, the ode pursues two strategies: first, it locates Melesias in a relationship of gift exchange with the victor and, second, figures his teaching as something other than the conferring of particular abilities on the victor. These two strategies represent two sides of the same coin, because the aristocrats viewed the kind of teaching offered by professional trainers as different from that offered by trainers who did not work for a wage. Professional trainers were thought to make their pupils great athletes, whereas nonprofessionals seemed rather to reveal the quality that was naturally there. Thus, if Melesias was not a professional, he was the right type of teacher, and, if he was the right type of teacher, he was not a professional.

Melesias' relationship with Alcimedon is described as one based on the exchange of gifts at the very moment at which his curriculum vitae might suggest otherwise, the moment at which his thirty victories as a trainer are mentioned: νῦν μὲν αὐτῷ γέρας Ἀλκιμέδων/ νίκαν τριακοστὰν ἑλών· "Now Alcimedon has given him an honor, winning for him his thirtieth victory" (65–6).[12] Melesias' thirtieth victory as a trainer is itself represented as a gift (γέρας, 65) that is given by the victor to his coach when he wins; indeed, γέρας is an appropriate term for an especially enduring and significant gift.[13] The transformation of Melesias' wage into a large gift does not only hide that wage; it also entirely refigures Melesias' relationship to the victor's family. Melesias must have been hired by the head of Alcimedon's family, presumably his grandfather Timosthenes, to train his grandson,[14] but the exchange as it is depicted here is primarily between Melesias and Alcimedon. Furthermore, as a wage earner, Melesias was under an obligation to provide training to Alcimedon, but here it appears that Alcimedon is in the trainer's debt: the victory he wins for him appears to be a return for the gift of training that Melesias gave Alcimedon.

The ground has already been laid for the representation of the relationship between Melesias and Alcimedon as friendly rather than commercial. From the beginning of the ode, athletic victory has been carefully insulated from commodity exchange. Olympic victory is described there as a "bright honor" (γέρας . . . ἀγλαόν, 11) conferred by the Olympic grove, while the preceding gnome declares that success of any sort is a return for a man's piety toward the gods: ἄνεται δὲ πρὸς χάριν εὐσεβίας ἀνδρῶν λιταῖς· "Men's prayers are accomplished in gratitude for their piety" (8). Melesias' own victories at Nemea are described in the same terms: each victory is referred to briefly and simply as a "gift" (ταύταν χάριν, τὰν δ' ἔπειτ' [χάριν], 57–8). As often in Pindar, the precise nature of the exchange is left vague to emphasize the range of the relations that the victor belongs to: the victory is both a gift to the victor from the gods and a gift from the victor to his family, his friends, and the spectators.[15]

The relationship between Melesias and Alcimedon is also specifically foreshadowed in the mythical narrative of Apollo and Aeacus. Collaboration is certainly a major theme of this narrative. Aeacus, in some sense, helps his descendants capture the city through his fine, but fallible, construction,[16] but the most telling collaboration is the one that builds the walls. As the story is told in Homer, it is a tale of wage-earners cheated of their pay: Poseidon builds the walls under the direction of Laomedon while Apollo herds his cattle, all for a set wage (μισθῷ ἔπι ῥητῷ, *Il.* 21.445), but when the time comes for the two gods to be paid (μισθοῖο τέλος, 21.450), Laomedon does not honor the contract (βιήσατο μισθὸν, 21.451) and drives them off. In the version offered by Pindar, however, no trace of a wage remains; indeed, there is no trace of Laomedon. The gods seem to be in charge of the project, and, far from being summoned themselves, summon (καλέσαντο, 32) Aeacus to help them fulfil the requirement of fate that the city be sacked. Aeacus himself does not come as a wage laborer but as a fellow worker (συνεργόν, 32). Given that Apollo prefigures Melesias, who is represented as having some knowledge of the future later in the ode (62–4), whereas Aeacus as the founding hero of Aegina prefigures the Aeginetan Alcimedon,[17] it seems reasonable to see in the relationship between Apollo and Aeacus a representation of the relationship between Melesias and Alcimedon. It does not need adding how fanciful such a representation is: Melesias was a wage earner like the Apollo of the Iliadic version; he did not summon Alcimedon to work with him toward his thirtieth victory, but was himself summoned by Timosthenes.

That Melesias is not a professional also seems to be the implication of the ode's stress on Melesias' knowledge of wrestling. The mention of Melesias' two victories at Nemea may look like a claim that Melesias is an aristocrat, someone from a family with the quality to compete successfully at the highest levels, but, although his victories do indeed suggest this, their immediate function is to serve the gnome that follows: τὸ διδάξασθαι δέ τοι / εἰδότι ῥᾴτερον, "teaching is indeed easier for one who knows" (59–60). Melesias' success in Panhellenic competition provides the particular premise for an implied syllogism: given that the trainer Melesias knows his athletics and that proper teachers know what they teach, Melesias is a proper teacher.

It may seem otiose to insist that a successful trainer knows his discipline, but that Melesias' knowledge was real would have had a particular significance to Pindar's audience. Here Pindar taps into a nexus of associations that grew up in aristocratic discourse around the Sophists, the professional teachers in all parts of the Greek world who offered a vast variety of subjects to anyone who would pay for their instruction. Part of the Sophists' claim to fame was their professed polymathy. Hippias of Elis, who was perhaps active as early as 460, would apparently attend each Olympic festival and challenge all comers to question him about any subject. He was particularly known for his skills in mathematics, astronomy, poetry, and mnemonics, as well as for making everything that he wore on one occasion when he visited Olympia, including his cloak, tunic, shoes, ring, oil flask, and strigil.[18] Hippias was only the most extreme example of a general phenomenon: according to Plato, Hippias' older contemporary Protagoras found time among his studies of ethics and epistemology to write on wrestling.[19]

Such polymathy seems to have been condemned by aristocrats as a sham. The aristocrats certainly had plenty to fear from such teachers. Their philosophical speculations tended to undermine the idea that quality was inherited, and their practical teachings in rhetoric threatened the unity of the aristocratic classes by drawing students away from the traditional organs of aristocratic education and solidarity, the symposia and the gymnasia, and enabled some nonaristocratic students to challenge the power of the aristocrats in the various deliberative and judicial bodies in the cities.[20] Accordingly, the Sophists were attacked on various grounds, and one of these seems to have been that they did not really have knowledge of the subjects they professed. In Plato's *Sophist*, the stranger from Elea who leads the discussion lambastes the Sophists for their claim that they know and can teach everything, declaring that such knowledge is impossible and that those who lay claim to it must be fraudulent magicians.[21] This testimony comes from the fourth century, but this association between professional teachers and sham polymathy certainly makes sense of Pindar's stress on Melesias' knowledge. Melesias' genuine knowledge of wrestling does not so much mark him out as a master of his art as separate him from the class of professional teachers. That he is a teacher who knows his subject meant, at least to the aristocrats who dominated Pindar's audience, that he was not a professional.[22]

There was a certain logic to the association of a polymathy that was assumed to be a sham with professional teachers. The harder it is to master a given subject, the lengthier the relationship must be between pupil and teacher. Conversely, if a subject could be taught quickly, there was little chance of a lasting relationship developing between teacher and student, and it was precisely this brevity that marked the transaction between a professional teacher and his student as a commodity exchange. The focus on the objects of the exchange in preference to the parties to the exchange was obvious; a set fee was paid, and a lesson was provided in return for the fee. Given their presumption that a professed polymath's knowledge was either shallow or fake, aristocratic critics could thus conclude that polymaths were professionals.

At the same time as the ode separates Melesias from professional trainers, it also offers a picture of his training that is appropriate to a nonprofessional trainer. Initially, Pindar represents the training as a kind of examination: ἄγνωμον δὲ τὸ μὴ προμαθεῖν· / κουφότεραι γὰρ ἀπειράτων φρένες. "It is poor judgment not to learn beforehand, for more fickle are the minds of those who have not been tested" (60–1). Here learning is assimilated to being tested (πεῖρα): learning beforehand is a wise thing to do because testing in general is desirable, and learning constitutes one such test. This transformation may seem to misrepresent what a trainer does, but it does promote an idea of training that is clearly compatible with an aristocratic ideology of inheritance. Because all the trainer does is test what is present in his pupils, that which is responsible for a youth's victory is present in him prior to his training.

That these gnomes appeal to aristocratic sensibilities is clear both from the words that Pindar selects and from the implication that the desirability of testing is self-evident. The πεῖρα, or "test," was central to the aristocratic ideology of excellence. Although itself a performance, it reveals the underlying essence of the performer, providing a means to distinguish those who are really of high quality from those who only appear to be so through cunning, dissimulation, or learning. Pindar often refers to the games themselves as a "test,"[23] and an elegy that appears twice in the *Theognidea* praises "testing" (πεῖρα) as the best thing that exists because it can separate those who appear to be noble from those who really are.[24] The second time the elegy appears, this testing is illustrated by appeal to the touchstone's ability to demonstrate the purity of gold when rubbed against it, further underlining that what the test does is reveal who you are already, not demonstrate what you have learned.[25] ἄγνωμον ("poor judgment"), too, is resonant. On the evidence of the *Theognidea*, γνώμη was the usual term for an aristocrat's good judgment.[26] To declare that it is ἄγνωμον for a student "not to learn beforehand" is, therefore, to imply that such learning is fully consonant with the principles of aristocratic ethics, not just that it makes sense generally.[27]

Melesias' testing of his pupils allows him, Pindar suggests, to prophesy victory: κεῖνα δὲ κεῖνος ἂν εἴποι / ἔργα περαίτερον ἄλλων, τίς τρόπος ἄνδρα προβάσει / ἐξ ἱερῶν ἀέθλων μέλλοντα ποθεινοτάταν δόξαν φέρειν. "But that man, beyond others, may tell of those deeds, that way which will advance a man who intends to win from the holy games the glory that is most desired" (62–4). As Kevin Crotty notes, this description of the trainer fits him into a sequence of prophets that begins with the prophets at Olympia in the proem:[28]

> Μᾶτερ ὦ χρυσοστεφάνων ἀέθλων, Οὐλυμπία,
> δέσποιν᾽ ἀλαθείας, ἵνα μάντιες ἄνδρες
> ἐμπύροις τεκμαιρόμενοι παραπειρῶν-
>   ται Διὸς ἀργικεραύνου,
> εἴ τιν᾽ ἔχει λόγον ἀνθρώπων πέρι
> μαιομένων μεγάλαν
> ἀρετὰν θυμῷ λαβεῖν,
> τῶν δὲ μόχθων ἀμπνοάν.

Mother of gold-garlanded games, Olympia, queen of truth, where mantic men, judging from burnt offerings, make trial of Zeus of the bright lightning, to see if he has any word about mortals who strive in their hearts to win great distinction and a rest from their toils.

(*Ol.* 8.1–7)

The similarity between Melesias and these prophets, as Pindar presents both, is clear. Both test someone (ἀπειράτων, 61; παραπειρῶνται, 3) to gain information (εἴποι, 62; λόγον, 4) about the success of athletes who eagerly desire glory (μέλλοντα ποθεινοτάταν δόξαν φέρειν, 64; μαιομένων μεγάλαν / ἀρετὰν, 5–6) at the games. The differences are also clear: the prophets at Olympia are presented as a group and struggle to obtain accurate information through their testing, whereas Melesias rises above his group (περαίτερον ἄλλων, 63) because his testing is productive. In this respect, Melesias is much more like Apollo in the central mythical section of the ode. When three snakes leap on the walls of Troy that Apollo, Poseidon, and Aeacus have just completed, but only one succeeds in entering the city, the portent sent by Zeus speaks so clearly to Apollo that he is able to prophesy what will happen to the walls in the succeeding years (43–4).[29] Melesias' training is thus represented not only as a kind of prophecy, but as a particularly successful kind that elevates him above the struggling prophets at Olympia to an Apolline level.

Crotty comments that training can be thought of as a kind of prophecy "inasmuch as it provides some foreknowledge of the outcome, enabling athletes to be confident of their skills and strength,"[30] and this idea has a surface plausibility. This plausibility is, moreover, strengthened by the elegance with which the identification of training as a kind of prophecy is encouraged. The description of Melesias' activity is quite reasonable; a trainer would tell of "those deeds, that way which will advance a man" (κεῖνα . . . / ἔργα . . . , τίς τρόπος ἄνδρα προβάσει, 62–3). But the use of the simple future (προβάσει), rather than an indefinite or potential construction ("those deeds, that way which would/could advance a man"), and the centrality of the theme of prophecy to the ode, encourage an unthinking identification of this activity with prophecy. Yet although on the surface the identification is plausible, it is, in fact, incoherent and misleading. To effect this identification, Pindar must elide two different types of knowing, knowing how to win and knowing who will win. A good trainer gives an athlete confidence by teaching him how to win, but knowing how to win in no way constitutes a foreknowledge of the outcome.

By eliding these two types of knowledge Pindar sustains the idea of training conveyed through its representation as a form of testing. Training is stripped of content; the job of a wrestling trainer is not to teach a pupil the moves that might enable him to win, but to test the pupil to see when he will win, if indeed he will. A trainer must scrutinize his charge – the signs he reads are not burnt offerings, but the external physical form (εἶδος, 19) of the athlete[31] – yet there is certainly no work to perform on the body of the athlete; indeed, it is up to the athlete to pass the test of training as much as that of competition. The trainer is no more responsible for an athlete's success at Olympia than are the prophets who try to predict it.

The praise of Melesias in *Olympian* 8 is thus organized around the troubling fact that Melesias is a professional teacher of wrestling. The praise seeks to hide this fact by depicting Melesias as the sort of trainer appropriate to an aristocrat, a trainer bound to his pupil through a relationship of gift exchange and a trainer who tests and scrutinizes his pupil, rather than making a winner out of him. One further anxiety that shapes the representation of Melesias' training, and of wrestling itself, in this ode has yet to be noted, however, and that is the central importance of skill to a successful wrestler, both in competition and in training. A good technique was important in all the events, but it was most important in the combat sports, and among the combat sports it was wrestling that "maximized the role of skill and science."[32] This was widely recognized. Pindar's usual term for wrestling was πάλα, but in later times, when manuals of instruction were also produced, wrestling was also referred to by the terms παλαιστική and παλαιστρική, in both cases adjectives in which the noun τέχνη is to be understood;[33] as befits an art, mythology supplied it with an inventor, although accounts varied between Theseus, Phorbas, and Athena.[34]

A skilled technique was thus crucial to wrestling, but nowhere in *Olympian* 8 is this admitted. No mention is made of any grips, turns, or other maneuvers in Pindar's spare description of the contest: ἐν τέτρασιν παίδων ἀπεθήκατο γυίοις / νόστον ἔχθιστον, "on four bodies of boys he pushed away a hateful homecoming from himself" (68–9). Although Pindar regularly resorts to such brevity in his descriptions of fights,[35] what it leaves out is made clear by his description of Epharmostus of Opuntian Locri defeating his opponents "with quick-falling trickery" (ὀξυρεπεῖ δόλῳ, *Ol.* 9.91) and Bacchylides' description, in an ode to a pancratiast, of Heracles setting his "neck-breaking hand" on the Nemean lion "with all types of skill" (δύσλοφον . . . / χεῖρα παντοίαισι τέχναις, 13.46–9). Pindar certainly gives a number of reasons for Alcimedon's victory, a desire to win (4–6; 64), piety (8), a fine physique (19), hard work (7), determination (67), and the divine favor accorded to his clan (15–16) and to himself (67), but Alcimedon's skill is not among them.[36] This lack of reference to skill complements Pindar's representation of Melesias as someone who tests and scrutinizes his pupils. By excluding skill from his account of victory, Pindar represents as insignificant to victory that ability that was most easily seen as portable and thus reinforces the idea that inherited qualities determined the victory, not any qualities added to the athlete by a trainer.

While at points it also hides the importance of skill to wrestling, *Nemean* 4 addresses its use more overtly than *Olympian* 8; at the same time, like *Olympian* 8, it seeks to represent Melesias as something other than a professional teacher. The date of *Nemean* 4 is relatively uncertain: all agree that it is earlier than *Olympian* 8, but estimates range from the early 470s through to the 460s.[37] Like Alcimedon, the victor celebrated in this ode, Timasarchus, is an Aeginetan wrestler who has won a victory in a youth category after being coached by Melesias, although his victory was at the least prestigious of the four Panhellenic contests. The trainer is mentioned briefly and at the end, soon after the victor's grandfather is remembered (or imagined)[38] celebrating the victor's maternal uncle Callicles:

> τὸν Εὐφάνης ἐθέλων γεραιὸς προπάτωρ
> σὸς ἄεισέν ποτε, παῖ.
> ἄλλοισι δ' ἅλικες ἄλλοι· τὰ δ' αὐτὸς ἀντιτύχῃ,
> ἔλπεταί τις ἕκαστος ἐξοχώτατα φάσθαι.
> οἷον αἰνέων κε Μελησίαν ἔριδα στρέφοι,
> ῥήματα πλέκων, ἀπάλαιστος ἐν λόγῳ ἕλκειν,
> μαλακὰ μὲν φρονέων ἐσλοῖς,
> τραχὺς δὲ παλιγκότοις ἔφεδρος.

Euphanes, your aged grandfather, once willingly celebrated [Callicles] in song, boy. Different people have different friends among their contemporaries. But each person expects to give the best account of what he encounters. Praising Melesias, what a twisting fight would he wage, binding his words, an invincible wrestler, not dragged down in the telling, having a kindly disposition towards the good, but a combatant harsh to the spiteful, and fresh after a bye.[39]

(*Ne.* 4.89–96)

As in *Olympian* 8, Melesias is located in a relationship of gift exchange and friendship. The gift he receives in return for his training is praise (αἰνέων, 93), and this praise is given by someone who has intimate knowledge of Melesias' work (τὰ δ' αὐτὸς ἀντιτύχῃ, 91), that is, someone who has a close relationship with him. Indeed, the ode suggests that the relationship between trainer and encomiast is as close as the relationship between Euphanes and Callicles, a father and son. The two relationships are clearly represented as parallel. They both involve praise and are further joined together by the gnome between them. As Bury observes, ἅλικες (91) must be understood expansively; it must include not only people of the same age, but people alive at the same time.[40] Understood thus, ἅλικες can be seen to cover, and bind together, the two relationships: both Euphanes and his son and Melesias and his encomiast are ἅλικες in the simple sense that they are friends.

The close relationship envisaged between Melesias and his encomiast obscures the structure of the relationship between trainer and patron that a wage would have dictated. As in *Olympian* 8, the training seems to be offered freely by Melesias, not under contract, and as in *Olympian* 8 also, the relationship is not between Melesias and the patron (here, Euphanes, both as head of the family, and as the victor's only surviving ascendant).[41] Who the exchange involves is rather vaguer, however. Taken precisely, the ode suggests that anyone who has real knowledge of Melesias' work could do the praising. Many commentators assume that Pindar, as the poet who is actually praising Melesias in this ode, is the only referent here.[42] As such, Pindar is claiming more knowledge of Melesias than he probably had a right to claim, but such misrepresentation is central to his strategy of denying his own professional status.[43] The unique vagueness of this formulation should be taken seriously, however,[44] and given the insistence on firsthand experience as well as the fact that the praise is described in a wrestling metaphor that refers to the wrestler as "invincible" (ἀπάλαιστος, 94), a second possibility surely presents itself: Melesias' pupils, Timasarchus to the fore. What the close of this ode suggests, therefore, is that Melesias gives his training to his pupils and is compensated with praise from whatever quarter that praise comes, whether from a famous poet or from a victorious pupil.

The end of *Nemean* 4 also offers an idea of what Melesias does when he teaches that fits with the aristocratic ideology of excellence. As argued earlier, Timasarchus must be included among those who praise the trainer (αἰνέων κε Μελησίαν, 93), but as a translation "praise" does not fully convey the meaning of αἰνέων here. αἰνεῖν in fact seems to be occasionally used to represent a relationship of learning in which the praise is in part constituted by an active effort to follow in a master's footsteps.[45] This is clear from another of Pindar's odes, *Isthmian* 7, in which the victor's uncle, who died in battle, is twice described as "praising" (αἰνέων, *Is*. 7.32) the warriors of the epic cycle:

> τὺ δέ, Διοδότοιο παῖ, μαχατάν
> αἰνέων Μελέαγρον, αἰνέων δὲ καὶ Ἕκτορα
> Ἀμφιάραόν τε,
> εὐανθέ' ἀπέπνευσας ἁλικίαν
> προμάχων ἀν' ὅμιλον.

But you, son of Diodotus, praising the warrior Meleager, and praising Hector and Amphiaraus, breathed out your flowering youth, fighting among the forefighters in the throng.

(*Is.* 7.31–5)

As the scholiast rightly observes, the uncle, Strepsiades, "praises" these three heroes insofar as he emulates them (ζηλῶν) and deems them worthy examples to follow.[46] That the praise of Melesias in *Nemean* 4 should also be thought of as a form of emulation is made clear by the use of the wrestling metaphor to describe that praise: it is indeed by imitating Melesias that Timasarchus praises him.

Such emulation is a form of education – by following Meleager's example, Strepsiades became a better warrior, and by following Melesias' example, Timasarchus became a better wrestler – but because it does not involve a teacher introducing anything from outside into the student, emulation is fully compatible with the aristocratic belief that excellence is inherited. Strepsiades' aristocratic credentials are certainly impeccable – like the heroes of epic, he died young and in battle, fighting as a champion, or forefighter (προμάχων, 35); the *Iliad*, in fact, suggests that learning from, and being inspired by, is the premier mode of learning in aristocratic ideology.[47]

Melesias is thus represented as a stimulus that revealed Timasarchus' natural quality. In this respect, the trainer is much like Chiron, who appears briefly earlier in the ode. Chiron is an obvious model for the trainer. He was known to Pindar's audience as the teacher of a number of heroes, including Jason, Achilles, and Asclepius; moreover, he put his name to a collection of ethical maxims, the *Precepts of Chiron*, that was an important element in aristocratic education.[48] In *Nemean* 4, Chiron does not, however, appear as an educator; his role is rather to aid Peleus in his struggle against Acastus. What is significant in his appearance, however, is that he is represented as an agent of the order decreed by Zeus and fate: ἄλαλκε δὲ Χίρων, / καὶ τὸ μόρσιμον Διόθεν πεπρωμένον ἔκφερεν· "Chiron warded off [the danger], and carried out the destined fate of Zeus" (60–1). Like Melesias, Chiron helps to reveal the order of things determined by the gods, fate, and nature.

What Melesias' pupils emulate is something of a surprise, however. Unlike *Olympian* 8, *Nemean* 4 explicitly recognizes the centrality of skill to wrestling. The metaphorical description of the praise of Melesias as a wrestling bout concentrates on the twists, turns, and grips needed to secure or avoid a fall and so characterizes wrestling as a contest of skill rather than of speed or strength: στρέφειν, πλέκειν, and ἕλκειν are all technical terms for wrestling moves, ἕλκειν denoting when one wrestler drags some part of his opponent's body forward to trip him up.[49] Yet, although skills are admitted to be crucial, they are not represented as things that can be passed on to anyone who can pay for them; the pupil who has such skills does not receive them from a professional trainer but possesses them, first, by virtue of his birth and, second, by virtue of his studious emulation of his trainer, a man represented as a friend as close as a family member (ἅλικες, 91). As one might expect from the skills developed in such a context, they obediently serve an aristocratic moral code: the skillful wrestler has "a kindly disposition towards the good" (μαλακὰ μὲν φρονέων ἐσλοῖς, 95) that is, the aristocrats, but to their enemies he waits "fresh after a bye, a combatant harsh to the spiteful" (τραχὺς δὲ παλιγκότοις ἔφεδρος, 96).[50]

The close of the ode reverses its earlier treatment of skill. In the main body of the ode, aristocratic models are mostly represented as fighting against skill with determination and strength. Thus, in his wrestling, or perhaps more properly pancration bout with Thetis, Peleus is merely said to hold Thetis fast (σχάσαις, 64), while Thetis is associated with the use of skill when she transforms herself into a "bold-devising lion" (θρασυμαχάνων . . . λεόντων, 62). Similarly, Pindar describes himself as gripped around the waist by an imaginary opponent whose tactics are described as "plotting" (ἐπιβουλίαις, 37) but advises himself merely to "strain against" it (ἀντίτειν', 37).[51] In both cases, the opponents stand in the way of the proper course of things, which is pointedly articulated through gift-exchange relationships: Pindar's excellence, which his opponent challenges, is the gift (ἔδωκε, 42) of "lord Fate" (Πότμος ἄναξ, 42) and will be accomplished to its "fated end" (πεπρωμέναν τελέσει, 43), while Peleus' victory secures his wedding to Thetis, which is attended by the gods and sealed with gifts for him and his descendants (δῶρα καὶ κράτος . . . ἐγγενὲς, 68).[52]

In the narration of his conflict with Acastus, Peleus again seems to be the victim of skill but again emerges victorious. Acastus plants an ambush for him (λόχου, 60), while Acastus' wife Hippolyta in the only actual use of the word τέχνα in any of the odes that name Melesias, seems to deploy "crafty skills" against him:

> Παλίου δὲ πὰρ ποδὶ λατρίαν Ἰαολκόν
> πολεμίᾳ χερὶ προστραπών
> Πηλεὺς παρέδωκεν Αἱμόνεσσιν
> δάμαρτος Ἱππολύτας Ἀκάστου δολίαις
> τέχναισι χρησάμενος·

By the foot of Pelion, turning against Iolcus with hostile hand, Peleus gave it over to the Haemonians to be their servant, using the crafty skills of Hippolyta, wife of Acastus.

(*Ne.* 4.54–8)

In fact, this is a confusing moment, as the translation suggests. χρησάμενος actually associates Peleus with skill, suggesting that he himself used the "crafty skills" of Hippolyta and conjuring up strange visions of a Peleus who made common cause with an adulteress against her husband.[53] It is only an audience's attachment to the traditional version of the story, in which Hippolyta finds her advances rejected and then tells her husband that Peleus had attempted to rape her, that ensures a more comfortable meaning for χρησάμενος, such as "using as an excuse" or "using to his own advantage the crafty skills of Hippolyta," is found.[54] Such an interpretation maintains the negative portrait of skill by suggesting that Peleus does not himself use skill; rather, skill is used against him by an adulteress who seeks to punish him for his virtue, but he is himself able to punish such actions by capturing Iolcus.

The suggestion that Peleus used skill is, therefore, only temporary, but, insofar as the association is made at all, it suggests that skill also plays a key role in aristocratic victories, in wrestling or war. The moment thus resembles the extended praise of the charioteer Nicomachus in *Isthmian* 2: it is a moment that challenges customary aristocratic ideology, in this case, its position that skill was not of primary importance to victory. The challenge is brief but real, and prefaces a significant change in the ode's ideology of skill. The end of the ode does not hide the use of skill by aristocrats but insists that the skills they employ are the right sort of skills, inherited and transmitted through the emulation of appropriate models.[55]

However the central narration of Peleus' exploits is understood, it is clear that skill is nearer the surface of *Nemean* 4 than of *Olympian* 8. Both odes combat the damaging notion that Melesias is a professional teacher, but while *Olympian* 8 suppresses any suggestion of skill, *Nemean* 4 admits that skill is central to wrestling but represents it not as a portable commodity, but as an ability acquired through inheritance and developed through emulation.

Of Melesias' three appearances in Pindar's odes, the one in *Nemean* 6 is the most enigmatic. The ode celebrates Alcimidas, another young Aeginetan wrestler, and seems most likely to date from the 470s.[56] At the end, after a recitation of the many victories won by the victor's family, Melesias is compared to a dolphin:

> δελφῖνί κεν τάχος δι' ἅλμας
> ἶσον εἴποιμι Μελησίαν
> χειρῶν τε καὶ ἰσχύος ἁνίοχον.[57]

He is equal to a dolphin in swiftness through the sea, I would say – Melesias, a charioteer of hands and strength.

(*Ne.* 6.64–6)

Comparing a trainer to a dolphin may at first sight seem strange, and even inept,[58] but, when considered as a response to the various anxieties that attended Melesias, these final lines, including the image of the dolphin, are revealed as a coherent and economical effort to project an idea of the trainer in accord with the aristocratic ideology of excellence.

First, like *Olympian* 8, the lines promote a partial idea of wrestling that obscures the importance of skill. Despite having spent the majority of the ode describing various family victories in boxing and wrestling, Pindar has so far not offered any indication of the qualities required of a good wrestler beyond general references to inheritance and the favor of the gods.[59] In comparing Melesias to a dolphin, however, he focuses explicitly on speed (τάχος, 64). Speed, in the sense of agility, was certainly of great importance to a wrestler, and there is no need to think that Melesias is being praised for the speed with which he turns out victors;[60] indeed, given that trainers attracted anxiety precisely because they seemed to produce victors, such a point would be grotesque. Yet agility is not the most obvious quality to focus on in a wrestler, and the focus on speed must be seen as a way of precluding a focus on some other quality, as the description of Melesias as the charioteer of his pupil's "hands and strength" (χειρῶν τε καὶ ἰσχύος, 66) confirms. One scholiast paraphrases these lines, rather carelessly, as saying that Melesias is equal "to a dolphin in speed, strength and skill" (τῷ ταχεῖ δελφῖνι τῇ τε ἰσχύϊ καὶ τῇ τέχνῃ),[61] but the paraphrase is useful because it exposes precisely what Pindar does not say. χειρῶν is not equivalent to τέχνῃ, although it may indeed describe the same ability; rather, it seems designed to replace any reference to skill with something vaguer that might encompass skill but might also more readily suggest strength. χειρῶν and ἰσχύος are, in fact, almost synonymous, because in Pindar's odes χεῖρες are most frequently associated with strength.[62] Skill is thus excluded from the account of wrestling here, as it has been throughout the ode, and the focus on speed in the dolphin image furthers this tactic.

That Pindar focuses on speed does not, however, sufficiently motivate his choice of a dolphin for the comparison (although dolphins were proverbially fast).[63] It is possible that the comparison of a wrestler to a dolphin seemed rather less odd to an ancient audience (in the imperial period, δελφινίζειν, or "doing a dolphin," was the name of a specific wrestling maneuver),[64] but rather more seems to motivate this image. The comparison of Melesias to a dolphin in fact serves to domesticate him, to bring him close to the victor's Aeginetan family by representing him as one of them, and thus to suggest that he is a friend or kinsman of the family, not simply a stranger momentarily connected to them by a commodity transaction. The dolphin appears to have been a symbol of Aegina, and perhaps more specifically of the Aeginetan aristocracy. In the fragmentary *Isthmian* 9, Pindar compares the Aeginetans as a whole to dolphins for their excellent stewardship of the arts and athletics (οἷοι δ' ἀρετάν / δελφῖνες ἐν πόντῳ, ταμίαι τε σοφοί / Μοισᾶν ἀγωνίων τ' ἀέθλων, "Like dolphins in the sea in excellence, they are wise stewards of the Muses and of the contests of games" *Is.* 9.6–8), and that this image was not Pindar's invention is made clear by the fact that the local athletic festival was called the Delphinia.[65] Both references suggest that the image was endorsed by the Aeginetan aristocracy: the Delphinia must have been dominated by the local aristocrats, as athletes, priests, and officials, while in *Isthmian* 9 the comparison of the Aeginetans to dolphins is linked not only to an appreciation of art and athletics, but also to Aegina's Dorian constitution and its respect for the laws of the gods and of guests, all core aristocratic values (*Is.* 9.1–6). In *Nemean* 6, therefore, the comparison of Melesias to a dolphin is resonant, particularly because it occurs in the context of athletic achievement. It taps a traditional image for the Aeginetan aristocracy, an image associated especially with their pursuit of athletics, to suggest that Melesias belongs among them and is not a professional trainer answering the call of money.[66]

Finally, the ending of *Nemean* 6 also communicates a particular idea of teaching in the idea of Melesias as a charioteer, which, although different to those communicated by *Olympian* 8 and *Nemean* 4, is equally acceptable to aristocratic ideology. In the context of this study, there is some irony in the comparison of Melesias to a charioteer, but the image does not function to join the trainer to another mostly unrecognized professional from the world of Panhellenic competitions. The context in which the image must be evaluated is the leisure practices of aristocratic Aeginetans, and the primary reference is almost certainly to the informal riding of horses and driving of chariots by these aristocrats, rather than to competition at the Panhellenic or even local level. The stunning success that the Aeginetan aristocrats as a group enjoyed in the athletic events, especially the combat events, at Panhellenic festivals, seems to confirm that they did not divert any of their relatively diffused resources to competitive chariot driving; there is certainly no evidence that any of the eleven families known to have secured Panhellenic victories in the half century between 490 and 440 entered any chariot races, even at the local level.[67]

Although clearly respectful of Melesias' work, the image of the charioteer treads a careful line. Melesias is described as a director, not a producer or creator of athletes; as a charioteer, his job is more to check and restrain the athletes' natural power and speed, rather than to make them strong or fast. The actual phrasing even avoids framing the athletes themselves as the objects of his work because the trainer is said to work not on them, but on their "hands and strength" (χειρῶν τε καὶ ἰσχύος, 66).

The image taps into the kind of ideas of horse driving and horse training that appear in the aristocratic Xenophon's treatise on horsemanship. As this work makes clear, the primary ingredient in procuring a good horse is choosing a good horse; no amount of training can substitute for good breeding. A rider can teach a horse, for example, to leap a ditch or go down hill,[68] but such teaching will only work if the horse is "healthy and not base" (ὑγιεῖς καὶ μὴ κακοὶ, 3.8). Riders and trainers must in general accommodate themselves to the horse's natural propensities, whether in teaching a horse how to gallop or rejecting a horse because it is shy by nature.[69] The same rhetoric surely informs the image of Melesias as a charioteer in *Nemean* 6: particular exercises can be taught, but the ability to do them well, the basic quality of the athlete, is already present in him by nature. This idea follows seamlessly from the highly impressive record of Praxidamas and the other members of Alcimidas' family at the Panhellenic games. Indeed, just before praising Melesias, Pindar has revealed that the Bassids, despite recently missing out twice on the honor of Olympic victory because of an unlucky drawing of lots,[70] have still accrued twenty-five Panhellenic crowns.[71]

The enigmatic ending of *Nemean* 6 thus addresses, however briefly, the same anxieties concerning the trainer that structure the other odes that praise Melesias: that he is a professional with no relation to the victors he has trained and that, as a professional, he challenges the aristocratic tenet that inherited qualities are primarily responsible for success. Melesias' professional status was the central problem for those who employed him: those types of teaching that were anchored within familial and friendship relations were suited to aristocratic ideology, whereas those that were not, were not. Those aristocrats who sought to compete in the games could have tried to find adequate trainers among their family members or friends, but most preferred a different solution, to use professional trainers but memorialize the role they played in ways that obscured the true nature of the exchange.

The usual method of obscuring the fact that a trainer was hired to train an athlete was simply not to mention him in the memorial.

The reason Melesias was named must simply have been that he was so highly visible that the problems he posed for the meaning of the victor and his victory could not be adequately confronted with silence. Certainly by the time of *Olympian* 8, when his pupils had accrued thirty Panhellenic victories, he must have been well known, especially in Aegina, where, to judge by Pindar's odes, he did the bulk of his coaching,[72] but he was presumably prominent long before that grand total was reached. He may also have been prominent for reasons other than his success as a trainer. Many scholars identify Melesias with the Athenian Melesias who was father of the Thucydides who took over from Cimon the leadership of the aristocratic faction in its struggles against Pericles.[73] If this identification is accepted, and the balance of the evidence supports it, Melesias must have been a significant figure in his own right, without counting his successes as a trainer. Most trainers, like most athletes, came from aristocratic families, but few can have come from such prominent families as what Plato calls "the great house" of Thucydides.[74] A prominent Athenian may, moreover, have been especially marked in Aegina, given that relations between Athens and Aegina were mostly rocky between 490 and 450,[75] and a sense of hostility may have exacerbated the impression that he had little connection to the families he coached. This can only be speculation, however; nothing is known about Melesias' political dealings with Aegina. He may, in fact, have worked in support of a more friendly relationship with Aegina, like Thucydides after him, or he may simply have avoided a public role and focused on training athletes.[76]

Even though Melesias was probably a prominent Athenian aristocrat, it would be a mistake to think that the problems he posed for those who bought his training were unique. The fact that he was treated explicitly in three different memorials certainly indicates that he was considerably more visible than most trainers, but as a highly visible trainer he is representative of a group of trainers who had significant public visibility, whether because of their success as trainers, their social status, or even their success as athletes before they became coaches.

Melesias' treatment in Pindar's odes is certainly not unique. Three other trainers are named, Ilas, Orseas, and Menander, and the same patterns structure their representations. Menander's treatment is considered in the next chapter, but the treatments of Ilas and Orseas, in *Olympian* 10 and *Isthmian* 4, can be considered relatively briefly here. *Olympian* 10 celebrates a victory of Hagesidamus of Western Locri won in 476[77] and, much as *Olympian* 8, takes care to combat the idea that the trainer is a professional who endowed his pupil with skill:

> πύκτας δ᾽ ἐν Ὀλυμπιάδι νικῶν
> Ἴλᾳ φερέτω χάριν
> Ἁγησίδαμος, ὡς
> Ἀχιλεῖ Πάτροκλος.
> θάξαις δέ κε φύντ᾽ ἀρετᾷ ποτί
> πελώριον ὁρμάσαι κλέος ἀνὴρ θεοῦ σὺν παλάμαις.

A boxer victorious in the Olympia games, let Hagesidamus give thanks to Ilas, as Patroclus thanked Achilles. Whetting one who is born in excellence, a man may, with a god's help, set him after huge glory.

(*Ol.* 10.16–21)

First, the image of the trainer as a whetstone nicely captures the notion that the trainer does not add anything to his pupil but brings out what is there already. This idea is made explicit by the declaration that the pupil is already excellent by virtue of his birth; the trainer certainly has a job to do, but he cannot, even with the help of a god, produce a victor out of anyone.

Second, the importance of skill in boxing is met with silence here, as in the ode as a whole: when the fight is described at the close of the ode, it is the "might" of the victor's hand (χερὸς ἀλκᾷ, 100) that is highlighted.

Third, instead of the training being traded for a wage, the victor is represented as owing Ilas thanks (χάριν, 17) for his attention, much as Patroclus owed thanks to Achilles. The reference here is not to the Iliadic portrayal of Achilles and Patroclus, in which Patroclus was the older of the two and was counseled by Menoitios to advise Achilles,[78] but to the later idea of their relationship that appears in tragedy, according to which Achilles was Patroclus' older lover.[79] The relationship of trainer and victor is thus compared to a pederastic relationship, a relationship ideally constituted by mutual trust and respect and a long history of favors and returns. The relationship thus aligns itself with that between the poet and the victor, which the ode represents as rising above the terms of a "contract" (κοινὸν λόγον, 11) to become a requital of friendly thanks (φίλαν τείσομεν ἐς χάριν, 12), but against that of Heracles and the "guest-deceiving" (ξεναπάτας, 34) Augeas, from whom Heracles "forcefully exacted a mighty wage for his servitude" (Αὐγέαν λάτριον / ἀέκονθ' ἑκὼν μισθὸν ὑπέρβιον / πράσσοιτο, 28–30).[80]

Isthmian 4 was composed for the victory of Melissus of Thebes in the pancration at the Isthmian games.[81] The ode is unique in that it is the only memorial for an adult that names a trainer, and, as in *Nemeans* 4 and 6, the trainer appears at the end. Much of the treatment of the trainer is familiar from the Melesias odes, but the treatment of skill is rather more complex:

ἔνθα λευκωθεὶς κάρα
μύρτοις ὅδ' ἀνὴρ διπλόαν
νίκαν ἀνεφάνατο παίδων <τε> τρίταν
πρόσθεν, κυβερνατῆρος οἰακοστρόφου
γνώμᾳ πεπιθὼν πολυβούλῳ· σὺν Ὀρσέᾳ δέ νιν
κωμάξομαι τερπνὰν ἐπιστάζων χάριν.

[At the Ioleia], this man revealed a double victory, his head whitened with myrtle, and a third before among the boys, trusting the much-counseling judgment of the tiller-guiding helmsman. With Orseas, I will celebrate him in the revel, pouring out thanks.

(*Is.* 3/4.87–90)

As the ode closes, its focus narrows to Thebes: a Theban victor is celebrated for three Theban victories by a Theban poet. Presumably, Orseas, too, is to be thought of as local. Certainly, he is represented as a close friend of the victor: with Pindar, he will join the celebratory revel as an offering of thanks and respect for the victor's achievements (τερπνὰν χάριν, 90), a job that belongs to the victor's friends, especially his age-mates.[82] Moreover, that he is mentioned at all, a unique occurrence in Pindar's odes, is highly significant. Orseas' training could be understood to refer to all the victories at the Ioleia, but, given Pindar's practice elsewhere in the odes, it is surely wiser to take it as referring only to the victory among the youths.[83] Consequently, what is suggested here is that the trainer from Melissus' youth is celebrating the victory Melissus has just won at the Isthmian games as an adult. The relationship between victor and trainer is thus one that extends far beyond any simple commercial transaction from the victor's youth: Melissus and Orseas have been friends for many years; only for a short time within that span did Orseas act as his trainer.

As in *Nemean* 6, training is represented as giving direction, not adding or creating, but at the same time it is also represented as less specifically concerned with athletics. The image of the trainer as a helmsman is for the trainer a flattering image, commonly used in aristocratic discourse for a ruler, whether of a city or some other subordinate body,[84] and it may seem to project an unflattering image of the pupil as fully controlled by his trainer.[85] Pindar is careful to combat any such impression, however, by making it clear that the trainer gives advice, not orders. Indeed, the relationship between trainer and pupil strongly resembles the idealized relationship that Theognis hopes for, but does not get, with Cyrnus: what Orseas offers seems rather to be ethical and social advice (γνώμᾳ πολυβούλῳ, 90), not training in specific grips and maneuvers.[86] Yet the training Orseas actually offered was surely more of the latter than the former, if indeed any ethical advice was offered at all.

The emphasis on judgment and counsel in the final lines fits with the ode's earlier excoriation of skill: καὶ κρέσσον' ἀνδρῶν χειρόνων / ἔσφαλε τέχνᾳ καταμάρψαισ', "[Chance] has even caused the better man to fall, catching him through the skill of worse men" (*Is.* 3/4.52–3).[87] The immediate context for this reflection is Ajax's defeat at the hands of Odysseus in the contest for the arms of Achilles, but an obvious subtext is their wrestling bout at the funeral games of Patroclus.[88] In both cases, as Pindar represents it, Odysseus' skill, combined with chance, robbed the better man of victory. Yet as Thomas Hubbard recognizes, the overall treatment of skill in the ode is much more nuanced, although Hubbard's reading requires qualification.[89] Hubbard argues that *Isthmian* 4 ends up positively valuing τέχνα as a necessary addition to the qualities present in an athlete from birth, but, although some uses of skill are certainly valued positively, the skills that are valued thus are not represented as additions, imported from the outside, but as constitutive elements of the user's nature. *Isthmian* 4 distinguishes between two sorts of skill, the imported skill that helps the worse man (ἀνδρῶν χειρόνων, 52) defeat the better (this is the only skill that is actually referred to by the word τέχνα) and the inborn skill that reinforces the natural, aristocratic order.

To describe Melissus' pancration victory, Pindar turns to animals: τόλμᾳ γὰρ εἰκώς / θυμὸν ἐριβρεμετᾶν θηρῶν λεόντων / ἐν πόνῳ, μῆτιν δ' ἀλώπηξ, αἰετοῦ ἅ τ' ἀναπιτναμένα ῥόμβον ἴσχει· "In his spirit in toil he is like the boldness of loud-roaring wild lions, but in cunning he is a vixen, which lies on its back to check the dive of the eagle" (*Is.* 3/4.63–5). As Hubbard sees, "cunning" (μῆτιν) is used to refer to the skills needed for pancration, so that Melissus is here being praised, in part, for his skill. Hubbard assumes, however, that, in contrast to the natural qualities such as boldness, cunning is an imported quality. Yet the use of animal metaphors in both parts suggests that cunning is thought of as a natural feature, just like boldness; after all, the vixen is cunning by nature.

The context in which the comparisons occur confirms that Melissus' winning qualities are seen as inherited rather than learned. Immediately before the quotation, Melissus is referred to as the "shoot of Telesiadas" (ἔρνεϊ Τελεσιάδα, 63). The reference to his father certainly suggests that Melissus' inheritance is key, but the vegetal image is even more telling, because it taps into an image associated in this ode with the recurrent successes of Melissus' family, the Cleonymids. At the beginning of the ode, Pindar describes how the family "flourishes" (θάλλοντες, 22) because of Melissus' success, and, soon after, this brief image is filled out when the victory is described as a spring that followed the barren winter of four family members dying on a single day in battle: νῦν δ' αὖ μετὰ χειμέριον ποικίλα μηνῶν ζόφον / χθὼν ὥτε φοινικέοισιν ἄνθησεν ῥόδοις / δαιμόνων βουλαῖς. ("But now again, like the dappled earth after the wintery darkness of months, [the hearth] blooms with crimson roses by the counsels of the gods," *Is.* 3/4.36–7.)

Melissus' skill is, therefore, sharply distinguished from the skill that brought down Ajax. This is not the skill of "worse men" (ἀνδρῶν χειρόνων), which has to be imported, but the skill of better men that reappears continually within a family. Skill may thus be important to Melissus' victory, but its importance in fact confirms the aristocratic tenet that inherited qualities are what determined the outcome of the contest.

The distinction between skills surfaces only briefly, however; as in other odes, Pindar prefers to speak of other qualities as responsible for success. It seems as though Pindar will continue to speak of skill; he justifies the need to resort to any means to defeat one's opponent by noting that Melissus was not large (οὐ γὰρ φύσιν Ὠαριωνείαν ἔλαχεν, "For he did not get Orion's body," 67), but he then proceeds to offer Melissus' power and determination as compensation, not his skill: ἀλλ' ὀνοτὸς μὲν ἰδέσθαι, / συμπεσεῖν δ' αἰχμᾷ βαρύς ("Yet, though contemptible to look at, he was heavy to meet in his warlike spirit," 68–9).[90] This turn away from skill is repeated as the ode shifts to Heracles and then Thebes; in his fight against Antaeus, Heracles' short stature is counterbalanced by his unbending determination (ψυχὰν δ' ἄκαμπτος, "unbending in soul," 71), while the pancration competition held at the Ioleia is characterized simply as "a work of strength" (ἰσχύος ἔργον, 86).[91]

Isthmian 4 thus takes a complex approach to the representation of skill. Although it mostly downplays its importance, preferring to represent the pancration as a contest of strength and endurance, it also sets up a distinction between two types of skill, the portable skill available to those without natural ability and the skill that comes by birth. Certainly, Orseas had no role in transmitting skill to Melissus; his role, according to Pindar, was to provide a more general education in life for the Theban victor .[92]

The representations of Ilas and Orseas thus address the same anxieties as those of Melesias. This suggests that, even if Melesias was remarkably successful or unusually well connected, he was not alone in being so visible to the surrounding community that his training could not be easily met with silence in a memorial. As a group, trainers thus seem to have been more visible than charioteers, and further evidence of this is offered by the number of trainers' names recorded by other literary sources and vases. The anecdotes that name Eryxias, Tisias, and a Pythagoras of Samos as the trainers of Arrichion of Phigalia, Glaucus of Carystus, and Eurymenes of Samos have been treated in the previous chapter. Glaucus and Arrichion both date to the sixth century, although the anecdotes themselves are not attested, as one

12. Javelin throwers with trainers Simon and Ptoiodorus. Red-figure psykter from Orvieto, obverse, ca. 525–500. Photograph © 2004 Museum of Fine Arts, Boston.

would expect, until considerably later. From the fourth century, Plato speaks of two trainers from around the middle of the fifth century, Xanthias and Eudorus, as if they were well known; they were, he has Socrates say, hired by Thucydides, the son of Melesias, to train his sons.[93] Finally, vases offer contemporary evidence of the fame of trainers. Several trainers, including Ptoiodoros and Simon (Figure 12), Eudemos, Hipparchos, Orsimenes, and Sotinos, are named on early red-figure vases, suggesting that at least in Athens in the late archaic and early classical period, a number of trainers were well known.[94]

For the most part, these trainers must have become well known through their successes. Anecdotal evidence suggests that trainers attended the games with their pupils, and, although they were not able to stand near the fighters during the actual bouts, they must have gained some visibility when their pupils were victorious;[95] at home, a successful trainer's fame would quickly spread as pupils, and their families, sought his services. It is also possible that some trainers actively sought to increase their visibility through the commissioning of memorials. There is an example of this practice from the early fourth century: Pausanias describes a victory statue for a Samian boxer that was dedicated by his trainer Mycon.[96] According to Pausanias, the dedication declared that Mycon was the dedicant and boasted that the Samians were the "best of the Ionians with regards to athletes and naval warfare," but did not name the victor.[97] The celebration of Samos should be read within the immediate context of Ionian athletics and should not be used to suggest an official capacity for Mycon. Stressing his Milesian descent, Antipater of Miletus had recently proclaimed himself the first Ionian to dedicate his statue at Olympia,[98] and a memorial at Delphi from around 400, perhaps of a victory by Mycon himself, may have claimed that the victor was the first of the Ionians to win the boys' boxing at the Pythia.[99] The novelty in the dedication Pausanias describes is rather the substitution of trainer for victor: a trainer has found a way to get around the general exclusion of trainers from victory memorials by himself acting as the dedicant of the victory memorial.

Given the example of Mycon, we should consider the possibility that some of the artworks from the early classical period were also commissioned by the trainers, not by the athletes' families. The circumstances of production of the various vases that name trainers is obscure, but it is as likely that a trainer commissioned a piece with himself on it as that an athlete did. Among the victory memorials, it is possible that *Olympian* 10 was commissioned by Ilas. Thomas Hubbard argues that Ilas was actually Hagesidamus' lover, as the comparison of trainer and pupil to Achilles and Patroclus suggests, and if so, it would not be unusual for him to organize a celebration for his companion's victory.[100] *Olympian* 8 offers a second obvious possibility: like *Olympian* 10, *Olympian* 8 does not leave the praise of the trainer for the end, and it certainly makes sense that Melesias might have wanted to ensure that his thirtieth Panhellenic victory was remembered. If the trainer dedicated or commissioned a memorial, this very act would help to promote the idea that the trainer enjoyed a close, not commercial, relationship with the victor and his family because memorials were for the most part taken care of by the family.

This chapter has argued that the memorials that name Melesias, Ilas, and Orseas address the same web of anxieties. These anxieties were rooted in the basic fact that the training the trainers provided was traded as a commodity, not offered within some enduring and preexisting friendship with the victor and his family. For an aristocracy that defined itself against commodity exchange, an involvement in a commodity transaction was awkward in itself, but the commodification of training also threatened to alter the perception of what the trainer was doing and of what was important in the contest in ways that would undermine the aristocratic ideology of excellence. Once training was separated from the aristocratic context in which it had always been practiced, it, and not qualities that could be seen as inherited, might appear to be the primary ingredient in success, and the importance of skill, which seemed dangerously portable, might be underlined. The anxieties trainers raised were, for the most part, addressed in victory memorials by simply ignoring the role they played in victory, but a group of trainers, including Melesias, Ilas, and Orseas, achieved such high visibility that their role in the victories they helped to secure could not be passed over. Instead, Pindar attempted to figure their practice in ways that were compatible with the aristocratic ideology of excellence: the trainer is represented as closely connected to the victor and his family; his teaching is represented variously as a stimulus to, reining in of, or testing of his pupils' natural abilities; and the skills that are central to victory are suppressed or themselves represented as inherited qualities.

This argument assumes that the anxieties created by professional trainers for their aristocratic patrons shape, and so can be deduced from, their representation in victory memorials. It might be objected, however, that this assumption is unfounded, that it finds construction where there is description. On such a reading, Melesias (as also Ilas and Orseas) is represented as closely bound to the victors he coached because that was the nature of his relationship with them; other trainers may have been professional, but Melesias was mentioned because he was not. Thomas Figueira, for one, accepts Pindar's descriptions of Melesias at face value; he sees Pindar's treatment of Melesias as revealing that his training of young Aeginetans was much more than a "mere physical education," that it served as a vehicle for the "transmission of elite values" and an entrée for the Aeginetan elite into a "network of political friendships in Attica."[101] Figueira's argument is strongly bolstered by the evidence he offers that Melesias' son, Thucydides, had extensive connections on Aegina and seems to have represented the interests of the Aeginetan aristocracy in his political struggles with Pericles, perhaps as their proxenos after the death of Aristides in 467.[102]

Training with Melesias may indeed have served as an entrée into Athenian political friendships, but it would still be a mistake to accept Pindar's descriptions of Melesias' relations with his pupils and their families as definitive of reality. What such an acceptance misses is the struggles and divisions within a society; a practice like training is not a transparent activity with a meaning that is universally agreed, but a changeable discursive formation that is subject to constant appropriation and reinvention by different interests. Pindar represents one of these interests, and his invention of the trainer must be seen as part of a struggle to fix the meaning of the trainer in ways that benefit certain aristocratic clans.

The basic elements of Melesias' relations with his pupils certainly indicates that his training was traded as a commodity. The number of his pupils simply precludes the conclusion that he could have been genuinely closely connected to them all. To have had thirty Panhellenic victories, Melesias must have had a large number of pupils; it would take many pupils from many families to win that many victories, and not all his pupils could have been successful.[103] At the same time, there were probably several elements in the relationships that could support the idea that those relations were enduring connections based on the exchange of gifts. The overall goal of the training, victory, could not easily be considered a commodity because it could not be a guaranteed part of the exchange; training must have lasted some months at the least, during which time the trainer may have been entertained by the family; and, in some cases, the training may indeed have been part of a more enduring connection. To try to describe Melesias' relationship with his pupils as a friendship was thus not absurd, but nor was it obvious. Yet the stakes were high; if the training a family member received was perceived as a commodity, that family's sense of identity and influence within its local aristocratic community could have been threatened, as well as the basic power and social status of the aristocrats more generally. Families were therefore prepared to commit significant resources to securing a congenial description of the trainer, and at least three gave the job to Pindar.

Pindar, and the clans he represented, may have been at least partly successful in fixing the description of the trainer according to their desires. That Thucydides seems to have represented Aeginetan interests certainly suggests that much of the Aeginetan aristocracy and many conservative Athenian politicians considered there to be a lasting bond between the two groups. It would be a mistake, however, to see Pindar's description of Melesias as representative of public opinion as a whole: there must have been other groups on Aegina, both nonelite groups and aristocrats, as well as other groups in Attica, that offered different versions of the trainer.[104] No competing contemporary versions of the trainer survive, but a good idea of what was out there is offered by an anecdote recorded by Athenaeus.[105] The anecdote belongs to something of a subgenre of anecdotes, those that concern the barbed witticisms of prostitutes. In this case, the prostitute is the famous Gnathaena:

> When a man who had paid her daughter [her fee of] one mina kept coming back again without bringing anything more, [Gnathaena] said, "Little boy, do you think, after paying one mina, that you can regularly attend my daughter, as if you were attending the school of Hippomachus the athletic trainer?"[106]
>
> (Ath. 13.584c)

This is a good line; Gnathaena's belittling of the man as a schoolboy ignorant in the ways of the outside world is as elegant as it is cruel. At the same time, the joke reveals a casual scorn of the trainer as much like a prostitute, except cheaper. Such an idea of the trainer was surely current in Pindar's time also,[107] and it is likely, as the context in Athenaeus and the actually quite considerable sum of money involved suggest,[108] that in many cases it was aristocrats at their symposia who sustained and disseminated it. The anecdote thus suggests that aristocrats were divided over how to understand the trainer, and it is surely in such a context that we should imagine Pindar's odes competing to determine that understanding. While Pindar put considerable effort into representing the trainer as a friend and model to his pupils, there were aristocratic groups that could quickly dismiss the trainer's relations with his clients as no different to a prostitute's.

8

MENANDER

The previous chapter argued that the representation of those trainers who are named in victory memorials is, in each case, shaped by the same concerns: to disguise the fact that the trainer is a professional; to represent him as aiding or revealing already excellent athletes, not producing victors; and to portray skill either as unimportant to victory or as an inherited quality. Only one trainer remains to be considered, Menander, who is named in both of the odes composed for the victory of the young Aeginetan pancratiast Pytheas, and the way he is represented in the two odes may seem to challenge this conclusion. The two odes may seem to portray Menander as the producer of his successful pupils, *Nemean* 5 by referring to him as a "maker" (τέκτον', 49) and Bacchylides 13 by listing his considerable successes as a trainer without giving any credit to the pupils he coached, in contrast to the catalogue of Melesias' wins that appears in Pindar *Olympian* 8. In both cases, however, it would be wrong to conclude that there was no anxiety about the idea that trainers made their pupils. In *Nemean* 5, the description of Menander as a "maker" needs to be understood in the light of the idea of an elevated type of craftsman developed in that ode and does not, in fact, imply that the trainer makes the athlete. By contrast, Bacchylides 13 is indeed an awkward passage, but this awkwardness should be seen as evidence of the compromises that faced wealthy patrons who hired highly successful trainers: the more successful the trainer, the less the patron could ensure his anonymity.

Menander was certainly a successful trainer, perhaps even more so than Melesias. Bacchylides tells us that at the time of Pytheas' victory, he had "often" (θ̣α̣μὰ, 193) been victorious at Olympia as a trainer, and that his successes at all the games, even perhaps at only the Panhellenic games, were "countless" (μυρίων, 13.196).[1] Presumably Bacchylides exaggerates, but it must be true that Menander had more than one Olympic victory, as well as a fine record at other festivals. Such a record implies that Menander coached athletes from several locales, even if, as is probable, he trained wrestlers as well as pancratiasts. Pytheas' victory belongs to the 480s,[2] and although there were many successful Aeginetan athletes in the thirty years before Pytheas, none is known to have won at Olympia.[3] As an Athenian,[4] Menander may have trained many of Athens' successful pancratiasts, such as Melesias, the Hermolykos who distinguished himself at Mycale,[5] and the Acharnian Timodemus who added an Olympic victory to the Nemean win celebrated by Pindar.[6] An association with Timodemus' family could have brought many victories; Pindar's *Nemean* 2 credits the family with a total of nineteen Pythian, Isthmian, and Nemean crowns prior to Timodemus' Olympic victory, many of which were likely in the pancration, especially because Acharnae was particularly associated with that event.[7] Menander may have turned instead to Aknonios of Pharsalus, however; his sons Telemachus and Agias, whose elegant, but fourth-century, statues were discovered at Delphi, won many Panhellenic victories, including one Olympic victory each, in wrestling and pancration, respectively.[8]

Whoever he coached, Menander was highly successful, and this surely made him conspicuous in any athletic context. He may, however, have been especially prominent in Aegina because, as an Athenian, he was viewed by many as unwelcome there. *Nemean* 5 is unique among the odes that name trainers in also naming the trainer's city of origin, and it seems to do this because the use of a trainer from Athens needs particular justification.[9] This is surprising because Melesias, whether he is to be identified with Thucydides' father or not, was, as his name suggests, almost certainly Athenian,[10] and yet this is never brought up in any of the three odes for Aeginetan victors that name him. The discrepancy is presumably due to the time in which the two trainers were in Aegina: Menander practiced in Aegina in the 480s when there was significant tension between Athens and Aegina and, on occasion, open fighting.[11] At this juncture in the relations of Aegina and Athens, an Athenian in Aegina, particularly one without any Aeginetan connections, would likely need to explain his presence.

It is the fact that he was an Athenian that has generated what interest there is in Menander in recent scholarship. How his city of origin is treated may help to date the ode and certainly sheds some light on Aeginetan attitudes to Athens.[12] Menander is also of great interest as a trainer, however. He is one of only four trainers to be named in victory memorials, the only one to be named in two odes composed for the same victory, and the only one to be named by a poet other than Pindar. Moreover, to examine how, as a trainer, Menander is represented in *Nemean* 5 and Bacchylides 13 is not to turn away from the details of Aeginetan politics. Rather, it is to trace the efforts of one particularly wealthy Aeginetan aristocrat, Pytheas' father Lampon, to maintain and justify, in the wake of the democratic ructions of 488–486, his clan's position of power before both the demos and the other aristocratic clans on the island.

Nemean 5 and Bacchylides 13 were not the only odes that celebrated victories won by a son of Lampon's. Indeed Lampon was, for a private citizen, an unusually prolific patron of victory odes, matched only by the tyrants of Sicily. Two more of Pindar's odes, *Isthmians* 5 and 6, celebrate victories won by Pytheas' younger brother Phylacidas, and, although neither Menander nor any other professional trainer is named in either, the way the trainer is represented in the two odes supplies an important context for the treatment of Menander in the two odes for Pytheas. Like the Pytheas odes, those for Phylacidas confront the use of trainers explicitly, but they do so by representing Phylacidas' training as provided in-house by family members, not by naming the trainer.

Approximate dates for *Isthmians* 5 and 6 are easily established, but precision is elusive.[13] The later of the two odes, *Isthmian* 5 celebrates a victory won by Phylacidas in the open pancration competition at the Isthmia.[14] Because it speaks of the battle of Salamis as recent (νῦν, 48), it seems likely to date from 476, 478, or, if celebration of the victory was delayed until late in the year, 480.[15] *Isthmian* 6 celebrates a victory in the same event at the same festival when Phylacidas was a boy.[16] There is no mention of Salamis, and, given that at the Isthmia the age class of the "beardless" youths intervened between the boys and the adults, this victory must have occurred at least four years before the victory celebrated in *Isthmian* 5, in 480 or earlier.[17] Pytheas' victory at Nemea, which he won as a beardless youth, occurred before Phylacidas' first Isthmian victory.[18]

In *Isthmian* 6, Phylacidas' father Lampon is represented as Phylacidas' trainer:

> Λάμπων δὲ μελέταν
> ἔργοις ὀπάζων Ἡσιό-
> δου μάλα τιμᾷ τοῦτ᾽ ἔπος,
> υἱοῖσί τε φράζων παραινεῖ,
> ξυνὸν ἄστει κόσμον ἑῷ προσάγων
> καὶ ξένων εὐεργεσίαις ἀγαπᾶται,
> μέτρα μὲν γνώμᾳ διώκων, μέτρα δὲ καὶ κατέχων·
> γλῶσσα δ᾽ οὐκ ἔξω φρενῶν· φαί-
> ης κέ νιν ἄνδρ᾽ ἐν ἀεθληταῖσιν ἔμμεν
> Ναξίαν πέτραις ἐν ἄλλαις χαλκοδάμαντ᾽ ἀκόναν.

In applying himself to his work, Lampon honors this saying of Hesiod especially, and he repeats and recommends it to his sons, bringing to his city an adornment for all to share, and he is loved for his generosity to his guests. Moderation he pursues in his judgment and moderation he takes hold of; and his tongue is not witless. You would say that he, as a man among athletes, is a bronze-subduing Naxian whetstone among other stones.

(*Is.* 6.66–73)

It cannot be denied that Lampon ends up taking the place of Phylacidas' trainer here. The image of the whetstone is familiar from the later *Olympian* 10, where a trainer's work is described as "whetting" (θάξαις, *Ol.* 10.20) his pupils. Yet the idea that Lampon trained Phylacidas is, of course, absurd. He did not train Phylacidas' older brother, who competed in the same event, and there is no evidence that he enjoyed any distinction in athletics. Although the odes that describe his children's victories take some care to describe often quite minor family wins, none is ascribed to Lampon. Indeed, all the athletic talent in the family seems to come from Lampon's wife's side: her brother Euthymenes won a Nemean crown, as well as victories at Megara and in Aegina at the Delphinia, and her father Themistius won at both boxing and pancration at the Asclepieia in Epidauros.[19] That the idea that Lampon trained his son was not only false but easily recognized as such is perhaps indicated by the particular way in which Pindar puts him in the trainer's place. Although Pindar certainly leaves the impression that Lampon was the trainer, by changing from a first-person to a second-person speaker, and from the indicative to the optative (φαίης κέ, "you would say"), he does not actually say he was, only that someone else might say he was.

What is gained from this misrepresentation is clear. By replacing a professional trainer, who must remain unknown, with the victor's father, the victor's training is set within the closest of relationships, and any suggestion that it was bought is refuted. Lampon is repeatedly connected with the vocabulary and actions of gift exchange. He "honors" (τιμᾷ, 67) Hesiod's saying, "gives" (ὀπάζων, 67) application to his work, "brings adornment" (κόσμον . . . προσάγων, 69) to his city, and is "loved" (ἀγαπᾶται, 70) in return for "his generosity to his guests" (ξένων εὐεργεσίαις, 70). Furthermore, the training becomes just one element in a father's upbringing of his child: Lampon is primarily represented as directing the general conduct of his sons, and it is only within this context that the idea of training is introduced.

The embedding of athletic training in the more general education a father gives his sons also renders moot any worries that training might produce victors or that skill might be revealed as central to victory. Training is here not a process of transmitting skills but of inculcating moral behavior. It is the father's morals and moral advice that dominate his teaching, not athletic techniques: Lampon is described here as moderate, generous, in full control of his tongue, and as someone who applies himself conscientiously to his work and advocates such application to his sons. Although the word Pindar uses for "application," μελέτα, later comes to be used almost as a technical word for training, here, as in the maxim from Hesiod, its meaning is much broader, merely "care," "attention," "application," or "industry," stressing that much more than athletic discipline is at stake.[20] As both model and mentor, Lampon exemplifies an idea of training that supports an ideology of inherited excellence: through the various encouragements he provides, he brings out the quality that is already in his children. He is, in fact, the ideal aristocratic teacher, a Theognis or Chiron within his own family: moderation (μέτρα, 71), judgment (γνώμᾳ, 71), and control of one's tongue (γλῶσσα, 72) are all paradigmatic Theognidean virtues,[21] and the word used for the advice he gives to his sons, παραινεῖ (68), seems to be a marker of the specific genre of advice poetry that included the Theognidea and the *Precepts of Chiron*.[22]

The idea of training projected by the praise of Lampon fits easily with the basic explanation of excellence that structures the ode's myth and representation of victory, that it is passed down from generation to generation as long as the family has the support of the gods and its friends. When Heracles asks Zeus, on Telamon's behalf, for a "bold son from Eriboea" (παῖδα θρασὺν ἐξ Ἐριβοίας, 45) to be his "guest-friend" (ξεῖνον, 46), Zeus grants the request. Similarly, although Lampon's sons come from a "victorious family" (εὐαέθλου γενεᾶς, 3), their victories are also due to the favor of the gods that preside over the Nemean and Isthmian games (3–7), and their continued success is figured as the result of the poet calling on the Fates to vouchsafe a satisfying old age to Lampon, "a man dear to him" (ἀνδρὸς φίλου, 18).

The transformation of the trainer into the victor's father in *Isthmian* 6 thus effectively sidesteps the anxieties attendant on the use of a professional coach. Only one other extant victory memorial uses such a strategy to address these anxieties, and that is *Isthmian* 5, the memorial for Phylacidas' victory at the Isthmia as an adult. In this case, the trainer is transformed into the victor's older brother:

> αἰνέω καὶ Πυθέαν ἐν γυιοδάμαις
> Φυλακίδᾳ πλαγᾶν δρόμον εὐθυπορῆσαι,
> χερσὶ δεξιόν, νόῳ ἀντίπαλον.

I praise also Pytheas among those who subdue limbs, that Phylacidas' course of blows held straight forward, dextrous with his hands and hostile in his mind. (*Is.* 5.59–61)

Pindar has no need to resort to an optative or a change of person here; Pytheas is a much more plausible coach than Lampon, having won a victory in the same event at a Panhellenic festival, albeit at the Nemean games and in the beardless youth category. Nevertheless, we should not accept Pindar's testimony. Successful athletes do not necessarily make successful trainers, and, more important, it is unlikely that a man who hired one of the best coaches in the Greek world for an older son and who continued to celebrate any victories won in grand style would stint on a coach for a younger son who had already won a victory as a youth and was seeking a first victory as an adult.

By representing a brother as Phylacidas' trainer, the training is again protected from the taint of commodity exchange. As in *Isthmian* 6, Phylacidas' training is a family affair, given to him by a family member out of friendship, loyalty, and a shared commitment to family success. Pytheas is not paid a wage but receives instead the thanks and support of his family, as well as recognition (αἰνέω, 59) when his brother wins a victory.

What exactly Pytheas did as Phylacidas' trainer is left so vague that an accurate translation of this passage has proved elusive.[23] This vagueness is presumably intentional, and its effect is to avoid any vocabulary that might suggest that Pytheas made Phylacidas the successful athlete he was. Pytheas is praised because "Phylacidas' course of blows held straight forward," but we are not told exactly what role Pytheas had in ensuring this result. There is, however, considerable stress on Pytheas' own success as an athlete; he is praised specifically as a pancratiast, one of "those who subdue limbs" (ἐν γυιοδάμαις, 59) and commended for being "dextrous with his hands and hostile in his mind" (χερσὶ δεξιόν, νόῳ ἀντίπαλον, 61), and this suggests that he served as a model for his younger brother, rather than as his instructor. The ground for this idea is prepared a few lines earlier when Lampon's sons are offered as models to anyone who wishes to compete in the games: μαρνάσθω τις ἔρδων / ἀμφ' ἀέθλοισιν γενεὰν Κλεονίκου / ἐκμαθών· "Let a man learn well the family of Cleonikos before he strives to succeed in the games" (54–6).[24] Pytheas and Phylacidas will not, of course, train this person, but stimulate and encourage him by their example.

In representing Pytheas as Phylacidas' model, Pindar is, in fact, telling the truth: Pytheas did serve as his brother's model insofar as he was the first to win a pancration crown at a Panhellenic festival. What is deceptive here is that Pytheas' presence covers up the participation of the trainer whose instruction refined, developed, and perhaps instituted Phylacidas' technique. It is as if having an older brother for a model is sufficient training in the many moves and holds of pancration to win a major crown in open competition.

In support of the idea that Phylacidas' trainer only brings out what is already present in Phylacidas, skill is both downplayed and represented as something that is inherited. Earlier in the ode, that skill is important is simply denied as Phylacidas' victory is represented as the result of physical effort and strength. What earns him the right to be celebrated in song is his "toil" (πόνων, 25), while the gnome that concludes the initial address to Theia suggests that "strength" (ἀλκὰ, 11) is the primary determinant of victory in both combat and running events: κρίνεται δ' ἀλκὰ διὰ δαίμονας ἀνδρῶν, "the different strengths of men are distinguished by their fates."[25] This emphasis on strength and toil is repeated in the praise of Pytheas when pancratiasts are referred to as "subduers of limbs" (γυιοδάμαις, 59) and when the "blows" (πλαγᾶν, 60) that Phylacidas delivers are picked out as the central fact of his fighting, and also in the suggestion in πλαγᾶν δρόμον, "a course" or "a running of blows," that winning a pancration bout is much like winning a sprint, something generally seen as requiring rather less skill.[26]

The praise of Pytheas does, however, add skill to the reasons for a pancratiast's success, as well as aggression, when it describes Pytheas as "dextrous with his hands and hostile in his mind" (χερσὶ δεξιόν, νόῳ ἀντίπαλον, 61). Yet the word δεξιόν represents skill as something that is not learned. From *Olympian* 9, it is clear that "dexterity," with its obvious connections to the right side favored by the gods, is generally seen as a natural attribute, divinely given, rather than an ability that is conferred upon an athlete from outside. In speaking of Epharmostus of Opuntian Locri, a victor at all four of the crown-bearing games, Pindar exhorts himself to "take courage and cry out shrilly that this man was born by divine will with fine hands, dextrous limbs and strength in his eyes" (ὄρθιον ὤρυσαι θαρσέων, / τόνδ' ἀνέρα δαιμονίᾳ γεγάμεν / εὔχειρα, δεξιόγυιον, ὁρῶντ' ἀλκάν, *Ol.* 9.109–11). That dexterity belongs together with natural endowment and divine favor is underlined by the prior excoriation of success that is owed to teaching: τὸ δὲ φυᾷ κράτιστον ἅπαν· πολλοὶ δὲ διδακταῖς / ἀνθρώπων ἀρεταῖς κλέος / ὤρουσαν ἀρέσθαι· ἄνευ δὲ θεοῦ, σεσιγαμένον / οὐ σκαιότερον χρῆμ' ἕκαστον· "That which is by nature is wholly best, but many men have sought to win glory with taught virtues. Without a god, each thing is worse when not kept in silence" (100–4).[27] The initial contrast between natural and artificial quality is elaborated by the following gnome, where what is best is associated with divine favor and what is worse with the left: σκαιός most commonly means "awkward," "left-handed," or "on the left." By representing Pytheas as "dextrous," Pindar is thus not implying that he passed on his skills to his brother, but rather that the skills of both brothers were present in them by virtue of the favor of the gods and the family into which they were born.[28]

Both *Isthmians* 5 and 6, therefore, obscure the actual circumstances of Phylacidas' training by representing a family member as his trainer. Yet although common to these two odes, this strategy should still surprise us: no victory ode other than these two offers a family member as the victor's trainer, and no victory ode other than *Isthmian* 5 gives a trainer (whether fictitious or not) to an adult athlete.[29] The explanation for the unusual treatment of the trainer in these odes surely lies with Lampon, Phylacidas' father. He appears to have been unusually wealthy for someone involved in gymnastic rather than equestrian competition. Hiring Menander to train Pytheas must have been very expensive, given his impressive record, and, as noted earlier, the number of odes that Lampon commissioned seems to have been equaled only by the Sicilian tyrants, and they competed in the equestrian events. It seems to have been rare for families involved in combat or running events to commission more than one full-length victory ode for a given victor, even when he won a greater victory later on.[30] No other certain example survives, although, as well as a victory ode, Xenophon of Corinth commissioned a skolion from Pindar to commemorate the dedication of a hundred temple prostitutes in return for his victory, but then the scale of the offering indicates that Xenophon was also unusually wealthy.[31] It is surely also significant that among all the victory odes, the only two uses of the word δαπάνα to refer to the expenditures of someone who does not race horses come in *Isthmians* 5 and 6: δαπάνα seems to represent those expenditures that are so large, they could almost be thought of as constituting a dangerous financial sacrifice (at least, if the patrons involved were not so wealthy).[32] It thus seems likely that Lampon enjoyed a level of wealth more commonly associated with chariot racing than combat sports, and it is surely this that explains the unusual ways in which the problem of the trainer is confronted in these two odes. Why Lampon did not, in fact, compete for equestrian crowns is explained by the goals he aimed at in competing: he sought prestige primarily among Aeginetans, not among the Greeks as a whole, and competition between the Aeginetan aristocratic clans was played out in gymnastic events, especially in the combat sports, not in equestrian events; no Aeginetan family seems to have raced horses, even at minor festivals.[33]

What *Isthmians* 5 and 6 suggest, therefore, is that, although the use of professional trainers was always a matter of concern in the commemoration of gymnastic victories, Lampon's great wealth made the use of trainers by his children especially problematic. Lampon's wealth made it all too easy for his critics, whether from the demos or from other aristocratic clans, to suggest that Phylacidas owed his Panhellenic victories to Lampon's ability to hire proven trainers, not to inherited qualities such as strength or divine favor. Such suggestions must also have surrounded the earlier victory of Pytheas; indeed, they were perhaps even more insistent in that case, because Pytheas' trainer, Menander, must have been one of the most well-known and successful trainers of his time, and Pytheas' victory was the first victory won by Lampon's children at any contest, indeed the first won by Lampon's family, as distinct from his wife's.[34]

On a first impression, the treatment of Menander in *Nemean* 5 may seem very different from that of other trainers in Pindar's odes. The treatment is brief and comes toward the end of the ode, but in describing the trainer as a τέκτων, or "maker," the ode may seem to point to two ideas about trainers that the other odes carefully avoid or refute: that the trainer is a professional tradesman and that the trainer makes the athlete into the victor, rather than revealing him as such[35]:

> ἴσθι, γλυκεῖάν τοι Μενάνδρου
> σὺν τύχᾳ μόχθων ἀμοιβὰν
> ἐπαύρεο. χρὴ δ' ἀπ' Ἀθανᾶν τέκτον' ἀεθληταῖσιν ἔμμεν·

Know that it was by the grace of Menander that you won a sweet requital for your toils. Athletes should have a maker from Athens.

(*Ne.* 5.48–9)

On further consideration, however, it is clear that Menander is represented in much the same way as the other trainers. That he is a τέκτων does not imply that he sells his training for a wage, and, although a τέκτων certainly produces products, the ode is careful to avoid the suggestion that the athlete or his victory is what the trainer produces. The term owes its inclusion not to any desire to denigrate or demystify Menander's work, but to a need not seen in Pindar's other odes – the need to justify the trainer's city of origin.

Certainly, Menander is represented as as much a part of a gift-exchange economy as Melesias and the other trainers. Menander does not here earn a wage for his training of Pytheas; rather, Pytheas is repaid with happiness (γλυκεῖάν . . . ἀμοιβάν, 48) for the physical effort he put into his training (μόχθων, 48). Menander's own role in securing the victory is rendered rather vague. It cannot be described in a contract but is instead much like the role the gods or fate play in victory: on several occasions Pindar describes victors in combat sports as winning "with the favor of" a god (σὺν θεοῦ . . . τύχᾳ, *Ne.* 6.24; τύχᾳ . . . δαίμονος, *Ol.* 8.67), or simply "with fortune" (σὺν τύχᾳ, *Is.* 8.67; τύχᾳ, *Ne.* 10.25). That Menander confers "fortune" or "favor" on Pytheas indicates a special relationship between the two.[36]

The vague description of Menander's role helps to avoid any implication that Menander made Pytheas what he is. Nothing is said about what Menander did as a trainer or the skills he taught; Pytheas is clearly the agent of the victory (ἐπαύρεο, "you won," 49), and teaching becomes simply a vague process of favoring or helping more usually associated with divine powers. This idea of Menander's teaching is supported by the fact that the accounts of Pytheas' success in other parts of the ode make no mention of skill, focusing instead on his strength (εὐρυσθενής, 4; χειρῶν βίαν, 19; σθένει γυίων . . . θρασεῖ, 39) and "inherited fate" (Πότμος . . . συγγενής, 40). The one reference to anything that might suggest skill, the mention of "trickery" (δόλῳ, 27) in the myth, ascribes it to the negative exemplum of Hippolyta. Even Thetis' wrestling match with Peleus has been removed: Peleus wins his marriage through his virtue and through Zeus' advocacy on his behalf with Poseidon, Thetis' brother-in-law (34–7).[37]

Moreover, what Pindar does not say about Menander is as important as what he does say. As is clear from Bacchylides 13, Menander has a distinguished record as a coach; he can boast a large number of victories, including several at Olympia. But nothing of this is mentioned in *Nemean* 5, and this omission is surely guided by a desire to represent Pytheas as winning on the strength of his own native abilities and not because of the coaching from his trainer. From the evidence of *Nemean* 5, one would have to conclude that Menander was nothing special.

Moreover, the description of Menander as a τέκτων does, in fact, fit with the more general presentation of the trainer here. First, it is important to notice that Menander is not described as a "maker of athletes," as most commentators have assumed.[38] ἀεθληταῖσιν is a dative of possession, not an objective genitive. Pindar says, "it is necessary that athletes have a maker from Athens," not "it is necessary that a maker of athletes be from Athens." The distinction may seem trivial, but when the sentence is understood in this way, the athletes maintain the subject position accorded to Pytheas in the previous line: although not in the nominative case, the athletes possess the trainer rather than being the objects of his craft. It is certainly tempting to supply a genitive for τέκτον' to govern, perhaps the athletes ("it is necessary that athletes get their maker from Athens")[39] or perhaps their strength or ability, but this would be to misread as accidental or insignificant a silence that is purposeful. What Pindar offers us here is a craftsman with a patron (the athletes), but without a product. Much as σὺν τύχᾳ carefully avoids specifying what Menander actually does with Pytheas, so τέκτον' ἀεθληταῖσιν ἔμμεν avoids specifying what the trainer produces through his craft.

Second, his description as a τέκτων does not necessarily implicate Menander in commodity exchange. Pindar's use of this word is mixed: in *Pythian* 3, he describes Homer and the other poets of the epic cycle who have told of Nestor and Sarpedon as τέκτονες (113), and while earlier in the ode Asclepius, who is described as a "gentle maker of limb-strengthening painlessness" (τέκτονα νωδυνίας ἥμερον γυιαρκέος, 6), is tempted by "gold that constituted a lordly wage" (ἀγάνορι μισθῷ χρυσὸς, 55), this is a perversion (ἔτραπεν, 55) of his earlier altruistic ministry and the path on which Chiron set him. The primary implication of τέκτων is of craft or skill, not of a particular mode of exchange through which the objects of this craft are obtained.[40]

In addition, in *Nemean* 5 the term must be set within the context of the distinction Pindar draws at the opening of the ode between superior and inferior artists. Statue makers, Pindar makes clear, are inferior to poets because their products cannot move: Οὐκ ἀνδριαντοποιός εἰμ', ὥστ' ἐλινύσοντα ἐργάζεσθαι ἀγάλματ' ἐπ' αὐτᾶς βαθμίδος / ἑσταότ'· "I am not a maker of statues, to make dedications that stand motionless on the same pedestal" (1–2). Indeed, Pindar's product is of a very special sort; it has a life of its own and can deputize for Pindar much as Aeneas and Nicasipus are imagined doing so in *Olympian* 6 and *Isthmian* 2.[41] Pindar, in fact, seems more like the ode's teacher than its composer: ἀλλ' ἐπὶ πάσας ὁλκάδος ἔν τ' ἀκάτῳ, γλυκεῖ ἀοιδά, / στεῖχ' ἀπ' Αἰγίνας διαγγέλλοισ', ὅτι / Λάμπωνος υἱὸς Πυθέας εὐρυσθενής / νίκη Νεμείοις παγκρατίου στέφανον . . . , "Rather, on every merchantman and in every skiff, sweet song, go from Aegina and announce that Lampon's son, wide-mighted Pytheas, won the crown of pancration at the Nemean games . . . " (*Ne.* 5.2–5).

Menander is squarely allied with the makers of Pindar's sort. The objects he produces are not appropriately described either as objects or as products; they have a life of their own and are capable of independent action. Moreover, immediately following the passage on Menander, Pytheas is, like Pindar's ode, addressed in the second person and imagined making a voyage, here metaphorical, that announces an athletic victory, here the double victory of his grandfather Themistius in boxing and pancration at the Asclepieia[42]: εἰ δὲ Θεμίστιον ἵκεις ὥστ' ἀείδειν, μηκέτι ῥίγει· δίδοι / φωνάν, ἀνὰ δ' ἱστία τεῖνον πρὸς ζυγὸν καρχασίου, / πύκταν τέ νιν καὶ παγκρατίου φθέγξαι ἑλεῖν Ἐπιδαύρῳ διπλόαν / νικῶντ' ἀρετάν . . . , "But if it is of Themistius that you have come to sing, do not shrink back any longer. Give out your voice, and stretch up the sails to the sailyard, and declare that, in his victory at Epidauros as a boxer and in the pancration, he won a double success . . . " (*Ne.* 5.50–3). The linking of statue and athlete is in some ways a natural one: the statue imagined in the opening lines is a statue of Pytheas, probably at rest.[43]

Menander is thus represented as a very special sort of craftsman, a craftsman almost without a product, or at least a craftsman whose products are not governed or determined by him. Establishing this idea of craftsmanship is a central concern for the ode: although Menander himself appears only briefly at the end of the ode, it is clear that Pindar's opening declaration that he is not a statue maker (Οὐκ ἀνδριαντοποιός εἰμ', *Ne.* 5.1) is not, as the scholia famously suggest, a justification of the greater expense involved in commissioning an ode instead of a statue,[44] but an immediate effort to define an understanding of the trainer that does not threaten the value of Pytheas' victory. Just as Pindar rejects the role of "statue maker" (ἀνδριαντοποιός) for himself, so, as it were, he rejects the role of "man maker" (ἀνδροποιός) for Menander.

The description of Menander as a τέκτων is carefully managed to avoid the suggestion that the trainer produces athletes like a cobbler produces shoes, yet one might reasonably wonder why Pindar used the term at all when it had such potentially awkward implications. The explanation lies in a second problem with Menander: he was from Athens at a time when Athens was highly unpopular. *Nemean* 5 is unique among Pindar's odes in naming the trainer's city and seeking to justify the use of a trainer from there. That he was from a foreign city does not explain the attention; Melesias, too, must have been Athenian,[45] but this is not mentioned in any of the three odes, all also for Aeginetan victors, that name him. What made it a problem that Menander was Athenian must, therefore, have been that Aegina's relationship with Athens was especially poor at the time of *Nemean* 5's performance, although perhaps not so poor that the presence of an Athenian was unthinkable. This points to a date for the ode in the 480s, before the uneasy rapprochement that followed Salamis (but, presumably, after the open hostilities of 488–486 that included the democratic rebellion of Nicodromus that the Athenians tried but failed to support).[46]

The justification Pindar offers for Lampon's engagement of an Athenian trainer is simple: the best trainers come from Athens. Presumably this justification rang true. Certainly, the scraps of evidence that survive suggest that Athens produced many fine trainers. Of the trainers named in the victory odes, the two Athenians, Menander and Melesias, appear to have been the most successful, and a mythological tradition that circulated at least as early as the third century linked Athens with the invention and teaching of wrestling.[47] More important, however, the justification provides the reason why Athens was unusually successful in producing trainers: it is precisely because a trainer can and should be thought of as a τέκτων that a good one is likely to come from

Athens.[48] Athena was acknowledged across the Greek world as the patron of craftsmanship and technology. She taught men how to work with wood and metal and women how to weave; she bestowed artistic ability and was responsible for inventions such as the horse's bit.[49] It is through Athena's favor that a craftsman becomes successful, and consequently it might be expected that, when he is revealed as a type of τέκτων, a trainer should come from the city that Athena most favors.[50]

In his brief mention of Menander, Pindar thus has two goals: to represent the use of trainers generally in a light favorable to the victor and his family and to defend the use of an Athenian trainer specifically. To some extent the strategies Pindar selects to achieve his goals conflict. His portrayal of Menander as favoring Pytheas much like a god favors a victor does not fit easily with his representation of Menander as a craftsman. Pindar is careful, however, to articulate in the opening lines of the ode an elevated tier of craftsmen, including the poet himself, who do not so much produce as direct, so that Menander can be cast as a craftsman, but Pytheas' natural talents can still be understood as the primary factor in his victory.

In his ode for the same victory, Bacchylides treats Menander's achievements at much greater length:

> νίκαν ἐρικυ[δέα] μέλπετ', ὦ νέοι,
> Π]υθέα, μελέτα̣[ν τε] βροτω-
> φ[ε]λέα Μενάνδρου,
> τὰν ἐπ' Ἀλφειοῦ τε ῥο[αῖς] θ̣α̣μὰ δὴ
> τίμασεν ἁ χρυσάρματος
> σεμνὰ μεγάθυμος Ἀθάνα,
> μυρίων τ' ἤδη μίτραισιν ἀ̣ν̣έ̣ρ̣ων
> ἐστεφάνωσεν ἐθείρας
> ἐν Πανελλάνων ἀέθλοις.

Sing, youths, of the very glorious victory of Pytheas, and of the mortal-aiding care of Menander, which often by the stream of Alpheus has reverend great-hearted Athena of the gold chariot honored, and which has already crowned with bands the hair of countless men in the games of all the Greeks.

(Ba. 13.190–8)

This translation requires some defense. Athena is usually understood as the subject of ἐστεφάνωσεν ("crowned," 197), as well as of τίμασεν ("honored," 194), so that Menander's "mortal-aiding care" has no role in the final part of the sentence. Campbell's translation is typical: "Sing, youths, of the glorious victory of Pytheas and of Menander's helpful care, which by the waters of the Alpheus august stout-hearted Athena of the golden chariot has often honoured, when she garlanded with headbands the hair of countless men in the contests of all the Greeks."[51] This cannot be easily accepted, however, because, by linking the final clause with a "when," it ignores the basic structure of the relative clause introduced by τὰν (193) and articulated by the repeated τε. Both ἐστεφάνωσεν and τίμασεν belong within the relative clause, and the relative pronoun must participate in both parts. The problem is, of course, that in the second clause the object of ἐστεφάνωσεν is clearly stated (ἐθείρας, 197), but it is not at all uncommon in prose for a relative pronoun to change case in a second clause within a relative clause without that change of case being signaled, especially when the case to which it changes is nominative;[52] and this is surely what happens here. After all, the point is not that Athena has crowned countless athletes (that is, that Athenian athletes have been especially successful in the games),[53] but that the sum total of victors trained by Menander is too great to count; his "mortal-aiding care" is central to this sentence.

As it is usually translated, this passage of Bacchylides should seem shocking for its treatment of the trainer, but when it is translated in this way, it is quite extraordinary. It suggests what all the other odes studiously seek to avoid: that the trainer is responsible for his pupils' victories; that, by his training, he makes them into victors rather than revealing them as such. A catalogue of the victories won by a trainer's pupils is bound to be a dangerous moment in an ode that praises one of those pupils, but, as Pindar's *Olympian* 8 demonstrates, a catalogue can be included that does not undermine the value of the victor's achievement. In that ode, Pindar credits Melesias with thirty Panhellenic victories, but he also makes clear that Alcimedon was responsible for his own success, describing him as winning (ἑλών, *Ol.* 8.66) the thirtieth victory and giving it to his trainer as a gift (γέρας, 65). Moreover, Alcimedon is clearly one of Melesias' star pupils, if not the star pupil, because the victory he gives to Melesias is an Olympic one. By contrast, the catalogue of Menander's achievements makes it clear that Pytheas is not his star pupil: while some other pupils have won at Olympia, he is just one of the "countless" (μυρίων, Ba. 13.196) students that have won at lesser festivals. Like all these victors, Pytheas is denied an active role in his victory: unlike Alcimedon, the catalogue does not cast him or the other victors as "winning" their victories or even as doing anything. In the description of the countless total victories won by Menander's pupils, the pupils appear as the object of Menander's crowning, or, more precisely, the pupils are crowned by Menander's "mortal-aiding care." Trainer and athlete thus switch the roles assigned to them in *Olympian* 8: where Alcimedon gave the victory to Melesias, Menander brings the crown of victory to his students. The athletes do, at least, appear in this clause; they are missing from the earlier description of the victories won by Menander's students at Olympia. There, the only two players involved are Athena and the trainer.

That the training makes the victor may also be suggested by Menander's special relationship with Athena, which seems to cast him in the place previously occupied by Pytheas. Early in the ode, Bacchylides describes the combat of Heracles with the Nemean lion. Because the combat is offered by some speaker as the origin of the pancration contest at the Nemean games, Heracles' heroic achievements function, as we might expect, as a parallel for the more recent feats of Pytheas at Nemea.[54] Yet at the same time, Heracles also appears as parallel to Menander. The early parts of the ode are so incomplete that it is unclear who this speaker is, but the obvious candidate is Athena; she is depicted on a number of vases accompanying Heracles as he kills the Nemean lion.[55] If the speaker is Athena, however, the honor she pays to Menander later in the ode renders him a latter-day Heracles. Moreover, the description of his training as "mortal-aiding care" (μελέτα̣[ν τε] βροτωφ[ε]λέα, 191–2) seems to allow the trainer's work to parallel Heracles' work in making the world a safer place for mankind: at the end of a fragmentary line, it is said that Heracles will "put a stop to arrogant violence and bring laws to mortals" (ὕβριος ὑψινόου / παύσει δίκας θνατοῖσι κραίνων, 44–5). Coming toward the close of the ode, this linking of Menander to Heracles may seem to trump the earlier linkage with Pytheas and so to suggest that the real responsibility for the victory lies with the trainer; at the least, it sets the trainer in the place of a victor.

This elevation of Menander at Pytheas' expense is especially surprising because in his praise of Menander Bacchylides clearly also shares Pindar's goals in representing trainers: to suppress any suggestion that they are wage earners who teach a technical knowledge that makes victory possible for students who do not possess the natural talent to win. Menander is certainly represented as part of the gift-exchange economy. His training belongs within a network of gifts involving the gods as well as the athletes: Menander gives crowns to the athletes (ἐστεφάνωσεν, 197) and in return is honored by Athena (τίμασεν, 194) and praised in song (μέλπετ', 190). Just as in Pindar, the trajectory of the obligation is reversed: Menander does not provide training because he is paid to do so; rather, it is the athletes who owe him praise because he has cared for them. Moreover, while the results of Menander's training are given in detail, exactly what that training involves is left vague. His training is referred to simply as "mortal-aiding care" (μελέτα̣[ν τε] βροτωφ[ε]λέα, 191–2); the term μελέτα in such a context is familiar from Pindar's description of Lampon in *Isthmian* 6, and once again its meaning here is general, "care," "attention," or "application," suggesting that what Menander does is tend to his students so that they may fulfil their potential. Certainly there is no sense that Menander molds his students or teaches them anything concrete, let alone teaches them particular holds and maneuvers. The injunction that immediately follows the praise of Menander is particularly neat: ε̣ἰ μή τινα θερσι̣[ε]πὴς / φθόνος βιᾶται, / α̣ἰνείτω σοφὸν ἄνδρα / σ̣ὺν δίκαι. "If envy, bold in words, does not force a man, let him praise the wise man in accord with justice" (Ba. 13.199–202). σοφός can certainly refer to someone who is skilled, but when it does, there is usually some indication given of where their particular skill lies;[56] when it is used in isolation, it usually means simply wisdom.[57] The technical knowledge necessary to Menander's craft is thus here transmuted into a general wisdom in the ways of the world, and Menander the trainer becomes Menander the sage (σοφὸς ἀνήρ).

In line with this representation of the trainer, skill is given no part in Pytheas' victory, which is credited to Pytheas' "overwhelmingly mighty strength" (ὑπέρβι[ον] ἰσχύν, 75), an ability less easily seen as portable. Similarly, the ode characterizes the pancration contest at Nemea as a whole as a contest where the Greeks will suffer "sweaty toil" (πόνον . . . ἱδρώεντ', 56–7). The narrative of Heracles' battle with the Nemean lion is more nuanced, however. It gives a central role to Heracles' "manifold skills" (παντοίαισι τέχναις, 49), but because Heracles is the ultimate symbol of the workings of inheritance, it is clear that these skills are Heracles' by virtue of his birth, not any training.

Like Pindar in *Nemean* 5, Bacchylides also addresses the fact that Menander is Athenian, although in a rather different way. The fact that Athena is represented as honoring Menander at Olympia when his pupils were victorious there surely indicates that he is Athenian, because she had no particular role at Olympia, but it does so in a very guarded way. In effect, being Athenian is transformed from a political affiliation with a city demonstrated by citizenship and residence to a personal affiliation with a goddess demonstrated by her favor at a Panhellenic site shared by all the Greeks. It is as though being Athenian means being Athena's, not being from Athens. Both Pindar and Bacchylides, therefore, seek to make palatable for an Aeginetan audience the fact that Menander is from Athens, but whereas Pindar seeks to justify using a trainer from Athens, Bacchylides seeks to mystify exactly what it means to be from Athens.

There are, then, considerable continuities between the two treatments of Menander, but these should not disguise the basic difference in the way the two poets treat Menander's curriculum vitae: whereas Pindar suppresses all information about Menander's previous successes, Bacchylides describes these successes in such a way that they undermine the victor's ability to represent his native abilities as the primary cause of his victory. This difference requires explanation, and the explanation must surely lie with the particulars of the commission given to each poet. That both the odes that celebrate Pytheas' victory name his trainer suggests that, at least in this case, the decision as to whether to name a trainer was not left up to the poet, but was included within the commission given to him (along with, for example, the request that Euthymenes' victories be included). It does not require a great leap to assume that certain aspects of how the trainer was to be treated might also be specified.

Two possibilities present themselves. The first is that Lampon commissioned both odes, but specified that Bacchylides should briefly catalogue Menander's victories. Such a specification would have involved a serious compromise. It was certainly not in Lampon's interest to raise the profile of the trainer to this extent, but the promise of such praise might have been part of the bargain he struck with Menander when he engaged him to train his son. Menander must have been one of the most prominent coaches operating at the time, and, because his record cannot have been compiled from Aeginetan athletes, this may well have been his first engagement in Aegina. Lampon may have been able to entice the famous trainer by offering not only a significant wage, but also the promise that his distinguished career would be celebrated in song, should his new charge be victorious.[58]

The second possibility is more speculative, but I think more likely: *Nemean* 5 and *Bacchylides* 13 were both commissioned as part of the same celebration of Pytheas, but whereas the Dorian poet was commissioned by the Aeginetan Lampon, the Ionian poet was commissioned by the Athenian Menander. A second ode represented a considerable honor for Lampon and his son, but also, because of its more sustained celebration of his son's trainer, something of a threat; this threat should again be seen as the price that Lampon was willing to pay to secure the services of someone so successful. A coach with Menander's record was both more likely to secure a victory for the family at a Panhellenic contest and more likely to demand, and be able to finance, recognition for his work.

That Bacchylides' ode maintains much of the aristocratic ideology of training evident in Pindar's odes and that, as the close of the ode (223–6) makes clear, it was performed at a celebration hosted by Lampon does not mean that Menander cannot have commissioned the ode. Indeed, neither fact should be a surprise. On one hand, Menander would surely want to insert himself into the victory record that the aristocratic clans maintained; on the other hand he had an obvious interest in sustaining the aristocratic ideology of training because his lucrative career as a trainer of aristocrats depended on an idea of training being established that was consistent with their ethics. Moreover, the hypothesis that Menander commissioned the Bacchylides ode offers a plausible explanation of why, uniquely for a gymnastic victory, two odes were commissioned; an obvious parallel is offered by Pindar's *Pythian* 4, commissioned by Damophilus as part of Arcesilas of Cyrene's celebration of his chariot victory in 462.[59] Lampon is still without rival as a patron of odes for victories in the gymnastic events, but, like the majority of his fellow Aeginetan aristocrats, he stands revealed as committed to the Dorian poet from the start.[60]

If Menander did commission a victory ode to celebrate Pytheas' victory at a celebration hosted by Lampon, this would illustrate well how complex the relation between trainer and athlete must have been. As argued in the previous chapter, the central fact of the relationship between a trainer and an athlete was indeed commodity exchange, but at the same time there were a number of elements more easily described under the rubric of gift exchange. These elements were perhaps increased by some trainers' desire, and ability, to memorialize themselves: if Menander did indeed commission an ode on Pytheas' behalf, such an ode would be seen as a gift to Pytheas and his family, and Menander would in turn be an honored and celebrated guest at the victory celebration, so that a gift exchange would overlay the wage payment that formed the basis of their relationship. Given such situations, it would not be surprising that, although to some, like Gnathaena, the trainer looked like a prostitute, to others he appeared as a friend and mentor.

It is the complexities in the relationship between trainer and patron that explain why the epinician poets seek to link themselves to the trainer in the odes where they name him. The trainer offers a perfect model for the poets: like the poets, his work is commissioned, but at the same time he is someone who can be plausibly seen as a friend or confidant of the patron. It is thus not surprising that the poets consistently yoke themselves to the trainers they name. In *Nemean* 5, as argued earlier, Pindar assimilates himself to Menander by marking out a superior type of craftsman to which they both belong. Bacchylides too links himself to Menander by describing the trainer as σοφὸς (Ba. 13.201), a term more usually applied by the poets to themselves,[61] and, possibly, by representing his delivery of the ode as the bringing of a garland to Lampon (ν[εόπλοκον δόσιν, "newly-woven gift," 223), an image reminiscent of Menander's crowning of victorious athletes (ἐστεφάνωσεν, 197).[62] Pindar also joins himself to Melesias in the three odes where he names him: in *Olympian* 8, Melesias is represented as a sage (εἰδότι, 60), as well as someone whose function is to tell of events at the games (ἂν εἴποι, 62); in *Nemean* 4, his wrestling is offered as a model for any praise poet;[63] and in *Nemean* 6, the description of him as a "charioteer of hands and strength" (χειρῶν τε καὶ ἰσχύος ἁνίοχον, 66) links the trainer into the imagery of the chariot of song earlier used of the poet.[64] In *Isthmian* 4, Pindar links himself to Orseas as a fellow-celebrant of Melissus, and in *Olympian* 10 Pindar likens himself to Ilas, whom he portrays as the victor's lover, by portraying himself as overcome by a genuine appreciation of his beauty.[65]

Pindar and Bacchylides thus consistently link themselves to the trainers, and this is surely further evidence that, although the underlying structure of the relationship between the trainers and their patrons was one of commodity exchange, the relationship was more complex than the simple provision of a commodity would imply. This was not true of professional charioteers and mule-cart drivers, who seem to have been easily pigeon-holed as wage earners. As we have seen, it is only Carrhotus, who was not, in fact, a professional driver, to whom Pindar links himself; Phintis and Nicomachus, by contrast, are relegated to some subordinate level.

The four odes that celebrate victories won by Lampon's children confirm the conclusions of the previous chapter: first, that in the celebration and memorialization of a victory the trainer represented a problem on which considerable poetic effort was expended; second, that the goal of this effort was to suppress any suggestion that the trainer's service was a commodity purchased by a patron, that he made a victor out of someone who should have not been one, or that portable abilities such as skill were central to success; and third, that, while the training was, in fact, traded as a commodity, the relationship between trainer and patron was sufficiently complex that to represent it in other terms was convincing. There must have been a variety of descriptions of the trainer and the work he did, both within and outside of the elite, and the job of the victory ode was to make generally accepted a version of the trainer that was favorable to his aristocratic patrons.

The odes also offer a sustained picture of a particularly wealthy Aeginetan aristocrat seeking to defend or improve his standing on Aegina. On Aegina, perhaps even more than elsewhere, athletic success served to justify political privilege, and Lampon set about using his considerable wealth to secure such success. Although his own blood relatives could claim no victories, Lampon had joined himself through marriage to a family with some sucesses already to their credit: his wife's father had won two victories in boxing and pancration at Epidauros, and her brother a Panhellenic victory at Nemea.[66] There was, therefore, some expectation of athletic success for Lampon's children, but Lampon used his wealth to maximize his chances. For Pytheas he hired Menander, one of the most eminent coaches available, now toward the end of his career, and Pytheas did indeed win a Panhellenic victory for his father, a Nemean crown in the pancration for beardless youths. His younger son Phylacidas was even more successful, winning two Isthmian victories in the same event, the first as a boy and the second as an adult. That he, too, was trained by a relatively prominent trainer is suggested by the level of concern directed at training in *Isthmians* 5 and 6: in both odes, the training is explicitly represented as provided in-house, and *Isthmian* 5 is unique in attributing a trainer to an adult athlete. To be sure that these major successes were widely publicized, and, moreover, publicized in ways that were favorable to him and their family, Lampon again made use of his considerable fortune: where most families commissioned only one ode to record an athlete's, or even a family's victories, Lampon commissioned a new ode on each occasion.

Things seem to have gone roughly according to plan for Lampon. His sons did not win at the Olympics, but he was able to proclaim his family's excellence through his lavish celebrations of his children's Isthmian and Nemean victories. At the same time, the odes that celebrate these victories suggest that Lampon's efforts to spend his way to victory did not come without some compromises. Lampon was able to hire one of the most successful trainers, but the very record that made Menander so attractive to a patron looking for a win threatened to undermine the value of any victory won by a pupil under his care. For the most part, victory memorials were able to give credit to trainers of such prominence without undermining the idea that inherited qualities determined the victory, but in *Bacchylides* 13 there is a clear tension between the claims of inheritance and the claims of training. In contrast to *Nemean* 5, the trainer's career record is given, and, in contrast to *Olympian* 8, the way this record is described suggests that the trainer was the primary determinant in his pupils' victories, not their innate excellence. *Bacchylides* 13 suggests that the most successful trainers on occasion sought some control over their representation in the aristocratic victory record, either by requiring some celebration of their other successes in the memorials composed for their pupils or by commissioning a victory memorial themselves.

Lampon's victory odes thus suggest that the most wealthy patrons faced an awkward choice, to hire those trainers with the best records and lose some control over the representation of the victory, or to hire a lesser trainer and accept a lesser guarantee of success. Lampon seems to have made both choices: for the older Pytheas, he hired one of the best trainers and allowed him to be praised according to his due, at least in one of the odes that celebrated his son, but for Phylacidas he hired a trainer whom he could leave out of his victory memorials but who was still good enough to train his son to two Isthmian victories.

9

CHIRON AND ATHENA

The last two chapters have shown that those victory memorials that name trainers consistently demonstrate the same ideological goals: to represent their training as a gift of friendship that helps an athlete to fulfil his potential to be a victor and does not make him into that victor by importing into him new and crucial abilities. These goals are pursued not only in the specific passages that name the trainers; often they are a more general concern of the memorial, whether in the particular way in which the event is represented or in the development of a specific theme that is central to the memorial's representation of training, such as the theme of prophecy in Pindar's *Olympian* 8 or that of a special type of craft in *Nemean* 5. Trainers were a central ideological problem and, on occasion, perhaps the central ideological problem for these memorials, but it was not only the trainers who are named – Menander, Melesias, Ilas, and Orseas – that posed a significant threat to the value of the victory being celebrated; trainers whose names are not given in the memorials were also of enough concern that, even in their absence, their work was the focus of much of the memorial.

Most of the memorials that do not name a trainer, especially the dedications made at the site of victory, address the problems raised by professional trainers simply by excluding any idea of them and their work from the memorial: the line connecting athlete to trainer is obscured by the lines connecting the athlete to his family and to his city.[1] In three memorials, however, Pindar's *Olympian* 7, *Olympian* 13, and *Nemean* 3, the absent trainers are more obviously present: even though no trainer is named, and the idea of athletic training is never directly broached, professional trainers motivate large sections of the memorials, as they seek to shape an idea of training or of the acquisition of skill that does not conflict with the idea that what determines victory is inherited excellence. Such memorials demonstrate three points: first, that the trainer was of more general concern than is suggested by the small number of memorials that actually name one; second, that the trainer constituted a significant problem for adult victors, as well as youths; and, third, that although trainers were used in all gymnastic events, it was only in the combat sports and the pentathlon that they generated particular concern.

Two memorials that do not name the trainer who trained the victor but do spend considerable effort confronting the problems he raised have already been examined. The two odes for Phylacidas, Pindar's *Isthmians* 5 and 6, praise a family member for training Phylacidas and leave the real coach in silence. Similar to these is the Olympic dedication made for Glaucus of Carystus, at least as it was framed by the anecdote told to Pausanias at Olympia. Like the two Isthmian odes, this anecdote subordinates learned skills to natural ability and replaces the victor's trainer with a family member. Glaucus' skill, we are told, was acquired only after he won his Olympic crown; before that, his father took the place of his trainer, and his job seems to have been limited to identifying his son's talent, entering him in the Olympics, and reminding him of his brute strength.[2] In these cases, the trainer's work is explicitly treated, but the concern of this chapter is not with direct representations of trainers and training, but with the general models of teaching, learning, and development that are promoted by memorials. In such cases, the reference to the athlete's training is less immediate, but the goal is the same: to create an idea of training that will preserve the value of the victory in the minds of an audience that might understand the importance of skill for victory and might suspect that such skill had been acquired from a professional trainer.

Pindar's *Nemean* 3 offers the most sustained engagement of any memorial with the idea of teaching: the third of the four triads is wholly taken up with a description of the education of Achilles at the hands of the centaur Chiron. The ode celebrates another Aeginetan pancratiast, Aristocleidas, a victor in the adult division at the Nemean games.[3] In all probability, Aristocleidas had a trainer; most adult competitors did, and pancration was perhaps the most technically demanding of the events. The ode does not name the trainer, however. What it does do is model a very specific type of teaching that is acceptable within an ideology of inherited excellence.

The description of Achilles' education is prefaced by one of Pindar's most famous excoriations of teaching:

> συγγενεῖ δέ τις εὐδοξίᾳ μέγα βρίθει.
> ὃς δὲ διδάκτ' ἔχει, ψεφεννὸς ἀνὴρ
> ἄλλοτ' ἄλλα πνέων οὔ ποτ' ἀτρεκεῖ
> κατέβα ποδί, μυριᾶν δ' ἀρετᾶν ἀτελεῖ νόῳ γεύεται.
> ξανθὸς δ' Ἀχιλεὺς τὰ μὲν μένων Φιλύρας ἐν δόμοις,
> παῖς ἐὼν ἄθυρε μεγάλα ἔργα· χερσὶ θαμινά
> βραχυσίδαρον ἄκοντα πάλλων ἴσα τ' ἀνέμοις,
> μάχᾳ λεόντεσσιν ἀγροτέροις ἔπρασσεν φόνον,
> κάπρους τ' ἔναιρε· σώματα δὲ παρὰ Κρονίδαν
> Κένταυρον ἀσθμαίνοντα κόμιζεν,
> ἑξέτης τὸ πρῶτον, ὅλον δ' ἔπειτ' ἂν χρόνον·
> τὸν ἐθάμβεον Ἄρτεμίς τε καὶ θρασεῖ' Ἀθάνα,
> κτείνοντ' ἐλάφους ἄνευ κυνῶν δολίων θ' ἑρκέων·
> ποσσὶ γὰρ κράτεσκε. λεγόμενον δὲ τοῦτο προτέρων
> ἔπος ἔχω· βαθυμῆτα Χίρων τράφε λιθίνῳ
> Ἰάσον' ἔνδον τέγει, καὶ ἔπειτεν Ἀσκλαπιόν,
> τὸν φαρμάκων δίδαξε μαλακόχειρα νόμον·
> νύμφευσε δ' αὖτις ἀγλαόκολπον
> Νηρέος θύγατρα, γόνον τέ οἱ φέρτατον
> ἀτίταλλεν <ἐν> ἁρμένοισι πᾶσι θυμὸν αὔξων,
> ὄφρα θαλασσίαις ἀνέμων ῥιπαῖσι πεμφθείς
> ὑπὸ Τροΐαν δορίκτυπον ἀλαλὰν Λυκίων
> τε προσμένοι καὶ Φρυγῶν
> Δαρδάνων τε, καὶ ἐγχεσφόροις ἐπιμείξαις
> Αἰθιόπεσσι χεῖρας ἐν φρασὶ πά-
> ξαιθ', ὅπως σφίσι μὴ κοίρανος ὀπίσω
> πάλιν οἴκαδ' ἀνεψιὸς ζαμενὴς Ἑλένοιο Μέμνων μόλοι.

It is through inborn glory that a man has great weight. But he who has taught things, remains an obscure man, blowing here and there, and never enters the competition with sure foot, but savors myriad virtues in his vain mind. Blond Achilles, when he stayed in Philyra's home, did great deeds in play while he was a child. Casting a short iron-tipped javelin with his hands, frequently and as fast as the winds, in battle he wrought death for wild lions, and slew boars. He brought their expiring bodies to the Centaur son of Cronus, at first when he was six years old, and then all the time. Artemis and bold Athena were amazed at him, as he killed stags without dogs or crafty snares; for he beat them on foot. This story of mine was told by those before me. Deep-counseling Chiron reared Jason within his stony shelter, and then Asclepius, whom he taught the soft-handed way of medicines. In turn, he betrothed the bright-breasted daughter of Nereus, and fostered her supreme offspring among all fitting things, increasing his spirit so that, when sent by the marine blasts of the winds to Troy, he might await the spear-crashing war-cry of the Lycians, Phrygians and Dardanians, and, when mixing hands with the spear-bearing Ethiopians, he might fix it in his heart that their lord Memnon, the raging kinsman of Helenus, would not go back home thereafter.

(*Ne.* 3.40–63)

Although not, in fact, in contradiction with the gnome that introduces it, this narrative of Achilles certainly sits uneasily next to it: while the gnome scorns teaching, the narrative describes what must be a positive model of teaching, the education of one of the greatest Greek heroes. Thomas Hubbard considers this inconsistency to be the result of a typically Pindaric mode of expression: as is often the case in Pindar's poetry, the initial gnome represents only a one-sided idea of reality that must be "qualified" by the myth that follows.[4] Yet to see Pindar's compositional strategies as the cause of this inconsistency is to deny the political work attempted by Pindar's odes. The inconsistencies characteristic of Pindar's forms of expression are themselves rooted in basic inconsistencies between aristocratic practice and aristocratic ideology; in this case, Pindar must reconcile the aristocratic practice of hiring trainers with an ideology that disdains the sort of teaching that it involved. Rather than as a provisional statement on teaching that is later revised, the gnome should be viewed as a genuine condemnation of teaching that resonates with many in Pindar's audience (even if they themselves use trainers), and the narrative of Achilles' education must be read against this background. The narrative does not seek to defend all teaching, but to mark off one specific type of education as exceptional and thus appropriate for an aristocrat. Education in general is still to be scorned, as the initial gnome declares.

The model of teaching that the ode promotes has three particular characteristics. The first is that the teaching is not a commodity but occurs within the context of a long-term, familial relationship. Chiron is represented as Achilles' teacher throughout his youth; he looks after the child when he is as young as six but prepares him for his military exploits as a young adult. Achilles comes to live with Chiron's family, rather than Chiron going to live with Achilles'; Chiron, in fact, appears as a kind of father for the boy. His qualification for such a role is that he is closely related to Achilles. Although his teaching of Peleus is not mentioned, he is represented as betrothing Thetis at her wedding. This version of the story is peculiar to Pindar,[5] and, because such a responsibility would normally fall to a close male relative, it serves as a declaration of Chiron's close kinship with Thetis and her son. In addition, the dying animals that Achilles brings back to Chiron should probably be thought of as gifts: Achilles repays Chiron's gift of teaching with the spoils of his hunting.

Second, as has often been recognized, the teaching represented here is not a teaching that will stand on its own; it has such good results because it is given to someone already excellent by nature.[6] What commentators have missed, however, is that such an idea of successful teaching implies a very specific idea of what successful teaching involves. While the narrative states that Chiron's teaching is crucial to Achilles' ability to withstand the war cry at Troy (ὄφρα, 59), it also makes it clear that Achilles was all but able to do such things as a child. His hunting exploits closely foreshadow his martial ones: his hunts are described as battles (μάχᾳ, 46), and the emphasis put on his spear (ἄκοντα, 45) and swift feet (ποσσὶ γὰρ κράτεσκε, 52) clearly evoke the Achilles of the *Iliad*.[7] Consequently, Chiron's teaching of Achilles is described as a "fostering" (ἀτίταλλεν, 58) and an "increasing" (αὔξων, 58) of what is already excellent (γόνον . . . φέρτατον, 57), not the instructing, molding, or producing of a great warrior. Chiron is not a craftsman, and Achilles is not his product.

Third, the part played by technical knowledge in this education is represented much as it is elsewhere in Pindar's odes. In the narrative of Achilles' education, skill is not mentioned. His feats are represented as feats of speed, strength, and bravery, not cunning or good technique, and Chiron's teaching appears moral rather than technical: his teaching is described simply as the "fostering" of Achilles "among all fitting things" (ἀτίταλλεν <ἐν> ἀρμένοισι πᾶσι, 58). Moreover, that Achilles chased down stags without dogs or "crafty snares" (δολίων . . . ἑρκέων, 51) suggests that the use of those skills or techniques that can be taught is the mark of an inferior person.[8]

The representation of the part technique plays in a properly aristocratic education is rather more complicated than this, however, and contains something of a surprise. In addition to suggesting that technique has no place in such an education, the Achilles narrative, or at least the narrative of Asclepius embedded within it, also accommodates technical knowledge within such an education: βαθυμῆτα Χίρων τράφε λιθίνῳ/Ἰάσον' ἔνδον τέγει, καὶ ἔπειτεν Ἀσκλαπιόν, / τὸν φαρμάκων δίδαξε μαλακόχειρα νόμον· "Deep-counseling Chiron reared Jason within his stony shelter, and then Asclepius, whom he taught the soft-handed way of medicines," (*Ne.* 3.53–5). Asclepius' education is initially described in similar terms (τράφε) to those that will be used of Achilles' education, but the relative clause suggests a very different process. While Achilles' hunting abilities are innate and have no need of learned skills to make them successful, Asclepius' medical skills are all taught him by Chiron (δίδαξε).[9] These skills are thus clearly marked as portable; yet it is also clear that they are not very portable. There is a significant difference between the teaching (δίδαξε) that Asclepius receives and the "taught things" of the "obscure man" of the opening gnome. While Asclepius' education is clearly rooted in his long-term relationship with Chiron, the teaching referred to in the gnome seems to come without a teacher. Rather than having been taught by someone, the "obscure man" simply "has taught things." We may compare here Jason's declaration before the people of Iolcus in *Pythian* 4: "Φαμὶ διδασκαλίαν Χίρωνος οἴσειν," "I say that I bear the teaching of Chiron" (102). That the teaching is Chiron's is a crucial piece of information; it means that it was obtained in the proper moral context and that the teaching was a gift. Like a gift it maintains a connection with the person who gave it, continuing to bear his name.[10] By contrast, the unattributed διδάκτ' appear as commodities, discrete pieces of learning purchased from any one who could sell them.

The narrative of Achilles' education thus promotes four particular ideas about Chiron's teaching, three of which are familiar from Pindar's treatment of athletic trainers elsewhere in his odes, but the fourth of which is new: first, that the teaching is a gift, given over a long period to a kinsman, not a series of discrete commodities purchased from nameless sellers; second, that it enhances what is naturally good and does not create quality on its own; third, that technical knowledge plays little, if any, part in the education; but, fourth, that when such knowledge does play a part, its circulation is restricted to appropriate pupils.

Achilles' location in a sequence of heroes whose independence has been emphasized makes it clear that such teaching as that offered by Chiron does not undermine a pupil's glory or his right to be thought of as the prime cause of his actions. The first two heroes to be named, Heracles and Peleus, are explicitly represented as acting on their own: Heracles searched out the ends of the earth "on his own" (ἰδίᾳ, 24), and Peleus captured Iolcus "alone without an army" (μόνος ἄνευ στρατιᾶς, 34). Peleus' independence is particularly striking; in other versions, he is aided in this venture by Jason and the Dioscuri, as well as an army.[11] The third hero in the sequence is Telamon, and with Telamon, the notion of independent action is made more inclusive. Telamon has a helper – he is Iolaus' companion (παραστάτας, 37) – but he is no less glorious than Peleus for that. Both are part of the Aiacid catalogue that illustrates the weight of "inborn glory" (συγγενεῖ . . . εὐδοξίᾳ, 40). Moreover, he also appears as no less independent: although he has a companion, their deeds are represented as his deeds, as he is said to have "sacked" (ἔπερσεν, 37) Laomedon, "pursued" the Amazons (ἕπετο, 39), and not been subdued by fear (νίν, 39). By being linked to two heroes whose independence is stressed, a man with a comrade is assimilated to a man who fights on his own.

Achilles is the fourth and last hero in this sequence. Like Telamon, Achilles has a helper, but unlike Iolaus, Chiron is represented as a direct cause of Achilles' success: his feats at Troy are represented syntactically as the result (ὄφρα, 59) of Chiron's education. Again it is clear that this does not affect Achilles' glory; he, too, illustrates the glory attached to Aiacid descent and is so impressive that even goddesses watch him in awe. Beyond this, Chiron's axial role, the ode suggests, does not compromise Achilles' independence either. Like the earlier heroes, Achilles is the subject of his own actions (προσμένοι, 60; ἐπιμείξαις, 61; πάξαιθ', 62), and the many links to Peleus and Heracles ensure that he is thought of in the same way. His spear (ἄκοντα, 45) recalls Peleus' (αἰχμὰν, 33), his killing of lions and boars Heracles' own subjugation of "wild animals in the sea" (θῆρας ἐν πελάγεϊ, 23), and most significantly his hunting "without dogs or crafty snares" (ἄνευ κυνῶν δολίων θ' ἑρκέων, 51) echoes Peleus' sacking of Iolcus "without an army" (ἄνευ στρατιᾶς, 34). As Ilja Pfeijffer notes, "Achilles, like Heracles and Peleus, is emphatically said to have done things on his own, without the help of anybody or anything."[12] Just as Telamon is represented as someone who acts alone, despite having a comrade, so, too, is Achilles, despite having a teacher.

Nemean 3's insistent concern with teaching can only be explained as an effort to address the problems raised by a professional trainer. Chiron serves to mystify Aristocleidas' training by setting up an acceptable form of teaching to which it can be assimilated. The reference to the victor's trainer is certainly not explicit; as Stephen Instone notes, there is nothing in the description of Achilles' exploits that points outside the immediate context of a Homeric hero's hunting.[13] But this does not mean that Instone is right to see no reference at all to athletic training.[14] Such a position unduly restricts the reference of Pindar's mythical narratives, and furthermore, in this case the lack of explicit reference is indicative of the trainer's relevance. Although not mentioned, he is hardly absent; in fact, it is precisely because he is so central a problem for the meaning of the victor's victory that the trainer is not mentioned. Aristocleidas' trainer is the unspoken problem around which the narrative of Achilles' education is organized: the narrative serves as a direct response to this problem, a concerted effort to validate Aristocleidas' use of a hired trainer by framing the training in such a way that it appears compatible with the aristocratic ideology of excellence.

In his recent commentary, Ilja Pfeijffer recognizes that training is central to *Nemean* 3, but his interpretation is radically opposed to that offered here: he argues that Aristocleidas, in contrast to many adult athletes, did not use a trainer to gain his victory. His evidence for this is threefold. First, he notes that no trainer is named in the ode. Second, he accepts an earlier emendation that has the ode declare that Aristocleidas won "according to his own destiny" (γ᾽ ἑὰν/ . . . κατ᾽ αἶσαν, 15–16)[15] and proposes that this refers, at least in part, to the fact that he won without the assistance of a trainer. Third, he suggests that the emphasis placed on the independence of Heracles, Peleus, and Achilles, at least in his youth, serves to praise the victor's own independence in not using a trainer.[16] This argument cannot be accepted, however. First, it is a mistake to read the absence of a trainer's name as proof that there was no trainer. The trainer posed so many problems for his patrons that his treatment in a victory ode cannot be read at face value. Second, although Pfeijffer's emendation is plausible, it is far from clear that the emended phrase refers to Aristocleidas[17] or, if it does, that it means he did not use a trainer. Yet if the victor did indeed do without a trainer, this would surely have been made completely clear, just as *Isthmian* 1 leaves no doubt that Herodotus drove his own chariot. Third, and most crucially, Pfeijffer's interpretation of the theme of independence is unconvincing. It does not satisfactorily account for the fact that Achilles has a teacher, and Telamon a companion. Pfeijffer explains these intrusions as implying the hope or expectation that Aristocleidas may one day train other Aeginetans and so help them achieve the success he has enjoyed.[18] This suggestion is arbitrary and fails to give due weight to the fact that even though Telamon and Achilles have helpers, they are assimilated to the solo fighting Peleus and Heracles, not differentiated from them. Any interpretation of the theme of independence must account for this inconsistency.

Such inconsistency is, in fact, a reliable sign that *Nemean* 3 was engaged in an ideological contest. The idea of teaching that Pindar promotes in this ode is actually riddled with inconsistency: the teacher is represented as a cause of his pupil's success, yet he seems to do nothing more than allow his charge to fulfill his potential; the teaching does and does not involve the teaching of skills; and, although helped by his teacher, the pupil acts alone. Such inconsistency is typical of ideology insofar as it seeks not simply to establish a particular version of reality, but to establish a particular version of reality that recognizes and accommodates divergent versions of that reality.[19] The explanation of the inconsistencies in the idea of teaching that Pindar promotes in *Nemean* 3 should, therefore, be sought not in a supposed change of career for Aristocleidas from competitor to trainer, but in the politics of athletic training, in the fact that the ode molds the practice of athletic training to an ideology with which it is fundamentally at odds. These inconsistencies are not failings; rather, they are what make this idea of teaching a convincing ideology of athletic training. Through such inconsistency, an ideology that marks innate excellence as the dominant factor in success can be made to incorporate a practice that implies that the learning of specific, easily transferable skills and techniques is crucial.

Pindar's *Nemean* 3, then, defends the propriety of an aristocrat using a trainer in the pursuit of victory. *Olympians* 7 and 13 have a more specific focus: the skills taught by an athletic trainer. Their myths offer models for the transmission of skills and technical abilities that represent this transmission as a mysterious and capricious occurrence. In both odes, the new abilities that are acquired are gifts from a god, unexpectedly given and simply and immediately conferred, without a process of training or study. And in both odes it is Athena, rather than Chiron, who confers the new ability.

Perhaps Pindar's finest ode, *Olympian* 7 celebrates the impressive career of the Rhodian boxer Diagoras. He won victories at all four of the crown-bearing festivals, one at Olympia, one at Delphi, four at the Isthmus, and "one after another" at Nemea; he also won many victories at many local contests, including six at the Aeginetan Delphinia.[20] His Olympic victory, in 464, was also celebrated with a statue dedicated at Olympia.[21] This victory proved to be the first in an unprecedented sequence of Olympic wins in the combat sports by Diagoras' immediate family: three sons won six Olympic crowns between them, and two daughters each bore an Olympic victor.[22] Diagoras seems, however, to have been the first member of his clan, the Eratidae, to win significant fame in athletics.

The victor celebrated by *Olympian* 13, Xenophon of Corinth, also belonged to a family with a stunning record in competition. According to Pindar, the Oligaethidae had accrued sixty-nine Panhellenic victories by the time of the ode, including three Olympic and six Pythian crowns.[23] *Olympian* 13 celebrates two of the Olympic victories, a victory in the stadion and a victory in the pentathlon, both won by Xenophon at the same Olympic festival in 464, the year Diagoras won the boxing.[24] This double victory was, according to Pindar, an unprecedented achievement[25]: it was not unusual for pentathletes to specialize in the sprint,[26] but Xenophon must have been the first to win both events in the same Olympic festival, and perhaps simply the first to win Olympic crowns in both events. Despite his achievements at Olympia, he did not win at all four Panhellenic games; at the time of his Olympic success, he had also won two Isthmian crowns, and one Nemean, but a Pythian crown seems to have eluded him.[27] Xenophon's celebrations reveal that his clan was among the richest in Greece: in addition to commissioning an epinician ode, he dedicated as a thank offering a hundred slave women to serve in Aphrodite's temple in Corinth and recorded this act in a second work commissioned from Pindar.[28]

Pindar's odes for these distinguished athletes contain mythical narratives that describe how Athena confers a unique technical ability in return for worship. In *Olympian* 13, she gives Bellerophon an instrument, a "gold-filleted bit" (χρυσάμπυκα . . . χαλινόν, 65), that he can use to achieve a goal that had long frustrated him, to "harness" (ζεῦξαι, 64) and "mount" (ἀναβαὶς, 86) Pegasus, whereas in *Olympian* 7, she gives the inhabitants of the newly formed island of Rhodes every artistic "skill" (τέχναν, 50) so that they can adorn their streets with realistic statues, "statues that resemble living and moving things" (ἔργα δὲ ζωοῖσιν ἑρπόντεσσί θ' ὁμοῖα, 52). The Bellerophon narrative is the dominant narrative of *Olympian* 13, while the narrative of the Rhodian sculptors is one of three stories of Rhodes' foundation treated at equal length in *Olympian* 7, but in both cases the reference to athletic training and competition should need no demonstration. As the previous chapters have shown, the use of skill in athletics, and the way in which that skill was acquired, were sources of such anxiety to aristocratic victors, it can be assumed that references to skill in their memorials speak not only to a general aristocratic anxiety about the role of skill in excellence, but also specifically to their anxiety about the role of skill in athletic victory. *Olympian* 7 makes the connection explicit, however: it likens the skill of the Rhodian sculptors to Diagoras' skill in boxing by describing it as a skill "to conquer those on earth with hands excellent at toil" (ἐπιχθονίων . . . ἀριστοπόνοις χερσὶ κρατεῖν, 51).[29]

Both narratives represent the abilities Athena confers as anything but commodities. The abilities are Athena's gifts, given to the chosen few as recognition of a special relationship between them and Athena and not available to anyone who can buy them. In *Olympian* 7, Helios advises the Rhodians at the time of Athena's birth to be the "first to build her a conspicuous altar" (πρῶτοι κτίσαιεν βωμὸν ἐναργέα, 42) and "gladden" (ἰάναιεν, 43) her and Zeus by making sacrifice to her (39–43). The Rhodians mark out a precinct for Athena on the acropolis, but, having forgotten to bring fire, must make unburnt offerings (48–9). Despite this, they are handsomely rewarded, both by Zeus, who rains down gold, and by Athena, who gives (ὤπασε, 50) them every artistic skill, and their new-found skills bring them great fame (49–53). In *Olympian* 13, the gift comes before the altar. Frustrated in his desire to harness Pegasus, Bellerophon is advised by the prophet Polyidus to spend the night on Athena's altar (75–6). Athena appears to him, "gives" (ἔπορεν, 13.77; also ἤνεγκ', "brought," 66, and δέκευ, "receive," 68) him the bridle, and tells him to show it to Poseidon Damaios, the Horse Breaker, and sacrifice a bull to him (63–9). The gift should thus properly be thought of as also, in some sense, given by Poseidon. Polyidus then counsels Bellerophon to build an altar to Athena Hippia (79–82).

The ability given to the Rhodians and the implement given to Bellerophon possess mysterious properties that further mark them as gifts because they retain the divine powers of the giver even when deployed by human hands.[30] The bridle is described repeatedly in terms that underline its mystery: it is as a "marvel" (τέρας, *Ol.* 13.73), a "drug" (φάρμακον, 85), and a "magical charm" (φίλτρον, 68). What makes it magical is, as Keith Dickson notes, "that its mode of operation is seen to lie outside the normal order of cause and effect and so to resist explanation in ordinary terms," that is, that with its help Bellerophon is able to do something he could not do through normal human means. The bridle is thus not simply a tool that Bellerophon obtains and uses; it is "gold that breaks the spirit" (δαμασίφρονα χρυσόν, 78), taming Pegasus through its own mysterious powers.[31] This otherworldly power marks the bridle as a gift. Unlike a commodity, it still retains some connection to the giver. Its mysterious abilities mark it as Athena's,[32] and its ability to "break spirits" (δαμασίφρονα) shows that it contains some of Poseidon Damaios' powers also. Indeed, the bridle is much like the winged horse it harnesses: never fully possessed by Bellerophon, Pegasus retains a separate, divine identity and eventually settles on Olympus without him (92). In *Olympian* 7, the stress on the realism of the statues the Rhodians produce also characterizes the skills they have been given as magical: "statues that resemble living and moving things" obviously challenge the normal order of cause and effect, according to which the inanimate and the animate are clearly divided, but the association of magic and realism must have been especially live in a Rhodian audience. In Rhodian mythology, the production of such lifelike statues was more usually associated with the magic and wizardry of the Telchines.[33]

The different abilities that Bellerophon and the Rhodians possess are thus represented as gifts, or as the result of gifts conferred on them by the gods as part of a privileged exchange. Because they are gifts, Bellerophon and the Rhodians do not fully possess their abilities; these abilities are somehow external to themselves, endowed with a certain autonomy and mysterious power that enables their human holders to achieve nonhuman feats and connects them to their divine givers. This externality is particularly clear in *Olympian* 13 in which the ability conferred on Bellerophon is actually conferred through the gift of a magical object: his ability to harness Pegasus is dependent on having this object and is thus not fully his own. Pindar is, however, careful to maintain Bellerophon's agency. Despite the harnessing of Pegasus being dependent on Athena's gift, Bellerophon must still himself put the harness on the horse.[34] Thus, while technical ability is conceived of as lying partly outside the control of its possessor, the possessor is not a tool of his ability, but an agent in his own right.

In these narratives technical ability is certainly given a level of credit and attention that it rarely receives; in *Olympian* 13 it is even represented as an essential ingredient without which those physical, mental, and social qualities that are seen as inherited cannot be successful.[35] The goal of these narratives is not to suggest, however, that a portable ability is more important to success than those that are inherited, but to establish an idea of skill that avoids portraying it as portable, and thus as the sort of thing that a professional trainer might offer. In fact, these narratives represent the acquisition of technical ability as a process similar to the acquisition of inherited excellence: its circulation is tightly restricted, it is acquired only with the blessing of a god, and it is not acquired through teaching. Technical ability, which many considered to be acquired through learning and study, is here relabeled as something acquired through a brief, mysterious, and capricious blessing.

This is why the acquisition of a technical ability is represented in these odes not in terms of its transmission from user to user, but at the moment of its initial use or invention. The feats that Bellerophon and the Rhodians achieve have no precedent, and the gifts they receive have not previously been given; indeed endowing the Rhodians with their superior artistic skills must be Athena's first dealing with humans. Yet once the possessor of a technical ability is conceived of as the inventor or first possessor of that ability, it is easy to conceive of the acquisition of that ability without the learning of that ability, and technical ability, like an invention, is easily imagined to be something given by a god, not something learned from a teacher.[36]

Furthermore, although it is not quite labeled as an inherited ability, technical ability is certainly identified with one because it is closely associated with the ability to invent. Like athletic ability, inventiveness is represented as an inherited quality in the opening triad of *Olympian* 13:

> ἄμαχον δὲ κρύψαι τὸ συγγενὲς ἦθος,
> ὔμμιν δέ, παῖδες Ἀλάτα, πολλὰ μὲν
> νικαφόρον ἀγλαΐαν ὤπασαν
> ἄκραις ἀρεταῖς ὑπερελ-
> θόντων ἱεροῖς ἐν ἀέθλοις,
> πολλὰ δ᾽ ἐν καρδίαις ἀνδρῶν ἔβαλον
> Ὧραι πολυάνθεμοι ἀρ-
> χαῖα σοφίσμαθ᾽.

It is a hard battle to hide inborn character, and, to you, sons of Alatas, the many-flowered Hours have often given the glory of victory when men excelled in the peaks of excellences at the holy games, and they often cast in the hearts of your men ancient devices.

(*Ol.* 13.13–17)

As in the narrative of Bellerophon, technical inventions (σοφίσμαθ', 17), like athletic victories, are seen as the gift (ὤπασαν, 14; ἔβαλον, 16) of gods (Ὧραι, 17), but here it is made explicit that the receipt or invention of these devices, like the receipt of athletic victories, is also to be thought of as the manifestation of "inborn character" (τὸ συγγενὲς ἦθος, 13). (Here the character is not that of a family, but of a citizen body, the citizens of Corinth; these are, however, represented as the "sons of Alatas," as if they are bound by ties of blood rather than situation.)[37] Inventiveness is easily considered an inborn quality, but its inclusion paves the way for a more daring expansion of the inborn. When, in the story of Bellerophon, inventing or being the first user of a technical ability is identified with its simple acquisition, technical ability, as well as intelligence and excellence in war and athletics, also becomes inborn.

This is also, surely, the significance of the difficult gnome that concludes the section on the Rhodian sculptors in *Olympian* 7: δαέντι δὲ καὶ σοφία μείζων ἄδολος τελέθει (53). As David Young sees,[38] δαέντι refers to someone who has learned or been taught, especially someone who has learned a craft; Solon speaks of a craftsman as someone who has "learned the works of Athena and many-skilled Hephaestus" (Ἀθηναίης τε καὶ Ἡφαίστου πολυτέχνεω/ἔργα δαεὶς, 13.49–50). On the other hand, as Young argues, σοφία ἄδολος refers to innate wisdom. ἄδολος, "without trickery," when used of liquids, can mean "unrefined" or "pure," and the use of δόλιος in *Nemean* 3.51 (ἄνευ κυνῶν δυλίων θ' ἑρκέων, "without dogs or crafty snares") makes clear the association between trickery, skill, and teaching. Moreover, σοφία is used elsewhere in Pindar of that wisdom which is not learned.[39] The gnome should, therefore, be understood to mean that "inborn wisdom is also found to be greater in a man who has learned a craft." On one level, this is nonsense – the sum total of one's knowledge is increased by adding new learning to it, but the wisdom one is born with is not – but it makes good sense as a piece of ideology. What happens in this gnome is that learned, technical ability (δαέντι) is relabeled as inborn wisdom (σοφία ἄδολος): in effect, Pindar widens the scope of inborn wisdom so that, rather than being defined in opposition to learned knowledge, it somehow includes that knowledge and renders it nonlearned.

Pindar's representation of technical skill in *Olympians* 7 and 13 has much in common with primitive ideas of technology,[40] but its deployment in the odes has a pointed ideological goal: to frame the use and transmission of technical skill in such a way that it can be accommodated by traditional aristocratic ideas of excellence. Once it is conceived of as a divine gift, technical skill no longer seems to be an easily transferable commodity; moreover, once it is identified with inventiveness, it is even made to seem a quality that is inherited.

The immediate concern behind this representation of technical skill was athletic training, and, in particular, the commodification of that training and the consequent perception that skills were tradable commodities available to all. Like *Nemean* 3, *Olympians* 7 and 13 confront the problems posed by the hiring of athletic trainers, but, whereas *Nemean* 3 plays down the role of skill by transforming the trainer from a paid provider of isolated skills into a surrogate father who (mostly) enhances the natural strength, speed, and determination of his charge, *Olympians* 7 and 13 squarely confront the skills taught by a trainer. The trainer himself, however, disappears; the skills he teaches are represented as given by a god, much as strength and speed are commonly represented in the odes. Skill is thus admitted to be central to the athlete's success, but not a trainer. It was not through the expertise of a trainer that the victor acquired his skills; rather, they were born into him, a gift from the gods and a mark of their special favor. The victor's success is thus portrayed much as any success in aristocratic thinking, as achieved through the help of the gods, and it is the gods to whom he owes thanks.

Three general conclusions follow from this study of *Olympian* 7, *Olympian* 13, and *Nemean* 3. First, the three odes demonstrate that professional trainers were a source of anxiety not only to those few memorials that name one, but to others also. The silence of these memorials concerning the victors' professional trainers was a purposeful erasure: even though none of them names or even mentions an athletic trainer, each ode works to produce an acceptable idea of how a victorious athlete can have a trainer or display the skills taught by a trainer, and the effort dominates two of the odes, *Olympian* 13 and *Nemean* 3.

Second, the three odes demonstrate that it was not only for boys and youths that professional trainers posed a problem. Two other memorials, *Isthmians* 4 and 5, as well as the anecdotal tradition surrounding the statue of Glaucus of Carystus at Olympia, have suggested this, but *Olympians* 7 and 13 and *Nemean* 3 confirm it. Xenophon, Diagoras, and Aristocleidas, like Melissus, Phylacidas, and Glaucus, were all adults.

Third, together with the memorials considered in the previous chapters, the three odes also suggest that the trainers of the various different events were not an equal source of anxiety. Of the memorials considered in detail so far, almost all were for victors in the combat sports: Aristocleidas of Aegina, Melissus of Thebes, and Phylacidas and Pytheas of Aegina were pancratiasts; Diagoras of Rhodes, Glaucus of Carystus, and Hagesidamus of Western Locri were boxers; and the three Aeginetans coached by Melesias, Alcimedon, Alcimidas, and Timasarchus, were wrestlers. The one exception is Xenophon, the victor of *Olympian* 13, who won the stade and the pentathlon, but he may not be much of an exception. The pentathlon may have been more closely associated with the combat sports than the running events. Wrestling was one of the five events, and, as the final deciding event, it must have received more attention than the others.[41] Moreover, Xenophon's participation in the field events of the pentathlon may have been particularly marked because of his family's history of competing in the running. His father, Thessalos, won a running event at Olympia, as well as the stade and the *diaulos* on the same day at Delphi and three more running events later that month on the same day at the Great Panathenaea.[42] The fact that Xenophon was a pentathlete as well as a sprinter may therefore have seemed like a departure from the more natural abilities his father displayed, and thus the skills he needed to excel in the field events and the wrestling may have generated more attention than was usual for a victor in the pentathlon.

Certainly, what we do not see is consistent evidence of anxiety concerning training in the odes that celebrate runners. The sample is not small: seven odes survive intact, with another two in fragments.[43] Comparison of *Nemean* 3 with *Pythian* 9, which celebrates the victory of Telesicrates of Cyrene in the race in armor at Delphi in 474,[44] is illustrative. Telesicrates did not enter only hoplite races; he was also a sprinter, winning the stadion at Delphi eight years later in 466.[45] In the latter part of his career he was probably a competitor of Xenophon's; indeed, he was probably one of the athletes who prevented Xenophon from winning at all four of the crown-bearing festivals.[46] It was after his first major win, however, that Telesicrates sought to preserve his name for history. At Delphi, he dedicated a statue of himself wearing a helmet, a sign of the race in armor,[47] and for his celebrations at home he commissioned a long ode from Pindar. It is in this ode that Chiron plays a major role.

In his dealings with Apollo, the Chiron of *Pythian* 9 displays a number of similarities to the Chiron of *Nemean* 3: just as Chiron hardens Achilles' determination in battle, so he "girds" (ἔντυεν, 66) Apollo to complete his marriage; just as he gives the youthful Achilles moral instruction, so he instructs a youthful Apollo in the subtleties of love and seduction (39–41);[48] and just as he (while acting as Achilles' teacher) does not seem to be responsible for Achilles' quality or the excellence of his actions, so he does not enlighten the all-knowing Apollo (44–9) or affect his actions, which are already determined by fate (51–65). Yet to see training as the silent center around which the narrative of Chiron in *Pythian* 9 is organized would be a mistake. Apollo is not Chiron's pupil here. There is no tradition to support such a conclusion, and Apollo's contact with Chiron is represented as brief, not part of a preexisting tutorial relationship.[49] Indeed, as Chiron is related to Cyrene, the model for the contact is a betrothal ceremony, in which the bridegroom seeks legal consent for a marriage from a senior male member of the bride's clan.[50] Moreover, there is none of the emphasis laid on teaching that is evident in *Nemean* 3: where *Nemean* 3 offers a dense sequence of terms that describe Chiron's teaching (τράφε, 53; δίδαξε, 55; ἀτίταλλεν, 58; θυμὸν αὔξων, 58), Pythian 9 offers at most only one: ἔντυεν ("girded," 66), and this is a pun on the event in which Telesicrates competed.[51] The central concern of this narrative lies elsewhere, then, in the notion of fate: Pindar seeks to represent not only Telesicrates' victory as preordained, but also the foundation and settlement of Cyrene by Greeks. Both events are instances of the cosmic order, not the result of chance, and so the justice and propriety of each cannot be questioned.[52]

The lack of concern for trainers in the odes that celebrate victorious runners suggests that people in general needed little convincing that being a good runner was a natural talent. This was simply taken for granted; even though runners had trainers, people simply did not see them as crucial to their success, and so there was no need for the odes to direct their resources towards shaping the trainer in ways favorable to the victor. The same lack of concern is evident in the anecdotes that survive concerning natural athletes, those individuals who, after demonstrating unusual athletic ability in some rustic occupation, are entered, without any formal training, into a contest which they then win. That the story of Glaucus of Carystus was not the only one of its kind has already been noted; but of the four athletes Philostratus names – Polymestor of Miletus, Glaucus, Amesinas of Barce, and Polydamas of Scotussa – only one is a runner, Polymestor, who is said elsewhere to have run faster than a hare; Glaucus and Amesinas are boxers, and Polydamas was a pancratiast.[53] This is very strange; although to be a successful runner in competition certainly required training, the running events were much less technical than the combat events, and so it was much more likely (if still highly unlikely) that an untrained farmhand could triumph in the running events than in boxing or pancration. What explains the preponderance of such stories concerning boxers and pancratiasts is their ideological context: whereas the aristocrats' version of running was not contested, their version of combat sports was, and aristocratic memorials, and aristocratic discourse more generally, had to ensure that their version achieved dominance.

Thus, not all the silences that surround trainers in victory memorials are equal. The exclusion of trainers from memorials for victories in the combat sports was strained and anxious; it had to compete against different, and popular, versions of how much training and what sort of training was required for these sports. By contrast, the exclusion of trainers from the memorials for runners was, although certainly purposeful, more comfortable. Even though most runners, adults and youths, used trainers, most people, then as now, felt that victories in the running events were the result of the victor's natural talent, not his training, and so an account of the victory that did not recognize the work done by a trainer was unlikely to meet opposition.

CONCLUSION

When Callimachus arranged the victory odes of Simonides, he divided them up primarily according to the event in which each victor had won his victory, but when he arranged Pindar's he did so according to the festival at which the victories had been won.[1] Although it is impossible to determine how different the scholarship on Pindar's odes might have been had they been organized as Simonides' were, such an organization would surely have had a profound effect. Arranging the odes by event sets up the victor as, first and foremost, an athlete of a certain sort – a racer of chariots or a wrestler – and so puts the focus on the specific mechanics of how each victory was won; what personnel, animals, and equipment were involved; and so also on the ways in which each ode confronts and represents these particular facts. By contrast, the arrangement of Pindar's odes makes victory more a matter of the title that is won; Olympic victors are grouped together because they all won at the same festival, and the differences between how those victors won are pushed into the background.

This study has, in effect, applied Callimachus' arrangement of Simonides' odes to all victory memorials from the late archaic and early classical period. This has, I hope, made it clear that the event in which the victory was won shaped the representational strategies of each memorial. Memorials for equestrian victories do not display the concern over skill and teaching that is evident in memorials for gymnastic victories; memorials for chariot victories generally focus on erasing the charioteer, and those for horse races focus on elevating the horse; memorials for victories in the combat sports expend more energy confronting the issue of training than memorials for runners.

In representing these events in their different ways, these memorials all confront the same central ideological problem for their patrons: the fact that a professional of some sort was instrumental in each of their victories – a charioteer, mule-cart driver, or jockey in the equestrian events, and an athletic trainer in the gymnastic events. The involvement of these professionals in an aristocrat's victory was extremely awkward for two reasons. First, it threatened the aristocratic tenet that victory, and indeed all success, was largely determined by inherited abilities, and, second, it validated a mode of exchange that challenged the aristocrats' control over society and sense of their own identity. A few victors were able to win without the help of a professional. The odd chariot victor drove his own car or had a friend or family member do so, and the odd victor in a gymnastic event may have been trained by a relative or by a trainer who was genuinely attached to his family, or perhaps even not trained by anyone for many years. But the majority of victors had to rely on individuals with whom they had no prior connection and whose services they purchased for a fee.

Most memorials simply exclude professional charioteers, drivers, jockeys, and trainers from the victory record and create in that way a victory in which commodity exchange had no part; the few memorials that include them figure them in such a way that they appear either to be insignificant to the victory, not to be a professional, or both. Victory can then be understood as the result of the victor's inborn abilities and of aristocratic modes of transmission, such as inheritance and the exchange of goods and services among people who have an enduring relationship.

Most victory memorials paid little regard to the facts of competition in their representation of the victory. Many simply avoided any mention of how an equestrian race was won, or of how a competitor prepared for a gymnastic event and the skills he needed to win. These memorials must have presumed that their audiences would be largely ignorant of the details of athletic contests, or at least largely uninterested in interrogating the memorials' representations of them, but they also received some support from epic poetry, and, in the case of the equestrian competitions at least, from the leisure practices of the aristocrats and the institution of the victory parade. The most convincing representations, however, were surely those that paid more regard to the actual mechanics of victory and recognized the participation of professional charioteers, jockeys, and trainers. While seeming to be a truer account of the event, these memorials were also able to make use of certain facts about this participation – the lower status of the charioteers, the youth of the jockeys and the fact that the racehorses were not commodities, the higher status of the trainers and the relative length of their employment – to hide what was really damaging to aristocratic interests: that these figures were professional and had no enduring connection to the victors.

Various factors must have determined the approach taken in each memorial: the location of the memorial's display or performance, the memorials recently displayed or performed there, those expected to hear or view the memorial, the particular circumstances and needs of the patron, the constraints and opportunities presented by the medium, the artist's experience and creativity, and the freedom given to him by the patron. Moreover, in some cases, the prominence of the professional involved may have been a factor. It seems likely that some of these professionals, such as the charioteer Nicomachus and the trainers Melesias and Menander, were able to force themselves into victory memorials, either directly, by making their employment contingent on such recognition or by commissioning the memorials themselves, or indirectly, by becoming so famous that they could not be ignored.

The danger of studying these prominent few at length is that this focus creates a false idea of the extent to which these figures as a group, and in particular those professionals who came from outside the elite, had some power over their representation. Few of the professionals involved in Greek athletics had any power to determine their representation, and few of those who did came from outside the aristocracy. Certainly, many aristocrats sought to adapt their ideology of athletics to the changing demands and perceptions of many outside the elite in the late archaic and early classical periods, but few from outside the elite were able to influence the new shapes that ideology took. Just as it was the aristocrats' competitiveness that created the conditions under which charioteers, jockeys, and trainers became professional, so it was mostly the aristocrats themselves who, in jostling for position against each other, either locally or across the Mediterranean, created new and threatening representations of victory. Many aristocrats were prepared to expose the silences in the traditional representations of athletics, if, in naming their charioteers and trainers, they could, like Lampon and some of the other Aeginetans, secure the services of the best professionals, or, like Arcesilas of Cyrene, demonstrate how much greater their own victories were than those of other victors. Those few professional trainers, like Melesias and Menander, who were able by the weight of their records to force themselves into the victory memorials of their pupils, must also have been mostly aristocrats because they themselves were mostly successful athletes when they were younger. Finally, it was most likely aristocrats who, to devalue the athletic activities of some of their peers, generated and transmitted the stories that surface later of trainers being responsible for victories or cheaper than courtesans.

The basic silences that most memorials maintained concerning charioteers, jockeys, and trainers were thus for the most part contested by aristocrats, not outsiders. This should not be a surprise: the same advantages that allowed aristocrats to dominate athletic competition allowed them to dominate its representations. This dominance was not total, however, and one person who challenged it was the charioteer Nicomachus, who, although not an aristocrat, seems to have become so famous after driving the winning chariot in the banner Olympic games of 476 that a memorial that ignored his participation in that victory could not be convincing. Nicomachus was an exception, however, and even he was reduced by the end of Pindar's *Isthmian* 2 from a position of some equality with Xenocrates and Theron to the status of their servant. Most professional charioteers, jockeys, and mule-cart drivers could not even win recognition as servants from the memorials that celebrated the victories they helped to win.

The goal of this study is not, however, to bring recognition or justice to those professionals who came from outside the elite. There is no compelling reason why their contribution to victory should have been valued more highly than it was (the victor's contribution can with some justice be seen as more important), and, although rarely recognized in the memorials, they were presumably better remunerated and lived more comfortable lives than those who lacked the opportunities their skills had given them. Rather, the goal has been to trace one particular way in which the aristocrats of the late archaic and early classical periods sought, in response to an increasing hostility to the idea of aristocracy, to affirm their identity to themselves and justify their political privileges to the wider civic community. Athletics was one of the central pillars of the aristocracy, and it was crucial that, even as commodification altered the ways in which victory was won, it be represented in such a way that it continue to promote the superiority and rightness of aristocracy as a system of organizing society. The aristocrats were, in effect, engaged in two contests, the first against each other for the prize of victory, and the second, as a group, for the meaning of athletics. They were prepared to spend lavishly on both.

NOTES

INTRODUCTION

1 Paus. 6.5.4–9, Luc. *Deor. Conc.* 12, Moretti 1957.110. As Moretti notes, the statue must have been set up some years after the victory but before the destruction of Scotussa in 367. Parts of the relief have been discovered; see Treu 1966.209–12.

2 On the aristocrats' dominance of the games, see Pleket 1975.71–4, Crowther 1991.166, and Rose 1992.147–8. (Tyrants should be counted among the aristocrats, as Rose 1992.147 notes.) Although some victors were surely not aristocrats (see Young 1983a.49–50 and 1984.150–62), the majority were, and the few consistently successful athletes from outside the aristocracy were probably absorbed into the elite; cf. Rose 1992.146.

3 Rose 1992.160–3 argues that Pindar's odes represented excellence as inherited, but other memorials did also. See Sim. 519A *fr.* 21–2 (Barrett 1978.5–16), Ba. 13.190–1, and the dedications of Polypeithes (Paus. 6.16.6, Moretti 1957.87), Anaxander (Paus. 6.1.7, Moretti 1957.106), and the two Alcmaeonids (*IG* I^3 597, Moretti 1953 no.4, Raubitschek 1949 no.317).

4 Rose 1974.154–5 and 1992.96–8, 147–8, 162–3, and Kyle 1987.155–68.

5 Kurke 1989, 1991.85–159, 252–5, 1999.17–18, 41–64; Rose 1992.120–1, 144–6; Murray 1993.220–45; von Reden 1995a.6–8; 11–76; and Tandy 1997.141–65. The aristocrats' denunciation of commodity exchange did not mean that they did not trade; see Rose 1992.137, 146, Murray 1993.220–8, von Reden 1995a.6–8, and Tandy 1997.73–5.

6 Tandy 1997.113–17. Cf. Kurke 1991.253.

7 Xen. *Ages.* 9.6, Plut. *Ages.* 20.1 Agesilaus, in fact, had his cake and ate it too by having his sister, Cynisca, compete.

8 Gzella 1971.189–202, Webster 1972.270–300, Bell 1978.29–86, Gentili 1988.155–76, Kurke 1991.7, von Reden 1995b.30–50, and Boardman 2001.11–127, 153–69.

9 Golden 1998.40–1; *IG* 5.1.213 (Moretti 1953 no.16); Shear 2003.92n.17, 102–5. *IG* 5.1.213 probably dates to the early fourth century: see Golden 1998.40n.35 and Hodkinson 1999.152. The Panathenaea also offered various military contests

involving horses; see Gardiner 1910.237–9, Kyle 1987.186–9, and Shear 2003.92, 102–5.

10 Pi. *Is.* 1.52–9; the victories probably date to the 470s (cf. Bowra 1964.410).

11 *IG* 5.1.213; see n.9 to this Introduction for the date.

12 Pi. *Is.* 1.15 and *IG* 5.1.213 leave no doubt that the victors drove their chariots; *IG* 5.1.213 repeats the phrase αὐτὸς ἀνιοχίον, "himself driving," nine times. *Contra* Lefkowitz 1985.41–2, such explicit statements should be differentiated from the suggestions made by many memorials that the owners drove; see Chapter 1, and Bernadini in Lefkowitz 1985.65–6.

13 Golden 1998.40–3. The Oxyrhynchus victory list does not record victors in either event. Only one memorial is attested for the *kalpe*, a statue of the victor that omitted his name (Paus. 6.9.2). On the mule-cart race, see Chapter 4.

14 *Contra* Golden 1998.40–3.

15 Paus. 5.9.2. On the *apobates*, see Gardiner 1910.237–9 and Kyle 1987.188–9.

16 Golden 1998.3. Some equestrian events were restricted to "warriors," presumably Athenian ones; cf. Gardiner 1910.237 and Shear 2003.102–5.

17 Olympia did not offer the *hippios* race, although the Nemean, Isthmian, and Panathenaic games did (Paus. 6.16.4; *IG*^{3} 597, Raubitschek 1949 no.317, Moretti 1953 no.4); the hoplite race was introduced only in 520 (Paus. 5.8.10). Some festivals offered other events, such as the individual events of the pentathlon (see Moretti 1953 nos.1 and 6).

18 The Olympic games required athletes to train at Olympia before the festival (Crowther 1991.161–2), and their trainers probably accompanied them. Like the athletes, the trainers had to swear to respect the games (Paus. 5.25.9), and several anecdotes describe them encouraging athletes during the events (see Chapter 6).

19 In the archaic period, youths could only compete in boxing, wrestling, and the stadion at Olympia, but at other festivals they could enter all the events open to adult athletes, except the hoplite race (Golden 1998.110). Although Olympia offered only one youth category (παῖδες), other festivals, including the Nemean and Isthmian, offered contests for "beardless youths" (ἀγένειοι) as well. On these categories, see Golden 1998.104–16.

20 *Il.* 11.698–702, 9.123–4, Golden 1998.91.

21 Golden 1998.118–23.

22 Philostr. *Gym.* 21, Moretti 1957.70, and Young 1984.147. The text of Jüthner 1969 is used throughout for Philostratus' *De Gymnastica.*

23 Appadurai 1986.9–13, Bloch and Parry 1989.1–7. For some different meanings attached to the payment of money, see von Reden 1995a.195–216.

24 Gregory 1982.19; also Kopytoff 1986.68–70 and Tandy 1997.94–101.

25 Pl. *Meno* 94c; Kyle 1987.202, 208–9, 224, 226.

26 Pi. *Ol.* 8.65–6; the victors celebrated in *Ol.* 8, *Ne.* 4 and *Ne.* 6, all trainees of Melesias, were wrestlers. For the identification of this Melesias with Thucydides' father, see Wade-Gery 1932.205–27, Woloch 1963.102, Kyle 1987.207, Figueira 1993.199n.7, and Mann 2001.230–1, *contra* Wilamowitz 1922.398, Young 1984.148n.45, Race 1990.155, and Kirchner 1996.

27 Kyle 1987.220, but also Kirchner 1996.168–72.

28 See Pi. *Ol.* 8.54–66, *Ne.* 4.93–6, 6.64–6, and also Mann 2001.232–3.
29 Figueira 1993.197–230.
30 Young 1984.148–9 and Kyle 1987.144n.121, 145n.132, *contra* Figueira 1993. 205–11 and Woloch 1963.102. The career of the Crotoniate doctor Democedes, who was hired by the Aeginetans for an annual salary of one talent (Hdt. 3.131) and who may have specialized in sports medicine (Young 1984.145–6, Miller 2000.285–7, and Mann 2001.171–81), suggests that the Aeginetan clans would have been happy to pay Melesias for his service. Indeed, the size of Democedes' salary suggests that the clans clubbed together to fund their investments in athletics (Mann 2001.232–3).
31 Pi. *Ne.* 5.48–9.
32 Ba. 13.190–8.
33 On Melesias and Menander, see Chapters 7 and 8.
34 Gardiner 1910.111–12, Young 1984.140–9, Kyle 1987.144n.121, 145n.132, and Rose 1992.169.
35 Pi. *Py.* 5 and *SEG* XXIII 38 (*ad IG* I^2 472). See Chapter 2.
36 Pl. *Lysis* 208a. Socrates' surprise addresses the question of a parent's trust in his children, not the use of a hired charioteer. On the family, see Pl. *Lysis* 205c, Davies 1971.359–61, and Kyle 1987.199, 206.
37 Thuc. 6.16.2 specifies that Alcibiades was the first private citizen (ἰδιώτης) to enter seven chariots at the Olympics, which implies that he was imitating a king or tyrant. The various accounts of this episode agree that at least one of Alcibiades' chariots was purchased; see Moretti 1957.109, Kyle 1987.195–6, Mann 2001.103–4.
38 That Cimon and Evagoras won three consecutive victories with the same teams (Hdt. 6.103, Moretti 1957.71–2) suggests that one entry was the norm in the sixth century. Xen. *Hiero* 11.5 asserts that Hieron entered teams in many races, not that he made multiple entries.
39 Pi. *Is.* 2.12–29.
40 Schol. *ad* Pi. *Is.* 2.28b. The scholiast misunderstands *Is.* 2.19–20. On Nicomachus, see Chapter 3. The text of the scholia is taken throughout from Drachmann 1903, 1910, and 1927.
41 1986.13–16.
42 Young 1983a.48–9, Golden 1998.37, and Mann 2001.246–8. Young 1983a.49 argues that Croton was not the town of Astylus' birth. On his victories, see Moretti 1957.82–5, 87, 90.
43 Mann 2001.244–5.
44 Paus. 6.4.11; cf. Pi. *Ol.* 12.1–2, 13–16. For the dates of his victories, see Moretti 1957.91, 94.
45 Kyle 1987.160, Crowther 1994.132, and Gardiner 1910.463. Lefkowitz 1985. 41–2 sees many owners as driving, whereas Golden 1998.82 sees a mix of owners, slaves, and professionals.
46 See Chapter 5.
47 See n.8, this introduction. Repeat commissions could suggest and even create an enduring relationship (Nicholson 2000.246), but there was no expectation

that a single commission would inaugurate such a connection. Pythagoras served victors from Sicily, Italy, Libya, and the Peloponnese; see Hyde 1921.178–83.

48 On Pi. *Is.* 5.59–61 and 6.72–3, see Chapter 8, and cf. Gardiner 1910.111–12. For in-house poets, see Pi. *Ne.* 4.89–90.

49 Kroll and Waggoner 1984, Kurke 1991.7, 1999.6–7, and Murray 1993.237–40.

50 In the sixth century Athens, Croton and, at least in the latter part of the century, Aegina were disproportionately successful in equestrian events (Kyle 1987. 104–5), running (Young 1984.134–40, Mann 2001.164–91) and combat sports, respectively (cf. Pi. *Ol.* 8.76, *Ne.* 6.58–61, and Ba. 12.36–41), while Sparta's earlier dominance in gymnastic events evaporated (Mann 2001.121–4). Various factors surely contributed, but anecdotes such as those about Alcmaeon (Hdt. 6.125; see Chapter 1) and Democedes (Hdt. 3.131; see n.30, this Introduction) suggest that one common factor was the willingness of the local aristocracies to purchase the services they required. See also Young 1984.140–6.

51 As noted earlier, owners drove their own chariots much more frequently at local competitions.

52 E.g. [Pi.] *Ol.* 5; see Bowra 1964.414–20 and Hamilton 1972.324–9.

53 As Slater 1984.244 argues, the majority were performed in the victor's hometown.

54 Pi. *Py.* 4 was commissioned by a politician who had returned to the victor's favor (Chamoux 1953.187–198, Mitchell 1966.109, Carey 1980b.143–4, and Braswell 1988.5–6), while a youth's lover is also a plausible patron (Hubbard 2003.6–7).

55 Mullen 1982 and Heath 1988.184–8.

56 Kurke 1991.5.

57 Bundy 1986, Hamilton 1974, and Race 1990.

58 Kurke 1991.5 and Gorgon *FGrH* 515 F18 = schol *ad* Pi. *Ol.* 7. Although much later, Gorgon's testimony is probably sound; temples did not dispose of valuable dedications, and Gorgon wrote a work specifically on Rhodian sacred rites (*FGrH* F18–19).

59 See Pliny *HN* 34.16, Gross 1969, and Jacquemin 1999.197n.324 for "Pliny's law," which perhaps restricted the pose in which an athlete could be represented; Paus. 6.3.6 suggests that trainers could not be included in statue groups.

60 In the fifth century at Delphi, it seems to have been a regular practice for memorials for youth victories to be dedicated by their cities (Jacquemin 1999.84–7, 202–3), but at Olympia cities only seem to have been allowed to dedicate memorials for earlier athletes (Hodkinson 1999.165–7, Mann 2001.136–8).

61 Habicht 1985.147–51. Dedications could even include buildings: the Sicyonian tyrant Myron commemorated his chariot victory in 648 with a treasury (Paus. 6.19.1–6).

62 London B144 (*ABV* 307/59; figs. 8 and 9); Würzburg 215 (*ABV* 375/213; fig. 11); Plovdiv, unnumbered, from the third quarter of the fifth century, for a citharode (*ARV*[2] 1044/9; Webster 1972.49; Boardman 1989.62–3, pl.149).

63 Thompson 1956.63–4, Moretti 1957.80, but also 1987.68. Moretti dates Titas' victory to 504. On such insults, see Svenbro 1988.207–37.

64 The list of Webster 1972.152–7 includes many vases where the scene of victory is peripheral.

65 E.g., Copenhagen 109 (*ABV* 135/33); see Chapter 2.

66 On Panathenaic vases, see especially Beazley 1951.88–100 and Shear 2003.96–102.

67 E.g., Florence, unnumbered (*ABV* 110/33; figs. 2 and 3) and Nauplion 1 (*ABV* 260/27; fig. 10).

68 Munich 1517 (*ABV* 401; fig. 1).

69 See Chapter 3 for a discussion of Mainz 74 (*ABV* 716, *ARV*[2] 1602) and Louvre F283 (*ARV*[2] 1584, fig. 6).

70 On the price of vases, see Boardman 2001.156–9.

71 See Chapter 7, and fig. 12.

72 Miltiades: Seltman 1924.136–45, Kyle 1987.208; Gelon: Kraay 1976.210, cf. Rutter 1997.121–32; Anaxilas: fig. 7, Arist. *Rh.* 3.2.1405b, Arnold-Biucchi 1990.17–19, 26–9, and Rutter 1997.119–20. Whether the Syracusan coins issued after 485 refer to Gelon's Olympic chariot victory of 488 is disputed. If Rutter's dating (1997.121–32) is accepted, however, two striking changes in the coin types make such a reference likely: first, a Nike bearing a crown is added above the four-horse chariot of earlier coins; second, the reverse introduces, or gives new prominence to Arethusa, the spring that, according to legend, linked Syracuse to Olympia. *Contra* Farnell 1932.30, however, Psaumis of Camarina did not commemorate his Olympic victory of 452 with a coin issue (Farnell 1930, fig. 2; *LIMC* II.1.974). *LIMC* dates the issue to the late fifth century, and the design links Camarina not to victory but to the coin issues of the Deinomenids. Athena takes the charioteer's place to signify Camarina's identity as a Rhodian (and not Corinthian) foundation.

73 The coin types of Messana and Syracuse were not significantly altered after the fall of their respective tyrannies (although those of Rhegium were); see Rutter 1997.132–5.

74 On another purpose of Anaxilas' issues, see Chapter 4; and on the aura of victory, Kurke 1998.

75 Miltiades' coin issue dates from around 550; cf. Moretti 1957.71 and Davies 1971.299–300.

76 Ibyc. 282B, Barron 1984.20–2, Jenner 1986, Golden 1998.77, Hodkinson 1999.171–3. The Callias of Ibyc. 282B, S221 may be the Callias who won an Olympic victory in 564 (Moretti 1957.70, Kyle 1987.203).

77 Paus. 6.18.7, with Moretti 1957.71–2. The first portrait statue of an equestrian victor to be dedicated as part of a statue group at Olympia was that of Cleosthenes, in 516 (Paus. 6.10.6–8, Moretti 1957.76–7).

78 Paus. 8.40.1, Moretti 1957.70. The statue's appearance supports its early dating; see Lattimore 1988.252–4.

79 London B144 (*ABV* 307/59, figs. 8 and 9).

80 Kyle 1987.21–4. Vases were awarded at other games too, including those at Thebes and Argos; see Beazley 1928.20n.3 and Thompson 1956.64.

81 Pindar was active from 498 (*Py.* 10) to 446 (*Py.* 8); Simonides from 520 (Sim. 509) to the 470s or even to 468 (Sim. 506, and Athen. 1.3e, with Moretti 1957.93–4); and the sculptor Glaucias of Aegina from at least 500 to at least 476 (Moretti 1957.80).

82 *Py.* 8, from 446, is Pindar's last dateable ode; Ba. 6 and 7 date from 452. On Euripides' epinician for Alcibiades' victory of 416, see Mann 2001.102–13.

83 Davies 1984.88–131, Golden 1998.84–6.

84 Xenophanes *fr.* 2.1–22. Tyrt. *fr.* 12.1–14 (West); cf. Hodkinson 1999.157–60, Mann 2001.121–132. London E78, from around 480 (*ARV*[2] 401/3, Poliakoff 1987 fig. 53); a vase in Baltimore of similar date (*ARV*[2] 340/65, Poliakoff 1987 fig. 54); and Villa Giulia 477, from the late sixth century (Poliakoff 1987 fig. 89). Golden 1998.59–60 rightly warns that such vases could be celebratory. For later criticisms, see Xen. *Ages.* 9.6, Plut. *Ages.* 20.1, Isoc. 16.33, Kyle 1987.141–2.

85 As Davies 1984.103–5 notes, the institution or reorganization of the Pythian, Isthmian, Nemean, and Panathenaic games between 582 and 566 dramatically increased the opportunities for prestigious victories, and smaller festivals continued to be founded or given greater prominence over the next hundred years. See, on Attica, Kyle 1987.32–55.

86 Morris, 2000.113–91.

87 On the composition of late archaic society, see Rose 1992.142–51, Murray 1993.102–58, 181–202, and Tandy 1997.194–227.

88 On "cult-power," liturgies and voluntary forms of civic expenditure in Athens, see Davies 1984.88–114.

89 Morris 2000.187–90; Kurke 1991. Typical is Pi. *Is.* 6.69–72, which elides gift exchange, civic benefactions, and the pursuit of moderation.

90 For this idea of cultural production, see especially Althusser 1971.121–173, Williams 1977.75–141, Macherey 1978.3–101, 258–98, Macherey and Balibar 1981.87–97, Eagleton 1983.194–217, Frow 1986.1–82, Ryan 1989.200–13, and Rose 1992.33–42.

91 Diog Laert. 8.12–13, Paus. 6.7.10, Ath. 412d–414c, and Golden 1998.157–8.

92 New Historicists, such as Montrose 1989.15–36 and Gallagher and Greenblatt 2000.1–19, emphasize the importance of considering different types of products when interrogating a cultural formation.

93 On the use of anecdotes, see Fumerton 1999.4–5 and Gallagher and Greenblatt 2000.20–74.

94 See Chapter 6.

95 See schol. *ad* Pi. *Ol.* 7 inscr. a and c.

96 Another premise of New Historicism: see Sewell 1999.46–58, and cf. Howard 1986.27–30 and Montrose 1989.22–3.

97 See Chapter 7, n.67.

1. MISSING PERSONS

1 The text of Pindar is taken from Maehler 1987 and 1989, unless otherwise noted. That of Bacchylides from Campbell 1992.

2 κόσμον (10) must refer to the glory cast either on Hieron (as Lefkowitz 1976.14) or on the chariot (as schol. *ad Py.* 2.16a), rather than to a harness. Cf. *Ol.* 3.13, 8.83, *Ne.* 2.8, 3.31.

3 For the location of the victory, see Most 1985.61–5, but also Lefkowitz 1976. 164–5, who suggests the Isthmian games at Syracuse.

4 See Introduction. Herodotus of Thebes did, in fact, drive his chariot at the Ioleia (Pi. *Is.* 1.55–6).

5 *Contra* Lefkowitz 1985.41–2.

6 Pi. *Is.* 1 and *IG* 5.1.213 (Moretti 1953 no.16). For the dates of these memorials, see Introduction, n.9.

7 Golden 1998.121 puts Hieron at over age fifty in 478. For the age of late antique charioteers, see Cameron 1973.178–9.

8 Most 1985.65–8 dates the victory between 477 and 475, but there is no reason it could not date from the late 470s.

9 Pi. *Py.* 1.47–55, and schol. *ad Py.* 1.89b. The specific details in the scholiast's account suggest that he drew this information from an independent source, perhaps Timaeus, rather than inventing it to explain the parallel with Philoctetes. *Py.* 3.73 also seems to refer to this illness; see Bowra 1964.129–30. Which campaign is referred to in *Py.* 1.50–5 is unclear, although νῦν (*Py.* 1.50) suggests it is closer to 470 than Cumae (474) or Himera (480).

10 Hieron's close associates certainly used specialist drivers: Hagesias, a Syracusan supporter, used a driver in his Olympic mule-cart victory (Pi. *Ol.* 6.22), and Theron and Xenocrates, the leaders of the ruling family of Acragas to which the Deinomenids were closely linked, used a charioteer at the Olympics and the Panathenaea, respectively (*Is.* 2.19–28).

11 Throughout this chapter mule-cart drivers are included in the general category of charioteers.

12 The twenty-eight memorials consist of sixteen odes, ten dedications, one vase, and one funerary monument: Pi. *Ol.* 2–6, *Py.* 1–2, 5–7, *Ne.* 1, 9, *Is.* 2–3/4 (*Is.* 1 is excluded because the victor drove his own chariot); Ba. 3–4; Ebert 1972 nos.3 (Moretti 1953 no.5), 4, 8, 13, 17; Raubitschek 1949 nos.171 and 174; the Olympic dedications of Polypeithes (Paus. 6.16.6), Gelon (6.9.4–5), and Cratisthenes (6.18.1); Munich 1517 (*ABV* 401); and the monument of the elder Cimon (Hdt. 6.103). *Ol.* 5–6 are for mule-cart victories; on *Ol.* 5, see Hamilton 1972.324–9 and Gerber 1987.8. Memorials that are so fragmentary or poorly recorded that it is not clear whether the charioteer was named have been excluded from this list, as have memorials that may date outside 550–440, and memorials, such as coins or certain vases, that do not name the victor. Pi. *Py.* 4 has also been excluded for reasons that become clear in the next chapter. The four memorials that name a charioteer are Pi. *Ol.* 6, *Py.* 5, *Is.* 2, and *SEG* XXIII.38, *ad IG* I^2 472 (Ebert 1972 no.3).

13 Sim. 514 suggests that Simonides praised a charioteer from a victory at Pellene but, given that the charioteer is said to have won and to have received the cloak traditionally awarded to the victor, either the testimonium is being careless or the victor drove his own chariot.

14 Of the twenty-eight memorials listed in n.12, this chapter, there is insufficient evidence to be sure about two: Raubitschek 1949 nos.171 and 174. Of the remaining twenty-six memorials, nineteen do not represent the charioteer at all: Pi. *Ol.* 2–5, *Py.* 1–2, 6–7, *Ne.* 1, 9, *Is.* 3/4; Ba. 3–4; Ebert 1972 no.8; the Olympic dedications of Polypeithes, Gelon, and Cratisthenes; Munich 1517; and the monument of the elder Cimon.

15 For the coin issues of Miltiades, Gelon, and Anaxilas, see Introduction; Cleosthenes' memorial is recorded at Paus. 6.10.6–8 (Ebert 1972 no.4) and Hieron's, which was dedicated by his son Deinomenes, at Paus. 6.12.1 and 8.42.8–9 (Ebert 1972 no.17). For Polyzalus' dedication, see Ebert 1972 no.13, Chamoux 1955, Jacquemin 1999 no.449; Rolley 1990.291–2 argues persuasively that it, too, commemorates Hieron's victories. Only three other memorials certainly refer to a charioteer: Pindar *Ol.* 6 and *Is.* 2 (which describes a chariot race from an earlier win), and *SEG* XXIII.38, *ad IG* I^2 472 (Ebert 1972 no.3).

16 The following vases, all from the middle to late fifth century, depict a racing chariot with a Nike nearby and thus seem to indicate victory in a chariot race: Athenian Agora P9486, on which the Nike carries a Panathenaic vase (*ARV*^{2} 1040/18); Syracuse 26563 (1097/13); Ferrara T. 187 B VP (1097/14); Bologna 205 (1101/1); "Paris Market" (1101/2); New York 41.162.69 (1108/23); Syracuse 19842 (1109/26); Naples Stg. 694 (1112/2); Leyden 1952.1.1 (1112/3); Honolulu 3589 (1112/4); Lecce 600 (1115/20); Naples RC 125 (1115/21); Ferrara T. 44 B VP (1115/22); Villa Giulia 5386 (1118/22); Upsala (1118/23); once New York (1120/4); Ragusa (1112); Eleusis 602 (1155/5).

17 Munich 1517 (*ABV* 401). The inscription is not visible in this photograph (from the archives of the Archaeological Institute of the University of Munich), but no better photograph is available. When Beazley saw the vase, it had been heavily repainted, but enough of the inscription remained for him to read.]ΛKM.ON.

18 Beazley 1953/54.204–5; also Webster 1972.57. On Alcmaeon, see Kyle 1987.196, and, for this story, Hdt. 6.125, who wrongly names the Lydian king as Croesus, and Kurke 2003.90–2, who argues that the story was part of a popular critique of aristocratic practices.

19 *SEG* XXIII.38 (Moretti 1953 no.5, Ebert 1972 no.3); see Chapter 2.

20 Webster 1972.57.

21 The anxieties concerning the charioteer expressed by the vase were probably misplaced, the result of an anachronistic retrojection of later Alcmaeonid equestrian practice. Alcmaeon almost certainly used a kinsman, acquaintance, slave, or servant.

22 Florence, unnumbered (*ABV* 110); see also Beazley 1951.90–1 and pl.18.

23 Beazley 1951.90–1.

24 Nauplion 1 (*ABV* 260, fig. 10).

25 As Bury 1890.174 sees, this phrase refers to chariots.

26 For Baton, see *LIMC* I.1.694–6, 698–9, and, for Schoenichus, schol. *ad.* Pi. *Ol.* 6.21d.

27 For the date, see schol. inscr. *ad. Py.* 6, schol. inscr. *ad Is.* 2. Waele 1971.40 and Jacquemin 1999.71 suggest that the remains of a dedication at Delphi by an Acragantine may celebrate this victory.

28 *Il.* 8.78–117.

29 *Ol.* 1.108–11 implies an interest on Hieron's part in chariot racing in at least 476, and Gelon won the Olympic chariot race in 488 (Moretti 1957.84). There is no evidence that Polyzalus raced chariots, however; see Rolley 1990.291–2.

30 The mythical race also transforms Hieron's victory into a chariot victory, which misled many ancient scholars; see schol. *ad Ol.* 1.inscr. a, b.

31 For these different traditions, see Hansen 2000.19–26.

32 Gerber 1982.136.

33 For other examples, cf. Pi. *Ol.* 3.39, *Ol.* 4.1, *Ol.* 6.48, 85. Note also that *Ol.* 1.95–6 summarizes the Olympics as contests "where speed of foot and peaks of strength, bold in toil, compete" (ἵνα ταχυτὰς ποδῶν ἐρίζεται / ἀκμαί τ' ἰσχύος θρασύπονοι). The feet are not the horses' feet here (*contra* Gerber 1982.148; cf. Ba. 7.6–7, from an ode for a boy sprinter, and the more accurate Pi. *Ne.* 9.11–12), and so this summary represents all contests as contests in which the competitors must display physical prowess.

34 On the victory procession, see Slater 1984, Heath 1988, and Cole 1992.11–32.

35 For these wedding processions, see Sutton 1981.152, 166–8, 238–40, 1992.26, and Redfield 1982.188–9. On vases, chariots regularly replace the mule carts used in such processions.

36 Diod. 13.82.7.

37 Jenkins 1986.60–1 notes that Acragas' magnificent issue of decadrachms around this time looks back to the Syracusan series inaugurated by Gelon.

38 Racing chariots would have made poor ceremonial conveyances because they were lightly constructed and rarely seem to have survived a race without considerable damage. Moreover, not all victors would have won the chariot race; Exaenetus, after all, was a runner. Some chariot victors may have driven their own ceremonial cars, but this should be viewed as a conscious effort on the victor's part to misrepresent the race.

39 See previous note.

40 Lefkowitz 1985.41 accepts that Chromius drove his own chariots.

41 See Farnell 1932.33, Gerber 1987.17, and Mader 1990.39–45.

42 See Grenfell and Hunt 1899.90, Farnell 1932.30, Mader 1990.41, and the apparatus in Drachmann 1903.128–137. For the suggestion that ὀχέων is a participle, see Farnell 1932.33 and, by implication, Slater 1984.246.

43 Paus. 6.18.1. The rough dating is assured by the sculptor Pythagoras of Rhegium; see Moretti 1957.95.

44 The memorials of Timon of Elis (Paus. 6.12.6, Moretti 1957.113), Lampus of Philippi (Paus. 6.4.10, Moretti 1957.132), and an unknown victor, by Tisicrates of Sicyon and the unknown Piston (Pliny *HN* 34.89), all replace the charioteer with a young woman; as Paus. 6.12.6 conjectures, the woman is probably Nike. The memorial of Timon may date to the third quarter of the fifth century; see Chapter 5, n.74.

45 Sim. 519 *fr.* 79.12: ἑνὶ δ' οἶον] εἴκει θ[εὰ δίφρ]ον ἐς μέγαν θορέν. "To one man only does the goddess give the opportunity to leap into her great car." That the goddess is Nike is made clear by the previous line, and the restorations are guaranteed by Cyril's lexicon entry on νίκη, collected under Sim. 519.

46 Ferrara T. 695 B VP (*ARV*² 1340/5); Webster 1972.157.

47 Paus. 6.9.4–5, Moretti 1957.84, and Harrell 2002.451. Part of the base of this monument survives. Krumeich 1997.35 suggests that Nike might have been in the chariot, but Pausanias would have mentioned a charioteer had one been present, as he does at 6.10.6.

48 Paus. 6.16.6, Moretti 1957.87, Hodkinson 1999.163.

49 This strategy is also evident in Pi. *Ol.* 4, where the chariot victory is not only packaged by a representation of a victory parade, but also by a myth that describes the victory of an Argonaut in a race in armor. When the victory is likened to a victory in running, the absence of the charioteer is easily passed over.

50 Moretti 1957.72 and Kyle 1987.204.

51 Hdt. 6.103; also Plut. *Cato Maior* 5.4.

52 Aelian *VH* 9.32.

53 That the Elean officials recorded the names of the horses in some form is suggested by Hdt. 6.103, which notes that Evagoras had also won three consecutive victories with the same mares. These horses could also be named on an Olympic dedication, as that of Cleosthenes of Epidamnus, from 516, demonstrates (Paus. 6.10.6–8).

54 On this Megacles, who won his Pythian victory while in exile, see Davies 1971.379–80.

55 Raubitschek 1949.340 suggests these are not necessarily chariot victories, but the opening certainly implies that they are. Although it would not be unusual for Pindar to misrepresent a victory to its advantage (Cole 1987), one piece of external evidence suggests that only chariot victories are named. A grave stele from the middle of the sixth century mentions an Olympic victory and appears to name a [-]κλες; Davies 1971.372 and Kyle 1987.223–4 argue that an Alcmaeonid victory other than Alcmaeon's chariot win is commemorated. If this is so, given that only one Olympic victory is recorded, only victories in the chariot race can have been included in the victory catalogue of *Py.* 7.

56 Ebert 1972 no.8: Μνᾶμά με ΤΕ [ ] / [hí(π)]ποις νικάσα̣ς̣ ϝεξάκις ἐ̣[ ], "[ ] set me up as a memorial, having won six times in the chariot race at [ ]."

57 Because the line is almost certainly a pentameter, and ἐν Νεμέαι is attested as a pentameter ending in Ebert 1972 no.2, Ebert restores the line to read [hí(π)]ποις νικάσα̣ς̣ ϝεξάκις ἐ̣[(ν) Νεμέαι]. Someone with such success in one festival likely enjoyed significant success elsewhere; that these other successes are not mentioned suggests this dedication was made at the site of these six victories, either at Nemea (from where it was later moved) or at some local Tegean festival.

58 For the statue of a god on a pillar as a victory memorial, see *SEG* XXIII.38 (Moretti 1953 no.5, Ebert 1972 no.3), and for a possible bowl, Moretti 1953 no.4 and Raubitschek 1949.338–40. For horses dedicated on small pillars on

the Athenian acropolis (as tithe offerings), see Raubitschek 1949.43, 272–3, 480–1.

59 Most probably more than one set of horses was used in the six victories, although a ten-year career (the shortest time possible for six Nemean crowns) for an ancient chariot team is certainly possible: Pliny *HN* 8.162–3 declares that horses can race from five to twenty years old.

60 Paus. 6.1.7; Moretti 1957.106. Anaxander's dedication blurs the distinction between gymnastic and equestrian victors: it recorded that his paternal grandfather won the pentathlon, and Anaxander's pose may have been borrowed from the statues of victors in the gymnastic events. Athletes were sometimes pictured in neutral poses such as prayer, rather than engaged in their events (Hyde 1921.130–3); it is possible, however, that Anaxander was clothed, in contrast, presumably, to the athletes depicted in prayer. Cf. Fontenrose 1988.131–4.

61 Paus. 6.1.7, Moretti 1957.104. Compare also the memorials of the Spartan hippotrophs of the later fifth century mentioned together at Paus. 6.2.1–2: Lycinus, victor perhaps in 432 (Moretti 1957.106), who also seems to have dedicated a statue for his victory in the hoplite race; Arcesilaus, twice victor perhaps in the 440s (Moretti 1957.102–3); and his son Lichas, who set up a statue despite the fact that his victory in 420 was recorded as a victory of the Theban people (Moretti 1957.108). All the memorials seem to have consisted of a simple statue of the victor, although no details as to their poses are given. The description of Lycinus' memorial is confused, however, and may reflect the fact that an undersize chariot group was dedicated for his victory (Hitzig and Blümner 1984.2.535–6); if this is the case, Pausanias may be describing chariot groups in all three cases.

62 Xen. *Eq.* 2.1–5.

63 Pi. *Is.* 1.15, for Herodotus of Thebes, and *IG* 5.1.213 (Moretti 1953 no.16), for Damonon. On the date of these victories, see Introduction, nn.9 and 10. *Contra* Most 1985.50–1, *Is.* 1 implies that Herodotus is the equivalent of a superior gymnastic victor: the myth describes how Castor and Iolaos won not only chariot races, but sprints, races in heavy armor, and the javelin and discus as well.

64 See Introduction, nn.15 and 16. Literary works also demonstrate how much the aristocracy admired equestrian skills; cf. Hom. *Il.* 23.262–615 and [Hes.] *Scut.* 118–21, 305–9.

65 Xen. *Ages.* 9.6; cf. Plut. *Ages.* 20.1, *Mor.* 212B. There is clearly a pun here: according to Xenophon, Agesilaus sought to prove that chariot racing did not demonstrate ἀνδραγαθία, "manly virtue."

66 Shear 2003.95–6.

67 Far from an embarrassment, Cynisca's two victories, in 396 and 392, proved a cause for much celebration. She dedicated two bronze chariot teams at Olympia, one in the temple of Zeus itself (Paus. 5.12.5, 6.1.6); the verse inscription accompanying one dedication largely survives (*IG* 5.1.1564a, *AP* 13.16, Moretti 1953 no.17, cf. Paus. 3.8.1–2). In Sparta she also established a heroine's shrine (Paus. 3.15.1), which may also have commemorated the victory. Cf. Golden 1998.133 and Mann 2001.141–2.

2. CARRHOTUS AND CNOPIADAS

1 Cf. Ba. 5.42–5.

2 Golden 1998.83.

3 Dougherty 1993.109–10.

4 Kurke 1991.125–7. Kurke, as well as Lefkowitz 1985.37, suggest that Victory is Carrhotus' companion, whereas *Py.* 9.75 suggests it could be Glory.

5 See Carson 1982.121–8, Brown 1984.37–50, and Kurke 1991.116–34.

6 Lefkowitz 1985.38–9.

7 As Hurst points out in Lefkowitz 1985.64.

8 Paus. 6.1–18 records no instance where the actual chariot was dedicated at Olympia (portrait statues were the norm), and all the dedications he records are located within the Sacred Enclosure, the Altis, not in the temple of Zeus itself. One of Cynisca's monuments, the undersized bronze horse group, was, however, located in the pronaos of the temple (Paus. 5.12.5), which is perhaps where Carrhotus' chariot was hung at Delphi.

9 Lefkowitz 1985.38–40, followed by Dougherty 1993.109. Lefkowitz notes that Pindar does describe the particulars of some racehorse and wrestling victories, but neither offers an appropriate parallel to a chariot victory: unlike most charioteers, wrestlers were the victors, and, as Chapter 5 argues, it is the jockeys not the horses, that offer the real parallel to the charioteers.

10 Lefkowitz 1985.41–2 argues that many owners did their own driving.

11 *SEG* XXIII.38, Pi. *Ol.* 6.22–8, and *Is.* 2.19–29, which dwells on the prestige of the charioteer's victories not the manner in which they were won.

12 Crowther 1992a.99.

13 Crowther 1994.121–3; also 1993.46–8.

14 Soph. *El.* 723–48.

15 See Crowther 1994.128.

16 Schol. *ad Py.* 5.33, 34.

17 Schol. *ad Py.* 5.34, *FGrH* 470 F1.

18 It was presumably to the status of manager (and not that of hired charioteer, as Kyle 1987.159 suggests) that Pisistratus strove to demote the elder Cimon when he accepted his second Olympic win in return for his recall from exile.

19 The information on raising the army is repeated in schol. *ad Py.* 4.455e, which distinguishes four Euphemuses, but the scholion almost certainly also draws on Theotimus. Theotimus probably included a genealogical digression on Euphemus' family in his περὶ Κυρήνης, because schol. *ad. Py.* 4.64 (=*FGrH* 470 F2) cites him when it discusses the first Euphemus.

20 Lefkowitz 1985.40–1; also Lefkowitz 1991.147–60.

21 Didymus may be ill served here by his epitomators but his works appear full of such carelessness; see West 1970.288–96.

22 Schol. *ad Py.* 5.34: "Some say he was [Arcesilas'] charioteer. Didymus says that he was responsible for Arcesilas' Pythian victory, and that he gathered an army from Greece and brought it to him. He confirms these things by citing the words of Theotimus from the first book of his About Cyrene which go thus."

23 Schol. *ad Py.* 5.34: "Consequently Pindar, by joining the companions, has attached what was done by Euphemus to Carrhotus. For he says that he alone succeeded in gathering the army."

24 Schol. *ad Py.* 5.34. Lefkowitz 1985.40–1 suggests that the reference to Carrhotus being Arcesilas' benefactor (*Py.* 5.44) motivated the story that Carrhotus raised the army, but this cannot be the case for Theotimus' account, which derives from sources other than Pindar's ode. His concern is, after all, the garrison for the Hesperidae, not the manner of the victory at Delphi.

25 Theotimus' evidence is accepted by Chamoux 1953.173–4, 200, Mitchell 1966.108, and Braswell 1988.3–4. The Hesperidae, or Euhesperides, were colonized some time in the middle of the sixth century (Malkin 1994.186), but Theotimus' word for "settlers" (ἐποίκους) should not be taken to imply that he thought the town had not yet been founded. Didymus and the other scholiasts certainly understood Carrhotus and Euphemus to be raising a garrison for the city; moreover, schol. *ad. Py.* 4.455e (which n.19 to this chapter argued should be attributed to Theotimus) suggests that Theotimus also spoke of Euphemus "gathering mercenaries" (ξενολογήσοντα).

26 Lefkowitz 1985.41 notes that the victor's brother is referred to, but not named, in both *Ol.* 2.49 and *Is.* 2.23–9.

27 The literature on the differences between gift exchange and commodity exchange, and on the relationship between gift exchange and friendship or kinship, is considerable. See especially Sahlins 1972.185–275, Gregory 1982.10–24, Appadurai 1986.3–16, Kopytoff 1986.64–70, and, with a view to archaic Greece, Kurke 1991.92–7, von Reden 1995a.1–76, and Tandy 1997.94–101. Gift and commodity exchange should be thought of as lying on the same continuum: the more service and payment are separated in time and embedded in a series of exchanges, the more trust exists between the two parties; conversely, the more immediate the exchange and the more closely equivalent the objects, the weaker the relationship that exists between the parties.

28 Cf. Rose 1992.147–8, 160–6, Murray 1993.203–6.

29 This community could also be called the aristocrat's φίλοι. Blundell 1989.39–49 divides φίλοι into three rough groups, family and kin, fellow citizens, and personal friends created by exchanges of favor and perhaps affection, but fellow citizens would not automatically be φίλοι of the aristocrats; how far other members of a polis shared the aristocrats' interests varied according to time and place. On the identification of gift exchange with the aristocracy, see Kurke 1989, 1991.85–159; Rose 1992.120–1, 144–6; Murray 1993.220–45; and Tandy 1997.141–2.

30 See especially Kurke 1989.540. Sahlins 1972.191–6 argues that the association between trade and theft is a common one.

31 Tandy 1997.113–17. Cf. Kurke 1991.253.

32 The schol. *ad Py.* 5.34 notes that the language "would more properly be used of a kinsman than of a charioteer," presumably because he thinks of charioteers as wage earners.

33 On these images, see Kurke 1991.125–8, 149–50; cf. *Py.* 8.18–20 and *Is.* 2.18.

34 Kurke 1991.126.

35 Arcesilas is also praised for his own driving ability (115), and he may well have been a fine horseman. Cyrenean aristocrats seem to have had a strong tradition of horsemanship; see Pi. *Py.* 4.17–18, schol. *ad Py.* 5.34.16–17, and Lefkowitz 1985.42.

36 See Dougherty 1993.112–13. On the Aegidae, see Malkin 1994.98–106.

37 On the use of gift exchange to disguise the poet's wages, see Kurke 1991.135–59 and Nicholson 2000.235–59.

38 That Carrhotus is not mentioned in *Py.* 4 is not an obstacle to this hypothesis. Whether the ode was commissioned by Arcesilas or Damophilus (as Mitchell 1966.109, Chamoux 1953.187–198, Carey 1980b.143–4, Braswell 1988.5–6, and schol. *ad Py.* 4.467 contend), the ode was surely, as Braswell argues, officially sanctioned and should thus be understood as part of the larger celebration in which Carrhotus was named by *Py.* 5.

39 Golden 1998.5–6, 157–75.

40 Pi. *Py.* 4 also focuses on the colony's link to the mainland, but in the more distant past.

41 Paus. 10.15.6. The rough date is secured by the sculptor, Amphion of Cnossos, who was active around 470 to 440. Chamoux 1953.199–201 and Moretti 1957.98 conclude that the dedication was made by Arcesilas on the occasion of his Pythian victory. That the artist was from Crete may also be significant: perhaps as much as a sixth of Cyrene traced its roots to Crete and Battus himself was said to have had a Cretan mother (Hdt. 4.154–5, 4.161, Farnell 1932.174, Chamoux 1953.179–87); further, *Py.* 5.39–42 also forges a Cretan connection by saying that the statue of the god near which Arcesilas dedicated his victorious racing chariot was dedicated by Cretans. Pausanias says that the group was dedicated by the Cyreneans, but this does not necessarily mean that Arcesilas was not, in fact, seen as the dedicant. Treasuries, for example, were ascribed to peoples but could be identified with individuals, as the Treasury of the Athenians was identified with the Alcmaeonids or the Treasury of the Sicyonians with Myron (Paus. 6.19.1–6). Wilamowitz 1922.377n.1 argues from Theotimus that the people of Cyrene were announced as victor in Arcesilas' Pythian win, but this is surely to read too much into Theotimus' wording. Paus. 10.13.5 records that the Cyreneans also dedicated a statue of Ammon in a chariot, presumably of bronze (see Wilamowitz 1922.377n.2), by the Sacred Way near the east face of Apollo's temple, but there is no reason to connect this with Arcesilas' victory.

42 Moretti 1957.95 dates the victory to 464; that Pythagoras of Rhegium made the dedication (Paus. 6.18.1) secures an approximate date.

43 For Arcesilas' Olympic victory, see schol. *ad. Py.* 4.inscr.a and Moretti 1957.98. Surprisingly, no memorial seems to have been made of the Olympic win; indeed, some ancient commentators felt the absence so unlikely that they suggested that either *Py.* 4 or 5 celebrated the win (schol. *ad. Py.* 4.inscr.a).

44 Kurke 1991.20n.14 provides a list of examples in Pindar's odes; for others, see Introduction, n.3.

45 Pi. *Ol.* 8 (Kurke 1991.20, but also Carey 1989a.1–6) and, presumably, *IG* I[3] 597 (Moretti 1953.8–10).

46 Ebert 1972 no.7 (Paus. 6.13.10) and Simonides 511.

47 Kurke 1991.15–34.

48 The phrase Pindar uses to describe Herodotus of Thebes, ἀνία τ' ἀλλοτρίαις οὐ χερσὶ νωμάσαντ' (*Is.* 1.15), is telling. This does not mean "wielding the reins with no other's hands" (as Slater 1969 s.v. ἀλλότριος 1.a. and Race 1997.137). Rather, because, as Kurke 1991.30–1 argues, ἀλλότριος refers in Pindar's odes to people from another household, Herodotus is praised for ensuring that no one from outside his household drove his chariot.

49 That Carrhotus is depicted returning to the palace of the Battiads with his bride (27–9) may suggest that that is his place of residence, but the image is surely structured by the logic of the transfer of the victory from Carrhotus to Arcesilas.

50 On this inscription, including its date, see Bizard 1920.227–36, Friedländer and Hoffleit 1948.154–5, Jeffery 1961.73, Bicknell 1970.129–31, Ebert 1972.38–42 and Schachter 1997.291–306.

51 The text is taken from *SEG* XXIII 38 (*ad IG* I² 472).

52 Friedländer and Hoffleit 1948.154–5 and Ebert 1972.40–1. Schachter 1997.291 translates the genitive [Φοί]β̣ο . . . Λ]ατ̣[ο]ί̣δ̣α̣ as "for Phoebus, son of Leto," surely incorrectly.

53 Something of a parallel is offered by Phayllus of Croton's commemoration of his Pythian victories on the acropolis (Raubitschek 1949 no.76, Moretti 1953.25–9); the location is appropriate because the dedication also commemorates Phayllus' service in the war against the Persians (on which, see Hdt. 8.47). Phayllus may, however, have taken up residence in Athens; as Kyle 1987.153n.174 notes, Phayllus was famous enough to be mentioned in comedy, and several vases suggest that he trained in Athens (Webster 1972.55–6).

54 If Cnopiadas, the lacuna would be restored ℎ̣ὰς Κνοπ̣ι[άδα]ς̣ ἔλαυν', and if Cnopis, ℎ̣ὰς Κνōπ̣ι[ς εἰ]σ̣ έλαυν'); see Ebert 1972.41.

55 Bizard 1920.230–1, Ebert 1972.41, and Schachter 1997.292.

56 Ebert 1972.41–2 suggests that a participle might also fit.

57 Gernet 1981.114–31 and Kurke 1991.94–7. There is no reason to distrust this presentation of the relationship of Alcmaeonides and Cnopiadas, because, as is argued later, part of the point of the monument was for the Alcmaeonids to proclaim a connection to a prominent local family. There would have been little point claiming a relationship with Cnopiadas if he had been a local wage laborer.

58 For example, Moretti 1953 no.9, Raubitschek 1949 no.156 and perhaps no.171.

59 Gernet 1981.121–31, 140–3.

60 Bicknell 1970.129–31 and Ebert 1972.39 convincingly refute the hypothesis of Jeffery 1961.73 that the location of the dedication is to be explained by the fact that the Alcmaeonids were exiled so soon after Alcmaeonides' Panathenaic victory (perhaps in 546) that they were unable to commemorate it in Athens.

61 Schachter 1997.291–306; cf. Bizard 1920.235–41. The Alcmaeonids were awarded the contract to rebuild the temple of Apollo at Delphi when it burned down in 548 and rebuilt it in greater style than the contract required; see Hdt. 5.62.

62 We may compare here the dedication of Hipparchus, *IG* I^3 1470, for which no motivation is offered. On *IG* I^3 1470, see Schachter 1997.292–3 and Bizard 1920.235–6.
63 For the date and a possible dedication at Delphi, see schol. *ad Py.* 6 inscr., schol. *ad Is.* 2 inscr., Waele 1971.40, and Jacquemin 1999.71.
64 The past tenses in *Is.* 2.37–41 make this clear; the ode was commissioned some time after the Olympics of 476. See Bowra 1964.125, 410, Norwood 1956.152, Woodbury 1968.527–9, and Nisetich 1977.139.
65 On why Pindar addresses himself to the victor's son, see Schein 1987.237–8, Kurke 1990, and Nicholson 2000.242–6.
66 *Il.* 23.262–613.
67 Nagy 1990.206–14 suggests that Thrasybulus' name alludes to Antilochus' conduct during and after the race.
68 ἄγω is a word properly used of marriage; see Carson 1982.122. νιν refers forward to ἐφημοσύναν, as the schol. *ad Py.* 6.19c sees; others, such as Nagy 1990.208, take it to refer backward to Thrasybulus' father in *Py.* 6.15, but this makes for a crowded and confused group.
69 These cues would have been obvious to an audience familiar with the vocabulary and iconography of Greek marriage.
70 Chamoux 1955.55, Lefkowitz 1985.41, Bell 1995.16–17. Some ancient scholars (schol. *ad Py.* 6.15) believed this also, whereas others (schol. *ad Py.* 6.13e) thought that Thrasybulus managed the team.
71 See Pi. *Is.* 2.18–29. *Contra* schol. *ad Py.* 6.15, *Is.* 2 does not name the charioteer used in the Pythian victory; see Chapter 3, n.1.
72 Copenhagen 109.
73 That the vase ended up in Vulci cannot preclude the possibility that it was intended for purchase by an equestrian victor. Although some vases depicting athletic scenes, such as the *perizoma* group of vases, were certainly intended for immediate export to Etruria, others must have arrived there through resale (see Webster 1972.289–95, Boardman 2001.58–60, 153–67). The Florence prize Panathenaic discussed in the previous chapter ended up in Orvieto, another Etruscan city, whereas London B144, an inscribed vase commemorating a victory in a horse race (discussed in Chapter 5), and Würzburg 215, an inscribed vase commemorating a victory in the pentathlon (Chapter 6), were, like Copenhagen 109, found in Vulci. Munich 1517 also certainly passed from its patron's hands to another owner: although it celebrates an Alcmaeonid victory, it was found in South Italy.
74 The vase was in the collection of the Marchesa Isabella Gugliemi when it was catalogued by Beazley (*ABV* 135). Beazley 1931/32.5 notes the connection, as does Webster 1972.153, but it passes unremarked in *ABV* 135.
75 Webster 1972.153. The design of the wheeling chariot appears on Panathenaics found in Sparta (*ABV* 369, Gardiner 1910 fig. 165) and in Taranto (9887, *ABV* 369, Boardman 1974 fig. 299); see Beazley 1951.93.
76 The charioteers of war chariots can be depicted on vases in an identical manner to the charioteers of racing chariots (e.g., Munich 1492), but usually there is some

distinguishing feature, such as a shield (New York 06.1021.161, *ABV* 192/3, Boardman 1974 fig. 126; Toronto 295, *ABV* 129/2, Robinson, Harcum, and Iliffe 1930 pl.32; Würzburg 192, *ABV* 259/23), or a dark or patterned tunic (Athens, Acr. 606, *ABV* 81/1, Boardman 1974 fig. 47; Berlin 1716, *ABV* 137/62, Blümel 1936.51; Munich 1404; Munich 1553).

77 Cf. Munich 1553 and New York 06.1021.161.

78 *Il.* 8.66–334 illustrates the diversity of charioteers used: Diomedes' henchman (cf. θεράποντε, 113), Sthenelus, leaves Diomedes' chariot to look after Nestor's with Nestor's own henchman, Eurymedon (113–14), while Nestor takes the reins of Diomedes' car (116–17); Hector loses two charioteers, a henchman Eniopeus (ἡνίοχον θεράποντα, 119) and Archeptolemus, who is not designated as a henchman (ἡνιοχῆα, 312), and then for his third charioteer picks up his own brother Cebriones (318–19). For the honor in which a henchman was held, see *Il.* 16.144–54, on Automedon.

79 It may not have been as uncommon in the middle of the sixth century as in the last quarter of that century for owners to use relatives or bondsmen to drive their chariots; if that was so, the vase may have been intended to represent accurately, through the merging of the two pictures, the relationship between charioteer and victor.

80 *Il.* 11.698–702.

81 Chariot racing was probably part of the original Olympic program and not a later addition; see Golden 1998.40–5.

82 The loosening of the aristocratic clans' control of the economy was the result of many factors: the increasing strength of the cities, the gradual spread of coinage, easier travel (cf. Murray 1993.102–23, 220–45, Morris 2000.257–306), and aggressive competition from the tyrants who had accumulated great wealth in more liquid forms (Ure 1922.290–306, Gentili 1988.160–6, Murray 1993.150–1, 239–40).

83 Paus. 6.10.6–7, who dates the monument to 516.

84 Gzella 1971.189–202, Bell 1978.29–86, Gentili 1988.155–76, Kurke 1991.7, and von Reden 1995b.30–50.

85 See Chapter 5.

3. NICOMACHUS

1 Maehler 1987.143 and Turyn 1952.200 accept the emendation of Bergk 1878, "καὶ τόθι κλειναῖς τ' Ἐρεχθειδᾶν," "And there, and in shining Athens." The emendation is of some importance: if it is accepted, the ode reveals that Nicomachus drove in the Pythian victory of 490, celebrated in Pi. *Py.* 6. But, although the emendation is somewhat supported by the scholiast *ad Py.* 6.15, who reads these lines as proving that Nicomachus did drive at Delphi, it seems safer to reject it. First, it would make Nicomachus a champion charioteer of considerable, although not inconceivable, longevity (because the Olympic victory was that of Theron in 476); second, if Nicomachus had been driving chariots for the Emmenids since 490, it is hard to explain why he did not take the reins in the

Isthmian victory (*Is.* 2.12–17). The resulting sense of καὶ τόθι is certainly awkward, but it should be noted that the emendation would strengthen the argument being made here.

2 The ode dates from the second half of the 470s. It is certainly after 476 (the date of Theron's Olympic victory), and most commentators date it after Theron's death in 472; see Bury 1892.30–2, Wilamowitz 1922.311, Norwood 1956.152, Bowra 1964.410, and Woodbury 1968.527–9.

3 Bell 1995.21n.118 suggests that Nicomachus drove in the Isthmian win because no other charioteer is mentioned, but Nicomachus enters the ode only with the Panathenaic victory.

4 Critics have missed how odd the presence of Nicomachus is; see Norwood 1956.152–7, Woodbury 1968, Nisetich 1977, and Kurke 1991.240–56.

5 Golden 1998.83, Farnell 1932.345, and Bell 1995.20–1.

6 Kurke 1991.152–4. The qualifying particle πού and the indefinite article τι also suggest that an actual event is not being recorded here.

7 On cosmetics, see Grillet 1975.33–6 and Vanoyeke 1990.37.

8 This evaluation of the image has been disputed by Woodbury 1968.540–1 and Nisetich 1977.141, but see Simpson 1969.471–2 and Kurke 1991.242–5. On the significance of gold and silver in aristocratic discourse, see Kurke 1999.41–64.

9 Kurke 1991.245–56. For other interpretations, see the works listed under n.4, this chapter.

10 See Introduction, n.8. The change is not from the spontaneous production of poetry, as Woodbury 1968 claims, but from the production of poetry that looked spontaneous.

11 Kurke 1991.245–56.

12 For this notion of a structuring silence, see Macherey 1978.3–101, 258–98, Macherey and Balibar 1981.87–97, Jameson 1981.281–99, and Rose 1992.33–42.

13 This epithet perhaps suggests that he is to be thought of, at least momentarily, as riding the chariot, like the older poets.

14 Kurke 1991.146–54.

15 Kurke 1991.152–4.

16 Schol. *ad Is.* 2.28b recognizes that the Olympic chariot win was not Xenocrates'.

17 Even though it is not mentioned in *Ol.* 2.48–51, the Panathenaic victory could have been won in 478 (*contra* Bury 1892.30–1); *Ol.* 2 was for Theron, and, although it includes two of his brother's victories, the catalogue limits itself to Panhellenic victories. 474 is also a possibility; see Bell 1995.18–21.

18 Rose 1992.159–63.

19 Nisetich 1977.143–4.

20 The relative pronoun ὅν in line 23 cannot here refer to Xenocrates: Nicomachus is the natural antecedent, and, as the schol. *ad Is.* 2.28b note, Xenocrates did not win a victory at Olympia.

21 It was not unusual for a relative's name to be suppressed to create the impression that the victor had a hand in more victories than he did. The same thing can be seen in *Ol.* 2.48–51 and 3.9 where Xenocrates is not named as the victor in the Pythian and Isthmian races. *Ol.* 3.9 is especially slick, because the transition to

the Pythian victory is achieved through the description of Theron as "a son of Aenesidamus" (Αἰνησιδάμου παιδὶ).

22 See Pi. *Ol.* 5.7–9, *Py.* 1.29–33, Ba. 10.26–30, and Nash 1990.

23 Equestrian entries could be made by brothers, however; see Ebert 1972 no.7 and Sim. 511.

24 The substitution of the charioteer for the victor in the actual victory announcement constitutes a much more aggressive elevation of the charioteer than was evident in *Py.* 5.

25 See Chapter 2, n.64.

26 See n.2, this chapter.

27 As Kurke 1991.35–61 argues, victories were perceived in aristocratic ideology as family heirlooms; the Isthmian win would thus have been seen by aristocrats as passing to Thrasybulus after Xenocrates' death.

28 Kurke 1991.247–56.

29 Schol. *ad Is.* 2.68, Bury 1892.49, Farnell 1932.346, Nisetich 1977.147–8, and Kurke 1991.251.

30 Nisetich 1977.147–8 sees Nicasippus as a doublet for Xenocrates, the victor, but that this is unlikely is shown by the subordinate position Nicasippus occupies in his relationship with the poet. Bell 1995.26–7 notes that Nicasippus seems to have been a common name for a charioteer and argues that the name is an "affectionate allusion to [Nicomachus'] athletic success" and that Nicomachus himself is being asked to deliver the ode.

31 This is not to imply that Pindar had a large aristocratic household, only that, in the imaginary of this ode, he is represented as having one.

32 Von Reden 1995a.6–10 notes that a payment of money could be part of a gift exchange.

33 For example: Deinomenes' dedication at Olympia for Hieron's Olympic victories, which included a chariot and two racehorses (Paus. 6.12.1 and 8.42.8–9, Ebert 1972 no.17); Polyzalus' dedication at Delphi (Ebert 1972 no.13), which, Rolley 1990.291–2 argues, was similar; and Pi. *Ol.* 5.4–7, which celebrates Psaumis' entries in all types of equestrian competition.

34 Pellizer 1990.183 and Kurke 1996. Bowie 1986 and Stehle 1997.221 note that symposiasts were able to adopt the roles of women in poetry. This model of the symposium owes much to New Historicist work on carnivals; cf. White and Stallybrass 1986.1–26.

35 The inclusion of potters in aristocratic scenes from vases of the late sixth and early fifth centuries suggests that the imaginary inclusion of nonelite personnel in an aristocratic group was a recognized rhetorical strategy of the symposium. On these vases, see Neer 2002.87–134. Neer argues, however, that these inclusions, like the epinician poets' presentation of themselves as their patrons' guest-friends, served aristocratic interests by representing a piece of flattery as freely given and not purchased. Such an explanation does not, however, sufficiently account for the shock inherent in this elevation, a shock much greater than that constituted by the epinician poet's elevation, as Neer 2002.89–91 makes clear.

36 Schol. *ad Ne.* 1.8. On Chromius, see Freeman 1891.491–5.

37 Arion (1.23–4) and Democedes (3.129–37). According to Hdt. 3.131, Polycrates paid Democedes two talents for a year of his medical services, a sum that could pay the salaries of four hundred sailors for a month.

38 Alcibiades was sued for either five (Isoc. 16.46) or eight (Diod. 13.74.3) talents for the chariot; see Golden 1998.169–71. Such sums dwarf even the prizes on offer at the Panathenaea (on which, see Young 1984.115–27).

39 The Olympics of 476 were the first to be held after the Persian invasion, and a confused story in Aelian *VH* 9.5 relating how Themistocles tried to prevent Hieron from entering the chariot race on the grounds that he had not taken part in the Persian war suggests that they were seen as a celebration of the Greek victory. Golden 1998.63–4 argues that this festival may have been so important that it influenced the traditional date of the festival's foundation.

40 On the adulation accorded Roman charioteers, see Cameron 1973.244–5 and Rawson 1981.8.

41 1995.2–4.

42 Bell 1995.2–4. Note that the Delphic charioteer is, in fact, unusual in two respects: the band is both thinner and worn slightly lower down the chest, and the tunic has sleeves.

43 Steiner 1998, Scanlon 2002.199–273, and cf. Hyde 1921.275n.7, who notes that charioteers were occasionally represented nude. Steiner 1998.135–7 discusses this statue but identifies victor and charioteer.

44 1995.10–15. Bode 1993.103–4 agrees with this dating.

45 1995.8–10.

46 1995.10.

47 Bell 1995.15–22 suggests, in fact, that the statue is of Nicomachus himself, but, although the statue may well have originally been located in Acragas, this seems too great a coincidence

48 Paus. 6.13.1. There are stories of other athletes' statues being damaged or destroyed in the late archaic period; see Lattimore 1988.245–6.

49 Bode 1993.104–10 argues that the statue was erected in Hamilcar's honor after he was killed at the battle of Himera in 480.

50 Mainz 74 (*ABV* 716, *ARV*[2] 1602) and Louvre F283 (*ARV*[2] 1584). Webster 1972.63–4 identifies Nikon and Mynnon as charioteers.

51 For the victor's name inscribed beside the charioteer, see Munich 1517 (*ABV* 401), treated in Chapter 1. Webster 1972.64 suggests, on the basis of a kalos-inscription, that Louvre F283 was a love-gift, but the Corpus Vasorum editor casts doubt on the legibility of this inscription.

52 An example is Berlin 1897 (*ABV* 293/8, Beazley 1951.78–9, pl.36.2), from 525–500, which depicts a harnessing scene. The vase seems to evoke real individuals because, in contrast to similar vases, such as Munich 1691 (*ABV* 267/6, Beazley 1927.88), it avoids generic names such as Kallippos for the charioteer and grooms, naming them instead as Euthos, Simon, and Sikon. Yet there is no evidence that it commemorates a chariot victory at a festival; the three may be aristocrats with a passion for horses.

53 See Thompson 1961.228–31, Crowther 1994.124–5.

54 Xen. *Eq.* 1.1, 11.6. For the location of the Eleusinium and its connection to the Panathenaic parades, see Thompson 1961.226–8.

55 His name may indicate that Simon's status was originally more lowly; see Alexander 1909.38, but also Davies 1971.359–61, 488–9. A second memorial of his own feats commissioned by a horse trainer may be Bologna 215 (*ARV*² 547/27), which depicts a man with a trainer's staff in the center of the vase, with Nike, behind a four-horse chariot moving left to right. The vase dates from the early classical period. Webster 1972.156 identifies the man as a trainer, but 1972.193 as a judge. The vase is not inscribed but is the only vase in Webster's list of vases showing Nike with athletes that includes such a figure.

4. PHINTIS

1 Paus. 5.9.1 dates the event's dissolution at 444, while the Pindaric scholia offer 440 (*ad Ol.* 5.6, *Ol.* 6. inscr.a) and 436 (*Ol.* 6. inscr.b).

2 Sim. 515 (Arist. *Rh.* 3.2.1405b); Golden 1998.43. The victory was, however, celebrated by Simonides, as well as by coin issues. The victory probably occurred in 480; the coins date from around then (Rutter 1997.119–20).

3 Sim. 515. The epithet "storm-footed" had an exalted pedigree: it was used of the horses of Tros in *Hymn. Hom. Ven.* 217 and probably of Pegasus in a poem by Ibycus, perhaps an epinician ode; see Barron 1984.17–19 and Jenner 1986.64–6.

4 [Pi.] *Ol.* 5.7, 21–3. On the date, see Gerber 1987.8, but also Bowra 1964.414–5; on the authorship, see Introduction, n.52.

5 Epinicians were commissioned by three of the four known victors, and *Ol.* 6 is one of Pindar's grandest odes. The fourth victor was the victor at the first contest, perhaps Thersias of Thessaly (Paus. 5.9.1), or Asandrastos (schol. *ad Ol.* 5.6b), possibly a corruption of the same name (*PW* s.v. Ἀπήνη).

6 This does not mean that tyrants and kings never entered. Anaxilas was a tyrant, but it was presumably the chance to win a cheap victory against a weaker field that motivated his entry.

7 *Ol.* 6.93–4. On Hagesias and his family, see Pi. *Ol.* 6.5–6, Hdt. 5.44, 9.33, Paus. 3.11.5–8, 6.2.4–5, schol. *ad Ol.* 6.7a–8b, 165, and Malkin 1987.93–7.

8 Hagesias must have won his victory between the foundation of Etna (*Ol.* 6.96), which occurred after the Olympics of 476, and the death of Hieron (*Ol.* 6.93) in 467; see Malkin 1987.93–7 and Farnell 1932.40. Pi. *Ol.* 1.108–11 suggests that Hieron intended to enter the chariot race in 472; he certainly entered the Pythian chariot race in 470.

9 Rutter 1997.119–20.

10 See Introduction n.72.

11 Minor chariot races were used also in this way. The entries of Chromius, another supporter of Hieron's, at both the Adrasteia at Sicyon (Pi. *Ne.* 9) and the Nemean games (*Ne.* 1) should be thought of as a way for him to compete for glory without competing against the tyrant of his city. Although he made the odd entry in a local contests such as the Theban Ioleia (see Chapter 1, n.3), Hieron focused his attention on Olympia and Delphi.

12 Golden 1998.40–3 discusses various reasons for the introduction of the mule-cart race.

13 Nothing is known about Phintis beyond the limited information provided by *Ol.* 6, but he was surely not an aristocrat. Neither his patronym nor his hometown are recorded, and his representation in *Ol.* 6 contrasts markedly with those of Carrhotus and Cnopiadas. His Sicilian-Doric name (Gildersleeve 1908.175) may also reveal his lower class; it certainly seemed strange to the scholia (*ad. Ol.* 6.37a, f). This was true also, however, for Psaumis' name (see Chapter 1, n.42), as well as for Carrhotus' (schol. *ad Py.* 5.33). The fact that Pindar gives the name in the nominative case and not the vocative demanded by the construction (schol. *ad Ol.* 6.37a), may also be explained by its oddness, although as the scholia point out, the practice has precedents in Homer.

14 Treatments of *Ol.* 6 have not examined the representation of the mules or the mule driver; cf. Woodbury 1955, Norwood 1956.86–7, 128–9, Ruck 1968.132–42, Stern 1970, Huxley 1975.28–30, and Kurke 1991.147–9.

15 Farnell 1932.41–2.

16 Cf. Harriott 1969.63–4.

17 Note also that the epic archaism, σθένος ἡμιόνων, presents the mules' strength as an epic virtue. The phrase specifically recalls the epic phrase σθένος ἵππων ([Hes.] *Scut.* 97; cf. *Py.* 2.12) and so also assimilates the mules to horses.

18 For the distances, see Gardiner 1910.457, Pi. *Ol.* 2.50, 3.33, *Py.* 5.33, 5.39, and schol. *ad Ol.* 2.92, 3.59. That two mules were used is made clear by Anaxilas' later coin issues (e.g., Jenkins 1986 pl.53).

19 Hdt. 9.33, Paus. 3.11.5–8.

20 E.g., *Il.* 23.111, 16.167.

21 For the Boeotian sow, see schol. *ad Ol.* 6.148b–c, Farnell 1932.48, and Bowra 1964.265–6. For the mule as comic, cf. Hdt. 1.55, Paus. 5.9.2, and Arist. *Rh.* 3.2.1405b.

22 Schol. *ad Ol.* 6.148a, 149a.

23 The victor reads the cipher-stick prepared by the poet (see Bowra 1964.266, but also West 1988) and consumes the wine he mixes in the bowl.

24 Hieron is asked to receive the victory revel, a task normally assigned to patron deities (*Ol.* 5.3, *Py.* 8.5, 9.73, 12.5, *Ne.* 11.3; cf. *Ol.* 4.9, 8.10, *Py.* 8.19).

25 1987.93–7; schol. *ad Ol.* 6.8a, b.

26 Schol. *ad Ol.* 6.165. The scholion is clearly misinformed in parts: Hieron was not deposed, although a year later his brother Thrasybulus was. Hagesias was perhaps killed after Thrasybulus was deposed.

27 On turbulence in Cyrene, see Chamoux 1953.173–5 and Mitchell 1966.108–10; on Cimon and Pisistratus, Chapter 2, n.18.

28 Paus. 6.2.4. Cf. also Paus. 8.10.5.

29 Cf. *Ne.* 4.89–90. *Contra* Farnell 1932.48, the two Aeneases should not be identified; Pausanias' belongs to the third century.

30 It might also be suggested that Phintis was a member of Hagesias' household and thus that he represented something of an added triumph for the victor, much as Carrhotus in *Py.* 5. Although possible, this is unlikely. Given that Phintis, unlike

Carrhotus, cannot have been well known, Pindar would surely have specified that he was a member of Hagesias' household.

31 On the Iamidae, see Pi. *Ol.* 6, Hdt. 9.33–6, Paus. 3.11.5–8, 6.2.4–5, 8.10.5, schol. *ad Ol.* 6.59b; on the Deinomenids, see Hdt. 7.153 and Bowra 1964.117.

32 *Ol.* 6.98–100.

5. PHERENICUS AND LYCUS

1 Gardiner 1910.458 concludes from this anecdote that riderless horses did count, but even this story implies that Elean officials had to decide whether to proclaim Pheidolas the winner.

2 Pi. *Ol.* 1, Ba. 5; Pi. *Py.* 3; Ebert 1972 no.17 (Paus. 6.12.1, 8.42.9). The Pythian victory of 482, while alluded to by Ba. 4.11–18, is not commemorated by any of these memorials (although it seems to have been commemorated by a dedication at Delphi; see n.16 to this chapter); Ba. 5.41 shows that Pherenicus had only won once at Delphi, and *Py.* 3 celebrates only the victories won by this horse. See also Gerber 1982.44–5. On the date of *Py.* 3, see Young 1983b.35–42.

3 Ebert no.5. Ebert 1972.44 dates the inscription to the end of the sixth century, whereas Moretti 1957.78 dates it to 508, before Cleander's overthrow of the Geloan oligarchy in 505.

4 Moretti 1957.78, Ebert 1972.44–5. Jeffery 1961.273 suggests that the dedication was a striding athlete.

5 Ebert 1972 no.7, Paus. 6.13.10.

6 Ebert 1972.48–9. On Pausanias' reliability, see Habicht 1985.64–94, 147–51. Moretti 1957.152–3 suggests that of the two victories referred to, one belongs to Pheidolas. This cannot be accepted, however, because Pheidolas' horse was a mare (a part of the Corinthian story that must have been supported by the dedication itself), whereas the horse of the sons of Pheidolas was a male.

7 Ebert no.6, Paus. 6.13.9.

8 Paus. 6.14.4. Moretti 1957.82 suggests 492, 500, or 504, but note that Moretti gives the sons of Pheidolas only one victory and puts Pantares' victory in the chariot race.

9 Moretti 1957.89.

10 Pi. *Py.* 3, Ebert 1972 no.7. *Is.* 3 may well celebrate a victory in the horse race at Nemea: as schol. inscr. notes, Pindar speaks ambiguously of Melissus "winning in the horse-running" (ἱπποδρομίᾳ κρατέων, *Is.* 3/4.13). Melissus and his family were, however, certainly engaged in chariot races, with victories at the Panathenaea and Adrasteia, as well as entries in the Panhellenic games (*Is.* 3/4. 15–17, 43–7), and the ode treats the victory as other odes treat chariot victories. *Is.* 3 seems to have been composed as a supplement to *Is.* 4, soon after the latter's composition; see Bury 1892.55–6, but also Hamilton 1974.111.

11 London B144 (*ABV* 307); Beazley 1951.92–3, Webster 1972.64, and Kyle 1987.200–1.

12 As Webster 1972.64. Many of the vases listed by Webster 1972.152–7 depicted victories in the horse race, but few were probably intended for purchase by those

wishing to commemorate such a victory: Cab. Méd. 364 (*ARV*[2] 646/9); a vase from Tutogi, Spain (1054/56 *bis*); Syracuse 6262 (1113/8); and Cambridge 43.8 (1164/47), all from the fifth century, are the most likely candidates.

13 The Pythian victory commemorated in *Py*. 10.15–16 was not won in the horse race, but in the hoplite race; Phrikias, a double Olympic victor, was the victor's father; see schol. *ad Py*. 10.22a-23, Farnell 1932.215–16, and Moretti 1957.78.

14 Sim. 511 (for a Pythian victory of the sons of Aeatius); 519 *fr*. 120 (for Athenaeus). Ath. 1.3e declares that Simonides wrote an epinician for an Olympic victor called Leophron and Moretti 1957.93–4 suggests that he won the horse race, but Ath. implies that he won the chariot.

15 Ibyc. 282B S221 (for Callias). That the Ibycus piece celebrates a victory in a horse race is not clear from the fragmentary remains, but the victor has been plausibly identified with the Athenian Callias who won the Olympic horse race in 564 and either the Pythian chariot or horse race before that; see Barron 1984.21–2, Jenner 1986.61, and, on Callias, Moretti 1957.70, Davies 1971.255–6, and Kyle 1987.203.

16 Ebert 1972 no.18. Peek 1958.43–59 argues that the dedication commemorates only Hieron's chariot victory at Delphi. Also note that Rolley 1990.291–2 argues persuasively that Ebert 1972 no.13, the dedication of Polyzalus, represents a memorial of Hieron's three Pythian victories, along the same lines as the Olympic memorial set up by Deinomenes, Ebert 1972 no.17; on Ebert 1972 no.13, see also Chamoux 1955 and Jacquemin 1999 no.449.

17 Pi. *Ol*. 1.18, *Py*. 3.74, Ba. 5.37, 184.

18 Ebert 1972 no.7 (Paus. 6.13.10).

19 As a possible parallel, Ebert 1972.49 offers Sim. 511, but the sons of Aeatius may well have been individually named in this ode.

20 See n.2. to this chapter.

21 Hdt. 6.103, Moretti 1957.71–2.

22 Ebert 1972 no.17 (Paus. 6.12.1, 8.42.8–9).

23 Ebert 1972 no.7.

24 Ebert 1972.46–7; *AP* 6.135: Οὗτος Φειδόλα ἵππος ἀπ' εὐρυχόροιο Κορίνθου / ἄγκειται Κρονίδᾳ μνᾶμα ποδῶν ἀρετᾶς, "This horse of Pheidolas from wide-plained Corinth is dedicated to the son of Cronus as a memorial of excellence of feet." Ebert suggests that, if Οὗρος was the first word originally, it could then have been corrupted both to Οὗτος in the epigram and Αὔρα in the Corinthian story.

25 Ebert 1972 no.4. Paus. 6.10.6–8 dates Cleosthenes' victory to 516.

26 Paus. 6.13.9 (Ebert 1972 no.6), 6.13.10 (Ebert 1972 no.7), 6.14.4. The excavations at Olympia have yielded numerous horses with jockeys (Hyde 1921.24), but there is no evidence that these were memorials for horse race victories from this period.

27 Jockeys: Paus. 6.2.8, 6.12.1 (Hieron), 6.14.12. Charioteers: Paus. 6.1.6, 6.10.6, 6.12.1

28 Ebert 1972 no.5.

29 Ebert 1972.44–5.

30 E.g., London B133 (*ABV* 395, Gardiner 1910 fig. 169) and Goluchow 164 (*ABV* 408, Gardiner 1978 pl. 206).
31 *Il.* 23.382–7.
32 *Py.* 1.91, 10.72, *Is.* 3/4.89b.
33 As Jebb 1905.275 and Campbell 1982.428, 1992.141.
34 Jenner 1986.64–6; also Barron 1984.19.
35 1976.47–8.
36 LSJ 1a, b. See especially Pi. *Py.* 4.28, *Is.* 1.15.
37 Ba. 5.39–40, 183; Ebert 1972 no.7.1, from Paus. 6.13.10; *Py.* 3.74; cf. *Ol.* 10.64 and 13.43.
38 Cf. especially Ebert 1972 nos.3, 8, 17, 18, Pi. *Py.* 1.32, 11.46, *Is.* 2.13, [Pi.] *Ol.* 5.8, Ba. 4.5, 14.21. The exception is Pi. *Is.* 3/4.43 where a chariot is described as winning.
39 Ebert 1972 no.3, *SEG* XXIII 38.3; Ebert 1972 no.17, Paus. 8.42.9. On the dedication of Alcmaeonides, see Chapter 2. It should be noted that, as in all equestrian inscriptions, the dative τεθρίππῳ is instrumental and indicates what the victor won with, not the event in which the victor took part. When the event is being indicated, it goes in the accusative, as in the memorials for gymnastic victors (e.g., Ebert 1972 nos.2, 9, 11).
40 Ebert 1972 no.5: Πανтάρες μ' ἀνέθεκ[ε] Μενεκράτιος Διὸ[ς ἆθλα] / [hίπ(π)οι νικάσας πέδο ἐ(κ) κλε]τ̣õ Γελοαίο, "Pantares, the son of Menecrates, from the famed plain of Gela, dedicated me after he was victorious in the games of Zeus with a horse." Ebert's restoration should be questioned, however, because it is based on contemporary memorials for chariot victories.
41 The way that Bacchylides testifies to Pherenicus' great feats mirrors his phrasing in Ba. 8.19–25, an ode for a gymnastic victor.
42 Akmatidas: Ebert 1972 no.9: ἀσσκονικτεί; Dromeus: Paus. 6.11.4, with 6.6.5.
43 1998.78.
44 London B144 (*ABV* 307).
45 For examples, see n.30 to this chapter. Kyle 1987.185n.55 lists Panathenaics for the horse race.
46 On the rendering of this name as Dysniketos, a name attested in Attic, see Kyle 1987.201.
47 Webster 1972.64. Webster's suggestion that the jockey is Dysniketos' son is unfounded.
48 Nauplia 1 (*ABV* 260); Beazley 1951.92 and Webster 1972.154.
49 The occasional memorial for a chariot victory, such as the funerary monument of the elder Cimon, obscured the charioteer by focusing on the horses, but this was rare, and Cimon's horses were indeed exceptional; see Chapter 1.
50 Ebert 1972 nos.6 and 7; the memorial of Crocon of Eretria, Paus. 6.14.4; Pi. *Ol.* 1 and *Py.* 3; Ba. 5. Although the memorial of Pantares, Ebert 1972 no.5, seems to privilege the owner, it should also be noted that, if Ebert's full reconstruction is accepted, the statue of the horse addresses the viewer, referring to itself as "me" (μ'). Deinomenes' dedication, Ebert 1972 no.17, privileges the owner as the common link between all the victories but betrays no concern about the jockeys,

focusing instead on Hieron's grandeur (on which, see Kurke 1991.163–94) and his personal connection with Apollo. This memorial is an anomaly, however, because it commemorates a victory in the chariot race.

51 Gardiner 1910.436, Beazley 1951.92, and Golden 1998.82.

52 Because it would have been hard to gain equestrian skills without an owner's interest, professional jockeys must have begun their careers closely tied to an owner. As long as they were not slaves, however, these connections would only be temporary, and the riders would later be free to circulate among different owners.

53 [Plut.] *Mor.* 839c tells of a statue on the Athenian acropolis of Isocrates as a boy riding a horse, presumably from around 420, and this has been understood as a dedication for a victory in the horse race (Hyde 1921.24). As Kyle 1987.222 notes, however, there is no evidence that this was a victory memorial, either for Isocrates or his father. Paus. 6.2.8 is discussed subsequently.

54 Although the victories probably date from the early fourth century (Introduction, n.9), it is perhaps significant that, although Damonon clearly thought it a worthwhile achievement for him to drive his own chariots, his son, a youth at the time and a gifted runner, is not said to have ridden any of their victorious racehorses (*IG* 5.1.213, Moretti 1953 no.16).

55 As has been common, at least until recently, in camel racing.

56 Laconia, for example, boasted at least nine such competitions in the early fourth century, although it may have been unusually keen on them; see Hodkinson 1999.152.

57 Appadurai 1986.13–16.

58 Golden 1990.33–5, 192–3.

59 The memorial at Olympia for Hieron's victories is an example (Ebert 1972 no.17); cf. also [Pi.] *Ol.* 5.7. Other owners who competed in both horse races and chariot races include Callias (n.15, this chapter), the people of Argos (Moretti 1957.89, 92), and Democrates and his father Lysis (Kyle 1987.199, 206).

60 E.g., Phintis, Aeneas, and Hieron in Pi. *Ol.* 6 and Nicomachus and Nicasippus in *Is.* 2.

61 *Py.* 1.58, 79, *Py.* 2.18.

62 See Pi. *Is.* 7.45, Hdt. 7.88, Eur. *Alc.* 490, 504.

63 See *LSJ* and Frisk 1955 s.v. δεσπότης.

64 *Il.* 8.185, 16.149–52, 19.400, 405, 420, 23.295, 346, 409. Horses are also named at *Od.* 23.246, [Hes.] *Scut.* 120, Alcman 25 PMG, Stesich. 178 PMG, and on Athens Acr. 611, which names Achilles' horses (*ABV* 82/1, Beazley 1951.40–1, Webster 1972.189–90) and London B 309 (*ABV* 364/56, Webster 1972.191). *Od.* 17.292, as some vases, names a dog; see Toynbee 1948.24.

65 *Il.* 8.185–190, 17.426–40. See also Redfield 1975.195.

66 *Il.* 8.185–97, 23.410–13.

67 See Kurke 1991.85–159.

68 Ebert 1972 no.17.

69 The sculptors were not included in this network; see Paus. 8.42.10, but also cf. Paus. 6.12.1.

70 There seems, in fact, to have been little attention paid to equine bloodlines. Only three of the literary passages that name horses also name a parent (*Il.* 16.149–50, 19.400, Stesich. 178 PMG), and in each case the same mare is involved, Podarge; further, only one names both parents, and the father is not a horse (*Il.* 16.149–50). Moreover, while Xenophon gives lengthy advice on purchasing horses, he never suggests checking their bloodlines (*Eq.* 1.1–17, 3.1–12).

71 Paus. 6.14.12. On the date, see Moretti 1953.76–8 and 1957.113. The dating of the memorial is complicated by a second Olympic dedication on behalf of Xenombrotus, dated to 330 by its letter forms and discussed by Moretti 1953.75–8. Moretti sees the dedication as the renovation of an earlier monument, set up before the one described by Pausanias, to commemorate only Xenombrotus' victory, but this seems needlessly complicated. More likely, the second dedication was made by Xenombrotus' hometown long after his death. As the first Olympic victor from Meropian Cos, Xenombrotus was a source of considerable civic pride.

72 Cf. the dedications of Anaxander (Paus. 6.1.7) and Polypeithes (6.16.6).

73 Paus. 6.2.8. On the date of the memorial and on Aegyptus' name, corrupted in Paus. 6.2.8, see Moretti 1957.113; the date is fixed by the sculptor, Daedalus of Sicyon, who worked on a number of Elean projects in the early fourth century (see Hyde 1921.120).

74 According to Pausanias, the dedication consisted of a statue of the victor's father Timon next to a statue of a horse ridden by a boy, who is named as Aegyptus. Pausanias' commentary suggests that the dedicatory inscription includes the information that Timon won the chariot race and Aegyptus the horse race, but there is much to be suspicious about here. First, this is not a memorial for Timon's victory, because that had already been commemorated (Paus. 6.12.6). Second, the representation of the victor as the jockey has no parallel among previous memorials. Third, for two victors to be given statues in a single memorial is, as noted earlier, exceptional. Fourth, there is no evidence that any youth prior to Aegyptus had won the horse race at Olympia; older men dominated the equestrian events (Golden 1998.117–23). The horse race may, however, have lost status with the introduction of the two-horse chariot race in 408 and (if early enough) the four-foal chariot race in 384; certainly in this period youths such as Damonon's son Enymakratidas did win horse races at local festivals with many equestrian events (Moretti 1953.36). Nevertheless, it seems more reasonable to reject Pausanias' account of the memorial. Although the memorial recalled Timon's victory, it probably did not represent him; rather, Aegyptus was the standing figure, while the boy seated on the horse was, in fact, a jockey, something novel enough but with some precedent in the memorial of Hieron's victories (Ebert 1972 no.17). *Contra* Moretti 1957.113, Timon was probably dead by the time of his son's victory and had won some years before his son.

75 The details were disputed, however. See Isoc. 16.1, 46, Plut. *Alc.* 12.2–3, Diod. 13.74.3, Golden 1998.169–71, Mann 2001.103–4, and also [Andoc.] 4.25–32, a reconstruction from a later period. The increasing use of multiple entries in the late fifth century may have contributed to the commodification of the horses.

76 Cleogenes: Paus. 6.1.4, Moretti 1957.116. Damonon: *IG* 5.1.213, Moretti 1953 no.16, and Hodkinson 1999.152.
77 Xen. *Eq.* 1.1–17, 3.1–12.
78 Paus. 6.10.6–8, Pi. *Ol.* 6.25–6.
79 Pliny *HN* 8.159–60. This strange anecdote surely offers evidence of a contrary discourse through which some elite Romans expressed scorn for the adulation most Romans gave to the charioteers.

6. MORE MISSING PERSONS

1 Sim. 509; Paus. 6.10.3. For the date of the victory, see Moretti 1957.75.
2 Glaucus' memorial is the only certain example from the fifth century of a combat athlete represented in motion in his victory dedication before the fourth century (cf. Hyde 1921.234, 243–5, 248–55). On Diagoras, see schol. *ad Ol.* 7.inscr.c, Moretti 1957.94, and on Acusilaos, schol. *ad Ol.* 7.inscr.c, Moretti 1957.102.
3 Paus. 6.10.3.
4 Philostr. *Gym.* 20.
5 Campbell 1991.373n.1 and Hyde 1921.243 both consider Glaucus a victor in the boys' contests. See also Moretti 1957.75.
6 From the same period Agiadas of Elis, Tellon of Oresthas and Epicradius of Mantinea (Paus. 6.10.9), Protolaus of Mantinea (6.6.1), Cyniscus of Mantinea (6.4.11), and Charmides of Elis (6.7.1) are all explicitly said to have won the boys' boxing.
7 Glaucus was so well known that Athenian orators could refer to him offhand in their speeches; see Moretti 1957.76.
8 Hamilton 1974.108. Cf. Pfeijffer 1998.32n.35.
9 *Ol.* 8.54 and 10.17, *Ne.* 4.93, 5.48, and 6.65. *Ol.* 11 is for the same victory as *Ol.* 10, and so the fact that it does not name a trainer is not significant.
10 As Pfeijffer 1998.28 recognizes, the inscription to the ode, which does not mark the victor as a youth, is therefore incomplete.
11 Pfeijffer 1998.30.
12 Hamilton 1974.107–8.
13 *Is.* 6.72–3. See also Chapter 8.
14 Ba. 13.192. The other odes are Ba. 1 and 2 (counted together because they celebrate the same victory), and Ba. 11. Ba. 1 has lacunae, however, so it is not certain that no trainer is named in that ode.
15 The memorials of Agiadas of Elis (perhaps Ebert 1972 no.23), Tellon of Oresthas (Ebert 1972 no.14) and Epicradius of Mantinea (Paus. 6.10.9), Protolaus of Mantinea (6.6.1), Cyniscus of Mantinea (6.4.11, Ebert 1972 no.21), Charmides of Elis (6.7.1, Ebert 1972 no.24), Theognetus of Aegina (6.9.1, Ebert 1972 no.12), and Pherias of Aegina (6.14.1, Ebert 1972 no.19). Moretti 1957.80 also dates the Olympic statue of Agametor of Mantinea (Paus. 6.9.9) to this period, but the evidence is thin.
16 Habicht 1985.147–51.

17 Ebert 1972 no.14, DP nos.147–8.
18 Ebert 1972 no.21, DP no.149.
19 Ebert 1972 no.24, DP no.156.
20 Raubitschek 1949 no.21. On Callias, see Kyle 1987.202–3.
21 Raubitschek 1949 no.154.
22 Pi. *Ol.* 8, 10/11, *Ne.* 4, 5, 6. Ba. 13 names the trainer, whereas Pi. *Py.* 8, *Is.* 6, 8, Ba. 1/2, Ba. 11, and the Olympic memorials of Agiadas, Charmides, Tellon, Epicradius, Protolaus, Cyniscus, Theognetus, and Pherias do not. See n.15.
23 On the mechanics of these events, see Gardiner 1978.144–76.
24 Webster 1972.201–3, 206–8 offers a list.
25 Boston 01.8020 (*ARV*[2] 321/22; Gardiner 1978 pl.105). Other examples include Florence, unnumbered (*ABV* 228/6); San Simeon 9931 (369/118); London B271 (375/212, 696, Gardiner 1978 pl.131); Munich 1892 (385/32, Jüthner 1968 fig. 36); Louvre F 264 (401/2, *CVA* He pl.55.6); Taranto, unnumbered (476/2); London B576 (480, Jüthner 1968 fig. 54); Berlin 2180 (*ARV*[2] 13/1, Hoppin 1917 pls.20, 21); Louvre G 42 (23/1, Gardiner 1978 pl.123); Boston 01.8019 (24/11, Hoppin 1917 pls.32, 33); Munich 2308 (26/2, Gardiner 1978 pl.124); Würzburg 509 (249/5, Richter and Milne 1973 fig. 11, Jüthner 1968 pl.59); Villa Giulia 50703 (281/34 *ter*); Arlesheim, unnumbered (351/8); Boston 10.176 (381/173, Gardiner 1978 fig. 102).
26 Barringer 2001.2–3.
27 Dedications for discus and long-jump victories survive; see Moretti 1953 nos.1 and 6, and Hodkinson 1999.153–5.
28 Boston 01.8019 (*ARV*[2] 24/11, Hoppin 1917 pls. 32–3). Phayllos seems to occupy an intermediate position between trainer and athlete because he wears the same fillet as the other trainers but is naked and has no forked stick. Fig. 12 is of the same vase.
29 Munich 2308 (*ARV*[2] 26/2, Gardiner 1978 pl. 124); Turin 4123 (28/11); London E 256 (168, Gardiner 1910 fig. 99); see Webster 1972.55–6.
30 On Phayllos, see Hdt. 8.47, Paus. 10.9.2, Gardiner 1910.309–10, Moretti 1953.25–9, Krumeich 1997.181–5, Golden 1998.60–2, and Neer 2002.94–5.
31 Paus. 6.14.9–10, Philostr. *Gym.* 55, and Hyde 1921.284–5.
32 Schol. *ad Ne.* 7 inscr.; Hamilton 1974.106.
33 Pfeijffer 1998. Neither of the two pairs of odes for gymnastic victors by Bacchylides, Ba. 1–2 and Ba. 6–7, mentions the age of the victors, although *IG* 12.5.608, an inscription from Iulis on Ceos that lists victors from Ceos, makes it clear that both won boys' contests. Pfeijffer does not address Ba. 1–2, but in response to the silence of Ba. 6 suggests that shorter odes may have been exceptions, or that Ba. 6 mentioned the age category in its small lacuna (Ba. 1 is also damaged). *Contra* Pfeijffer, most also consider *Py.* 11, which does not reveal the victor's age, to celebrate a youth (Hamilton 1974.106).
34 1998.30.
35 Würzburg 215 (*ABV* 375/213, Langlotz 1968.1.39, 1968.2 pl.59).
36 See the Introduction, n.19.
37 Gardiner 1910.272–84, 1978.135–40.

38 Cab. Méd. 252 (*ABV* 344/1, Gardiner 1978 fig. 182, Jüthner 1968 fig. 4); Würzburg 215 (375/213); Basle auction (386/7); Meggen, Käppeli, unnumbered (*ARV*[2] 868/45); Boston 28.48 (882/36, Gardiner 1978 pl.88). Cf. also Cab. Méd. 354 (*ABV* 345/2, Jüthner 1968 fig. 2) and Leipsic T 3599, T 3619, T 3712 (*ARV*[2] 38/5).

39 Orvieto, Faina, unnumbered (*ARV*[2] 260/14); perhaps Milan, Scala, unnumbered (271/1); Villa Giulia 50760 (279/1); London auction (279/8, cf. 1641); Cab. Méd. 523 (316/4, Gardiner 1910 fig. 54); Leipsic T 504 (363/35); Roman Market? (418/28, Jüthner 1968 fig.6); New York 56.171.40 (565/37). Cf. also, from the classical period: Naples 3083 (*ARV*[2] 1016/33).

40 Gardiner 1910.285, 1978.140.

41 Paus. 6.1.5. Moretti 1957.118 dates the victory to 380; the general date is fixed by the statue's artist, Cleon of Sicyon. ἄσκησις was a technical term for an athlete's training in the Roman period; see LSJ I.

42 Strabo 6.1.12, Young 1984.134–46, and Mann 2001.164–91. The victory in 484 may have been announced as Croton's also; see Young 1984.141n.35.

43 On the statue, which seems to have been transported to Rome in the first century B.C.E., see Hyde 1921.196–200. For Ladas' death, see Paus. 3.21.1. Moretti 1957.96 dates the victory to 460.

44 Paus. 2.19.7, 8.12.5, 3.21.1. Moretti 1957.96 tentatively suggests that Ladas was an Argive, whereas Hyde 1921.196 and Poralla 1985.80 see him as Spartan. The name Ladas is otherwise unattested for a Spartan, however, and Paus. 3.21.1 does not suggest that Ladas lived there.

45 Epicradius (Paus. 6.10.9; dated by Moretti 1957.87 to 484), Protolaus (6.61; dated by Moretti 1957.95 to 464), and Cyniscus (6.4.11; dated by Moretti 1957.97 to 460). Moretti dates the victory of Pytharchus of Mantinea in the stadion to 464 (Moretti 1957.95, Paus. 6.7.1) and of Agametor of Mantinea in the boys' boxing to 500 (1957.80, 6.9.9), but the evidence is weak. On the disproportionate success of Elis and nearby states, see Crowther 1989.207–10.

46 Pi. *Ol.* 14, *Py.* 10, Ba. 6, 7, and the victory statue of Socrates of Pellene (Paus. 6.8.1, 7.17.14, Moretti 1957.97). Ba. 7 is fragmentary. Moretti also dates, on little evidence, the Olympic statues of the runner Philo of Corcyra (Moretti 1957.79, Paus. 6.14.13), Meneptolemus of Apollonia (1957.80, 6.14.13) and Pytharchus (see n.45, this chapter) to this period. None appears to name the trainer, however.

47 Hamilton 1974.106, but see Pfeijffer 1998.36–7.

48 Pfeijffer 1998.33. Pfeijffer's other evidence for adults having trainers is weak, however: Pi. *Ol.* 8.56–9 does not indicate that Melesias trained adults, only that he won a victory himself in the open competitions, and, although *Is.* 3/4.87–90 does name a trainer in an ode that celebrates an adult victory, the trainer's input is restricted to the youth victory mentioned just before. Note also that Pi. *Ol.* 8.63 (ἄνδρα) and Ba. 13.196 (ἀν̣έ̣ρων) speak of a trainer's help leading to victories for "men" in various competitions, although it would be unwise to take the words too exactly.

49 Philostr. *Gym.* 21, also *Im.* 2.6. For the date, see Paus. 8.40.1 and Moretti 1957.70.

50 Philostr. *Gym.* 22 describes how a trainer secured victory for Promachos of Pellene in the men's boxing of 404 (Moretti 1957.111) by suggesting that the boy he was in love with would never refuse an Olympic victor. The victory was especially noteworthy because Promachos was said to have defeated Polydamas of Scotussa, on whom see the Introduction n.1 and Paus. 7.17.5–7.

51 Cf. Golden 1998.110.

52 Würzburg 215 (*ABV* 375/213); also Cab. Méd. 252 (*ABV* 344/1, Gardiner 1978 fig. 182, Jüthner 1968 fig. 4) and Cab. Méd. 354 (345/2, Jüthner 1968 fig. 2).

53 Cab. Méd. 354 (*ABV* 345/2, Jüthner 1968 fig. 2); Louvre F 240 (370/129); Munich 1892 (385/32, Jüthner 1968 fig. 36); and London B 271 (375/212, Gardiner 1978 pl. 131).

54 Vatican 414 (*ABV* 343/3, Gardiner 1978 pl.163, Poliakoff 1987 fig. 26); Cab. Méd. 354 (345/2, Jüthner 1968 fig. 2); Villa Giulia (345/3, Poliakoff 1987 fig. 62); Villa Giulia 50680 (394/10, Poliakoff 1987 fig. 83); New York 06.1021.49 (703, Gardiner 1978 pl. 200, Poliakoff 1987 fig. 56); Dartmouth C.959.93 (Poliakoff 1987 fig. 29); Castle Ashby (Gardiner 1978 pl. 185); Berlin 2159 (*ARV*[2] 24, Gardiner 1978 pl. 154, Poliakoff 1987 fig. 22).

55 For example: Berlin 1831 (*ABV* 274, 691, Gardiner 1910 fig. 144), NY Met. 16.71 (404, 696, Poliakoff 1987 fig. 57). Webster 1972.203–5, 213 offers a comprehensive list of Panathenaic amphorae in the combat sports.

56 Fourteen odes: Pi. *Ol.* 7, 9, 12, 13, *Py.* 9, *Ne.* 2, 3, 8, 10, *Is.* 4, 7, Ba. 9, 10, 12. Twenty-three dedications at Olympia, following the order of Moretti 1957: Praxidamas of Aegina (Paus. 6.18.4), Milo of Croton (6.14.5), Rhexibios of Opuntian Locri (6.18.7), Anochos of Taras (6.14.11), Glaucus of Carystos (6.10.1), Timasitheos of Delphi (6.8.6), Acmatidas of Sparta (Ebert 1972 no.9, Moretti 1953 no.8), the boxer Philo of Corcyra (Paus. 6.9.9, Ebert 1972 no.11), Hieronymos of Andros (Paus. 6.14.13), Theopompus and Demaretus of Heraea (6.10.4), Euthymus of Locri (6.6.6, Ebert 1972 no.16, Moretti 1953 no.13, DP no.144), Mnaseas of Cyrene (Paus. 6.13.7), Theagenes of Thasos (6.11.2, DP no.153), Ergoteles of Himera (Paus. 6.4.11, Ebert 1972 no.20), Callias of Athens (Paus. 6.6.1, DP no.146), Diagoras of Rhodes (Paus. 6.7.1, DP no.151), Leontiscus of Messene (Paus. 6.4.3), Timanthes of Cleonae (6.8.4), Alcaenetus of Lepreum (6.7.8), Pythocles of Elis (6.7.10, DP nos.162–3), Damagetus of Rhodes (Paus. 6.7.1, DP no.152), Cheimon of Argos (Paus. 6.9.3), and Acusilaos of Rhodes (6.7.3). Four dedications at Athens: Alcmeonides of Athens (Moretti 1953 no.4, Raubitschek 1949 no.317), Phayllos of Croton (Moretti 1953 no.11, Raubitschek 1949 no.76), Epicharinos of Athens (Paus. 1.23.9, Raubitschek 1949 no.120), and Callias of Athens (Raubitschek 1949 no.164, Moretti 1953 no.15). Six dedications elsewhere: Arrichion of Phigalia (Paus. 8.40.1), Aristis of Cleonae (Ebert 1972 no.2, Moretti 1953 no.3), Exoidas (Moretti 1953 no.6), Aiglatas of Sparta (Moretti 1953 no.9), Aeschyllus of Argos (Moretti 1953 no.10), and Agatha[. . .] of Sicyon (Moretti 1953 no.12). This list is conservative; a number of memorials with dates that may lie outside these boundaries or whose authenticity is questionable, or that are less intact, might be added. *Is.* 5.59–61 names a fictional trainer; see Chapter 8.

57 See the dedications of Euthymus, Theagenes, Callias, Diagoras, Damagetus, Pythocles, and Epicharinos listed in n.56.

58 Other memorials that mention victories won in the victor's youth include Pi. *Ol.* 9.88, and the dedications of Alcaenetus and, probably, Milo, listed in n.56.

59 Paus. 6.3.6. The date is roughly fixed by the artist, Cantharus of Sicyon; Moretti 1957.136 suggests 272.

60 Diog. Laert. 8.12–13. See also Moretti 1957.74.

61 Paus. 6.14.3. Even though Pausanias here records a victory in which the trainer was instrumental, his account still downplays the trainer's role, as it does elsewhere: he describes how Artemidorus of Tralles was pushed by "a trainer's encouragement" to his victory in the beardless youths' category but adds that it was the insult of an adult contestant that motivated him to win the open category.

62 Pi. schol. *ad Ol.* 10.19a, 19c, 20, 21a. The story that Hagesidamus would have lost without his trainer is clearly invented by the scholia to explain Pindar's choice of the Cycnus myth. Philostr. *Gym.* 22–4 offers three more stories from later periods in which the trainer is key to the victory.

63 Text of Turyn. See also *Ol.* 9.100–2, *Py.* 2.31–2, and Miller 1983.209–10.

64 Hubbard 1985.108–9.

65 This position conflicts with that of Kurke 1991.192–4, who argues, following Vernant 1983.260–1, that the shifting valuation of skill in Pindar's odes is more to do with which part of the process of production is considered and that the product itself was admired, whereas the producer was not.

66 Philostr. *Gym.* 43. Most of these stories are surely fanciful, but a few successful athletes could have come from modest backgrounds (Young 1984.147–57). Such athletes were presumably absorbed not only into aristocratic ideology but also into aristocratic families (Rose 1992.146–7). The anecdotal tradition in fact suggests that Glaucus ended life as Gelon's lieutenant, in charge of Camarina (see Moretti 1957.75–6, Dunbabin 1968.416); it may thus be more than coincidence that Glaucias of Aegina made Olympic dedications for both of them (Paus. 6.10.3, 6.10.5).

7. MELESIAS

1 "Trainer praise" is so regular in Pindar's odes that it has been marked as a component of the genre; see Thummer 1968.35–6 and Hamilton 1974.107–8.

2 Schol. *ad Ol.* 8. inscr.a, b.

3 The victory of Timosthenes, Alcimedon's grandfather (see Carey 1989a.1–6, *contra* schol. *ad Ol.* 8.16, 19b) is also celebrated in the naming complex (Kurke 1991.20), but, as *Ol.* 8.70–1 makes clear, Alcimedon is the primary honorand.

4 Moretti 1957.97 represents the general consensus in dating the ode to 460. This is the date offered by the scholia (*ad Ol.* 8. inscr.a) and is supported by the Oxyrhynchus victory list, POxy. 222. The list gives enough information to rule out 480, 472, 468, 456, 452, and 448. In 476 an Aeginetan won, and it is usually assumed that this was Theognetus; Alcimedon is also a possible supplement, although both names are somewhat too long for the gap (Grenfell and Hunt

1899.91). A date of 444 is probably too late for Pindar, whereas 484 seems too early for Melesias to have accrued thirty Panhellenic wins, given that this is not mentioned in *Ne.* 4 or 6; 464 and 460 remain, but the testimony of the scholia makes 460 more likely. Figueira 1993.84n.15 argues that the content of the ode fits this date.

5 Following the manuscripts, Turyn 1952 offers μάχαν, but the resulting sentence is extremely difficult to construe. μάχας or μαχᾶν make better sense and could easily have been corrupted to μάχαν because of the opening τὰν. Cf. Farnell 1932.65–6.

6 *Pace* Kirchner 1996.172–3. Carey 1989b.287–90 thinks, very plausibly, that this total includes Melesias' own victories as an athlete (but there is no evidence that these included an Isthmian victory in the beardless category).

7 Milo: Moretti 1957.72–3, Paus. 6.14.5; Glaucus: Moretti 1957.75–6, Paus. 6.10.3; Theagenes: Moretti 1957.88, Paus. 6.11.4–5, Ebert 1972 no.37, DP no.153.

8 For example, Ergoteles of Himera, a long-distance runner, won eight Panhellenic victories (Paus. 6.4.11; cf. Pi. *Ol.* 12.17–18). Cf. also Diagoras of Rhodes, who won six times at the three most important contests and "one victory after another" (Pi. *Ol.* 7.82) at Nemea; Epharmostus of Opuntian Locri, a wrestler who won five times at the big three and had "some joys at Nemea" (Pi. *Ol.* 9.87); and Xenophon of Corinth, a runner and pentathlete, who won twice at each of the other three and "was not resisted by Nemea" (Pi. *Ol.* 13.34).

9 *Ne.* 6.58–61, Ba. 12.36–41; Ba. 12.36–41 may include the local victories mentioned in 12.35. Cf. also the Timodamids of Acharnae who had won nineteen Panhellenic crowns by the time of Pi. *Ne.* 2 (19–23) and were soon to add another (schol. *ad Ne.* 2.1a, Moretti 1957.96–7). At *Ne.* 6.25–6 Pindar claims that no clan has won more boxing victories than the Bassids, and, although this was surely nothing more than conjecture and refers to local victories as well, it does show that the Bassids were considered highly successful.

10 Given that a youth would need to be near the upper age limit to stand a real chance, even with the extra age classes at the Isthmia and Nemea, few youths could have won more than two or three Panhellenic crowns. Indeed, it seems to have been rare to win more than once; as a youth Aristomenes of Aegina had six wins, but only one was Panhellenic (*Py.* 8.78–80), and Timasarchus of Aegina had only one Panhellenic win among his four wins as a youth (*Ne.* 4.13–22).

11 The identification with Thucydides' father would suggest that Melesias was around sixty-five or seventy in 460 (see Kirchner 1996.172).

12 There is some dispute as to how to understand these lines, with the scholia variously suggesting that Alcimedon provided the honor to Melesias (*ad Ol.* 8.86a, d) or himself constituted the honor (*ad Ol.* 8.86c). Although Race 1990.158 argues strongly for the latter, the former is surely more likely. The victory, as is usual in Pindar (see Kurke 1991.35–61), is figured in concrete terms as a valuable and movable possession that must be brought to its owner's home.

13 See *Ol.* 7.68, *Is.* 8.38.

14 On Timosthenes, see n.3, this chapter.

15 Kurke 1991.104n.65 sees χάριν as specifically indicating that the victory is a gift from the gods. Later in this ode, however, at *Ol.* 8.80, χάρις is used of the joy that Alcimedon's victory rouses in his dead relatives.

16 As Robbins 1986.320–1.

17 Robbins 1986.320–1 sees Aeacus as prefiguring Melesias, because Melesias, the father of Thucydides, seems to have been related to Miltiades, who himself claimed descent from Ajax and Aeacus (Hdt. 6.35, Paus. 2.29.4). If indeed Melesias the trainer was the father of Thucydides, the figure of Aeacus may thus have been selected to display a bond between the families of Melesias and Alcimedon.

18 Pl. *Hp. Mi.* 363c–8e.

19 Pl. *Soph.* 232d.

20 Rose 1992.273–8, 338–41.

21 Pl. *Soph.* 231a–5c.

22 Cf. also *Ol.* 2.86–8, which allows for knowledge of many things but is structured by the same underlying contrast between real and sham knowledge.

23 Pi. *Ol.* 4.18 (διάπειρά), *Ne.* 3.70, 4.76, *Is.* 3/4.48 (ἀπειράτων).

24 *Thgn.* 571–2, 1104a–b. Cf. also 1178.

25 *Thgn.* 1105–6. On the touchstone as a recurrent symbol of aristocratic ideology, see duBois 1991.9–18.

26 *Thgn.* 396, 408, 412, 453, 540, 554, 635, 895, 968, 1171–4. Cf. especially 895: γνώμης δ᾽ οὐδὲν ἄμεινον ἀνὴρ ἔχει αὐτὸς ἐν αὐτῶι, "A man has nothing better in himself than γνώμη." It is telling that Hes. *Op.* does not use γνώμη at all.

27 Figueira 1993.208 argues that Melesias is represented as a teacher not just of wrestling but also of aristocratic morals and manners, "more like a master of one of the oriental martial arts than a secondary school wrestling coach." This seems too strong a conclusion because every effort is made to avoid the question of the content of Melesias' teaching.

28 1982.23–26. See also Dickson 1988.115, 1990.110–11.

29 On the contrast between speaking and mute signs, see Dickson 1990.

30 1982.25.

31 Cf. Dickson 1988.119–21.

32 Poliakoff 1987.23.

33 LSJ s.v. παλαιστικός I, and, for ἡ παλαιστρική, schol *ad* Pi. *Ne.* 5.89b. On the manuals, see Gardiner 1910.374, Poliakoff 1987.52–3.

34 Schol *ad* Pi. *Ne.* 5.89a, b.

35 Cf. *Py.* 8.81–2, *Ne.* 6.11–16, 10.21–4.

36 τρόπος (63) does not refer to a wrestling move but to the general manner or method of victory (LSJ II), or perhaps the character of the wrestler (LSJ III.2).

37 Farnell 1932.263, Woloch 1963.104, Bowra 1964.409, Cole 1992.91–101, and Figueira 1993.208–9.

38 Due to the corruption of this passage, it cannot be determined whether this celebration is imagined as happening in the future (as Turyn 1952), perhaps in Callicles' presence in Hades or without him in Aegina, or recorded as having happened before Callicles died (as Maehler 1987).

39 For the translation of the wrestling terms, see Poliakoff 1982.137–142.
40 Bury 1890.79.
41 The patron is always named in a victory ode, and the other possible candidates, the victor's father Timocritus and uncle Callicles, are dead.
42 Bury 1890.234, Köhnken 1971.215–17, Poliakoff 1982.138, Bulman 1992.76, and Willcock 1995.109.
43 Nicholson 2001.50–1.
44 Pindar usually closes his odes with an emphatic reference to the quality of his own praise; see Nicholson 2001.50.
45 Bury 1890.234.
46 Schol. *ad Is.* 7.44.
47 Phoenix (*Il.* 9.432–605) and Nestor (11.654–802) offer stories of heroic exploits as a form of education for Achilles (διδασκέμεναι, 9.442; cf. ὑποθέσθαι, 11.788).
48 See *Py.* 3.45, 4.102, *Ne.* 3.53, and, on the *Precepts of Chiron*, Schwartz 1960.228–44 and Kurke 1990.89–94.
49 Poliakoff 1982.140–1.
50 On the strong aristocratic tone here, see, for example, Hubbard 1985.75–6.
51 On this opponent, see Miller 1983.202–11.
52 Not all accept the reading of Maehler 1987, but the majority of suggestions (for example, Bowra 1947 and Williams 1976.151, 206–7) preserve the idea of the gifts being family possessions.
53 The frequent emendations made to this passage testify to the awkwardness of its initial impression. For the emendations, see Gerber 1976.106, 1984.23, and Nicholson 2001.33n.3.
54 Nicholson 2001. "Using as an excuse" is the interpretation of the schol. *ad Ne.* 4.92c, whereas "using to his advantage" is that of Carnes 1996.22–3 and 1999.5–9.
55 In Nicholson 2001, I argued that the dissonance of *Ne.* 4.57–8 was generated not so much by a guiding intention as by the influence of contradictory ideologies on the narration of the Peleus myth.
56 Estimates of the date vary from 484 to the 440s, but the late dates are unlikely, given that the victor's grandfather, Praxidamas (*Ne* 6.15–17), won at Olympia in 544 (Paus. 6.18.7); see Bowra 1964.412, Cole 1992.92n.6, and Gerber 1999.34–6. Any date before the reconciliation of Athens and Aegina in 482 is also unlikely: although at least one Athenian trainer was active before then, the fact that he was Athenian had to be addressed in the victory ode celebrating his pupil; see Chapter 8, and cf. Figueira 1993.206.
57 Text of Turyn 1952. The mss. have an unmetrical κε in 64. Maehler 1987, following the schol. *ad Ne.* 6.108b, emends to . . . δελφῖνι καὶ τάχος δι' ἅλμας / ἶσον <κ'> εἴποιμι . . . , but the καὶ makes little sense, and the insertion of <κ'> is unnecessarily radical. See also Gerber 1999.86.
58 Cf. Bury 1890.235–8 and Farnell 1930.196–7.
59 See *Ne.* 6.8–26, 34–44, 57–63.
60 As schol. *ad Ne.* 6.108a, Farnell 1930.196–7.
61 Schol. *ad Ne.* 6.108b.

62 *Ol.* 4.24–5, 10.100, *Py.* 1.42, 10.23, 11.18, *Ne.* 1.45, 5.19, 10.48. Gerber 1999.87 sees χειρῶν τε καὶ ἰσχύος as equivalent to "of strong hands."

63 See Pi. *fr.* 234.2, and Gerber 1999.87.

64 Luc. *Lexiph.* 5, Bury 1890.235.

65 See schol. *ad Py.* 8.88, 91.

66 The fact that in both *Ne.* 6 and *Is.* 9 the dolphin is specified as "in the sea" (δι' ἅλμας, *Ne* 6.64; ἐν πόντῳ, *Is.* 9.7) perhaps indicates that there was a famous depiction of a dolphin somewhere on Aegina, perhaps in the temple of Apollo (Paus. 2.30.1). The Delphinia, like the Aeginetan month Delphinios (Pi. *Ne.* 5.44–5), were dedicated to that god (schol. *ad Py.* 8.88, 91, cf. *Hymn. Hom. Ap.* 3.399–401). Aeginetan coins featured turtles, not dolphins; see Kraay 1976 pl.6, figs.113–17, 123, 126.

67 The families are the Blepsiads (Pi. *Ol.* 8), the Meidulids (*Py.* 8, Ebert 1972 no.12), the Theandrids (*Ne.* 4), the Psalychiads (*Ne.* 5, *Is.* 5, 6, Ba. 13), the Bassids (*Ne.* 6), the Euxenids (*Ne.* 7), the Chariads (*Ne.* 8), and the families of Aristocleides (*Ne.* 3), Cleander (*Is.* 8), Teisias (Ba. 12), and Pherias (Paus. 6.14.1, Ebert 1972 no.19). The wrestlers Crius (Sim. 507, Cole 1992.47–8, Mann 2001.193–5) and Taurosthenes (Paus. 6.9.3, Moretti 1957.103) may represent two further clans involved in athletic competition or belong to one or more of the eleven listed here. That none of the odes mentions any chariot racing is significant; *Is.* 4 (= *Is.* 3/4.43–7), an ode to a pancratiast, speaks of his clan's hippotrophy.

68 Xen. *Eq.* 8.1–8.

69 Xen. *Eq.* 7.12, 3.9.

70 *Ne.* 6.57–63. The near misses at Olympia were by Alcimidas and Polytimidas, presumably a living kinsman. The suggestion of Cole 1987.556 that Alcimidas and Polytimidas actually missed out on the same crown, perhaps by being drawn against each other and then wearing each other out, is highly attractive. On the lottery, see Crowther 1992b.68–74.

71 As Bury 1892.113 and others have noted, ἁνίοχος is used figuratively in an epigram that records the victory of Theognetus of Aegina in the boys' wrestling contest at Olympia (Ebert 1972 no.12, *AP* 16.2, [Sim.] XXX (Campbell 1991)). The epigram may have accompanied the puzzling statue of Theognetus at Olympia (Paus. 6.9.1; Theognetus carried a pinecone and a pomegranate) and, if so, was roughly contemporary with *Ne.* 6. Theognetus' victory must predate 446 because it is mentioned in Pi. *Py.* 8.36, for a nephew's Pythian victory in 446, and it is usually assigned to fill the gap in POxy. 222 for 476 (Moretti 1957.90), but 484, 464, and 460 are real possibilities (cf. n.4, this chapter). Whatever its precise date, the epigram, if genuine, surely either tried to correct *Ne.* 6 or was itself corrected by it: in it, it is Theognetus, and not his trainer, who is described as "a skillful charioteer of wrestling" (παλαισμοσύνης δεξιὸν ἡνίοχον). If *Ne.* 6 came first, Theognetus' family should be understood as disclaiming the trainers used by other Aeginetan wrestlers. Such a claim, despite the fact that no trainer is mentioned for the nephew in *Py.* 8, should be understood as false. No wrestler could have done without training; the Meidulids may instead have used obscure trainers whose participation could be erased more easily than Melesias'.

If Theognetus' memorial came first, however, *Ne.* 6 should be understood as correcting the reference of the metaphor and exposing the use of trainers by Theognetus that his memorial tried to hide. A particularly intriguing possibility is that Theognetus was the beneficiary, at least in the Bassids' eyes, of the lottery that weighted the odds against Alcimidas and Polytimidas (see n.70, this chapter). Theognetus' Olympic victory, and Alcimidas' and Polytimidas' near misses, might then have come in 476, and Alcimidas' Nemean win in 475. *Ne.* 6, with its grousing about Theognetus' win and appropriation of the charioteer metaphor for Melesias' training, might thus have been a very specific response to the success of a rival clan, as well as the celebration of Alcimidas' success.

72 Mann 2001.232–3 suggests that Melesias was a kind of state trainer for Aegina, hired jointly by several Aeginetan clans.

73 See Wade-Gery 1932.205–27, Woloch 1963.102, Davies 1971.231, Kyle 1987.207, Figueira 1993.199n.7, and Mann 2001.230–31. Wilamowitz 1922.398, Young 1984.148n.45, Race 1990.155, and Kirchner 1996 argue against the identification.

74 Pl. *Meno* 94d. Figueira 1993.206 surmises that Melesias' son Thucydides was by 480 "on the verge of becoming one of the greatest men in Athens," having probably already held a generalship and being already linked to Cimon by marriage.

75 Cf. Cole 1992.33–111, Figueira 1993.205–11. Note that, as Kirchner 1996.173–4 shows, Melesias was almost certainly an Athenian.

76 For Thucydides and Aegina, see Figueira 1993.197–230.

77 See POxy. 222.1.16 and schol. *ad Ol.* 10, inscr.a, *contra* inscr.c.

78 *Il.* 11.785–8.

79 See Mullen 1982.186–7; Sergent 1986.250–8; Hubbard 2002.264n.25, 2003.1–2; and Aesch. *frs.* 134a-7 *TGF.*

80 On the myth of Heracles and its treatment of wage labor, see Golden 1998.146–57; on the treatment of the poet in *Ol.* 10, see Kurke 1991.232–5.

81 The date is unclear; cf. Bowra 1964.408. On the relationship between *Is.* 3 and 4, see Chapter 5, n.10.

82 See *Ne.* 11.3–4 (ἑταίρους), *Is.* 8.65b–6b (ἁλίκων), and cf. *Ol.* 4.4–5.

83 *Contra* Pfeijffer 1998.33.

84 Pi. *Py.* 1.86, 4.274, 5.122, 10.72, *Thgn.* 457–60, 667–682, Alcaeus *frs.* 6, 208.

85 *Thgn.* 457–60, for example, suggests that ideally a husband should act as the helmsman of his wife.

86 For the Theognidean resonance of γνώμᾳ, see n.26, this chapter; for πολυβούλῳ, cf. *Thgn.* 38.

87 Text of Turyn.

88 *Il.* 23.700–39.

89 1985.107–16.

90 Text of Turyn 1952. Maehler 1987 unnecessarily emends the manuscript reading to the weaker ἀκμᾷ, "in the peak of his strength" (which also turns attention away from skill). Bury 1892.74 translates αἰχμᾷ "in battle," but a translation that stresses character (LSJ III) is preferable.

91 *Contra* Hubbard 1985.111, who sees these lines as pointing to the use of skill by Melissus and Heracles.
92 Hubbard 1985.116 argues that Orseas, and athletic trainers in general, represent "for Pindar the synthesis of *physis* and *techne*, of physical prowess (insofar as he is himself an athlete) and technical skill (insofar as he is a trainer)." As argued earlier, however, the steersman image focuses not on skill but on moral guidance.
93 Pl. *Meno* 94c.
94 Ptoiodoros, Simon, and Eudemos: Boston 01.8019 (*ARV*[2] 24/11, Hoppin 1917.127–30; Webster 1972.55–56 assigns the names differently); a fourth trainer is pictured, but, *contra* Webster, his name has been lost. Hipparchos: Berlin 2180 (*ARV*[2] 13/1, Hoppin 1917.68–72). Orsimenes: Munich 2308 (*ARV*[2] 26, Hoppin 1917.13–15). Sotinos: Louvre G42 (*ARV*[2] 23/1, Hoppin 1917.123–6, Neer 2002.107–8). Trainers also seem to be named on the interiors of London E78 (*ARV*[2] 401/3, Gardiner 1910 fig. 134) and of Cab. Med. 523 (*ARV*[2] 316/4, Gardiner 1910 fig. 115).
95 The presence of trainers at Olympia is implied by the anecdotes of Eryxias and Tisias, as well as those of Peisirhodus and his mother (Paus. 5.6.7–8), Artemidorus (Paus. 6.14.3), and Ilas (Pi. schol. *ad Ol.* 10.19a, 19c, 20, 21a). The anecdotes of Eryxias and Tisias imply that trainers could encourage their charges while they were fighting, but as the anecdote of Peisirodus makes clear, at least at Olympia, trainers were kept away from the ring itself.
96 Paus. 6.2.9, Moretti 1957.118, 1987.69–70.
97 Paus. 6.2.9, which perhaps quotes parts of the inscription here. Ebert 1972.104 thinks that the victor's name appeared elsewhere on the monument.
98 Paus. 2.2.6, Moretti 1957.116.
99 Ebert 1972 no.31.
100 2002.260–1, 264n.25, 2003.1–16.
101 Figueira 1993.205–11.
102 Figueira 1993.197–230.
103 See n.10.
104 Cf. n.71.
105 The dramatic date of the Gnathaena anecdote is somewhere in the late fourth or early third centuries, as her acquaintance with the comic poet Diphilus shows (Ath. 13.579e–580a, 583e–f). A Hippomachus of Elis perhaps won a youth victory in boxing at Olympia around 300 (Paus. 6.12.6, Moretti 1957.132–3), but these two Hippomachuses should not be identified because the trainer must have resided in Athens.
106 The saying is structured around a pun on φοιτάω, which can mean both "have intercourse with" (LSJ I.3) and "go to school" (LSJ I.5): "παιδίον, ὥσπερ πρὸς Ἱππόμαχον τὸν παιδοτρίβην μνᾶν δοὺς οἴει αἰεὶ φοιτήσειν;"
107 Commissioned poets were certainly compared to prostitutes in some quarters; see Pi. *Is.* 2.1–11, and Chapter 3.
108 How large the sum involved was depends on the context in which it was evaluated. Around the dramatic date of the anecdote, one mina (100 drachmae) represented perhaps forty or fifty days of skilled labor (Kyle 1987.145n.131, cf.

Golden 1998.160). It was probably rather less in Athenaeus' time but must still have been a considerable fee, despite Gnathaena's scorn.

8. MENANDER

1 On the meaning of ἐν Πανελλάνων ἀέθλοις (Ba. 13.198), see Blass 1898.304, Jebb 1905.353, and Maehler 1982.285. Pindar's usage is inconclusive; see *Is.* 2.38 3.46–7.

2 On the date of Pytheas' victory, see Woloch 1963.102–4, Bowra 1964.407, Cole 1992.41–6, and Pfeijffer 1995.318–32 and 1999.59.

3 Crius (Sim. 507, Cole 1992.47–8, Mann 2001.193–5) may have won at Nemea, not Olympia.

4 That Menander was from Athens is clear from Pi. *Ne.* 5.49. The name is certainly a contemporary Athenian name; an early-fifth-century red-figure stamnos names a departing warrior as Menander (Louvre G 54 *bis*, *ARV*² 246/8, Webster 1972.61), and, although he is too young to be identified with the trainer, he may be a relative.

5 Hdt. 9.105, Paus. 1.23.10, and Kyle 1987.202.

6 Pi. *Ne.* 2, schol. *ad Ne.* 2.1a, Kyle 1987.211–12. Bowra 1964.407 dates the Olympic victory to 484, but Moretti 1957.96–7 to 460.

7 Aristotle records that an Acharnian invented the discipline (schol. *ad Ne.* 3.27a).

8 Moretti 1957.85–6 dates the victories to 484, but many slots in both events are open in this period. On the statue group, see Hyde 1921.286–7 and Fontenrose 1988.131–4.

9 Pfeijffer 1995.323–5 and 1999.81–2, 179.

10 Kirchner 1996.173–5.

11 For the history of Aegina in the 480s, see Gzella 1981.14–16, Cole 1992.33–71, Pfeijffer 1995.329–31 and 1999.59–61; for the early 490s, see Figueira 1993.113–149.

12 Cole 1992.33–71 and Pfeijffer 1995.318–32 and 1999.81–6.

13 Cf. Bowra 1964.407, Cole 1992.33–41, and Pfeijffer 1995.318–32.

14 Cole 1992.40n.10 is unique in arguing that *Is.* 5 celebrates a youth victory; cf. Hamilton 1974.106–10.

15 The Isthmian games occur in the spring, while the battle of Salamis took place in the early Fall of 480.

16 If the victory was won among the beardless youths, this would probably have been indicated. See Pfeijffer 1998.21–34, but also Chapter 6, n.33.

17 The precise boundaries of these age classes is unknown (Golden 1998.105–6), but the two-year cycle of the Isthmian games makes it more likely that each age class at the Isthmia contained two rather than four years.

18 Pi. *Is.* 6.1–7. Two plausible datings are therefore as follows: Pytheas' Nemean victory 485, Phylacidas' first Isthmian victory 484, and his second 480, with the celebration delayed for half a year; Pytheas' Nemean victory 483, Phylacidas' first Isthmian victory 482, and his second 478. The reference in *Is.* 5 to Salamis would be more poignant soon after the victory, but Cole's attractive suggestion

(1992.35–9) that the reference to Zeus Soter in the opening of *Is.* 6 refers not only to the (unfulfilled) hope that Phylacidas would win an Olympic title but also to fear of the Persians suggests a date for *Is.* 6 nearer 481. Cole himself dates *Is.* 6 to 480, but the fear of the Persians was surely very real two years earlier.

19 See Pi. *Ne.* 5.41–6, 50–3, *Is.* 5.57–62, and, on Themistius, schol. *ad Ne.* 5.91 and *ad Is.* 6.95. What Euthymenes won is disputed: see Cole 1987.553–4, Carey 1989b.290–5, Pfeijffer 1995.319–22 and 1999.172–6, and n.34, this chapter. The name of Lampon's father, Cleonicus, need not refer to an athletic victory.

20 Hes. *Op.* 412: μελέτη δὲ τὸ ἔργον ὀφέλλει, "Application makes work prosper." On μελέτη, see LSJ I.2a, b.

21 For μέτρον, see *Thgn.* 467–96, 497–8, 499–502, 611–14, 693–4; for γνώμη, see Chapter 7, n.26; for control of one's γλῶσσα: *Thgn.* 61–8, 421–4, 479–80, 757–60, 1185–6. All three virtues are closely related: *Thgn.* 479–80, for example, describes how immoderate drinking leads one to lose control of one's tongue and mind.

22 See Kurke 1990.91–2.

23 εὐθυπορῆσαι is usually understood as a transitive verb, with δρόμον as its object, and Φυλακίδᾳ as a dative of possession: "I praise Pytheas . . . for guiding straight the course of Phylacidas' blows" (Race 1997.181, also Bury 1892.103 and Farnell 1932.369–70). This is, as Fennell 1899.188–9 and Farnell 1932.369 recognize, an unprecedented use of εὐθυπορεῖν, which is elsewhere an intransitive verb, meaning "proceed straight forward." It is, therefore, preferable to take δρόμον as the subject of the infinitive: "I praise also Pytheas . . . , that Phylacidas' course of blows held straight forward." This is the understanding of the schol. *ad Is.* 5.75a (although he, unlike Pindar, specifies Pytheas' role in effecting this result). Bury 1892.59 and Farnell 1932.369 claim that αἰνεῖν cannot govern an infinitive in indirect statement, but this construction is not uncommon when αἰνεῖν means "recommend" or "promise," and it is surely wrong to think that in Greek these different meanings were sufficiently distinct to govern different constructions (cf. LSJ II.2, III). The variant form Φυλακίδαν can give a good sense ("I praise Pytheas also . . . , that Phylacidas held straight forward in the course of his blows"), but the scholiast did not read the accusative, and Turyn 1952, Maehler 1987, and Race 1997 prefer the dative. ἐν γυιοδάμαις may also mean "among limb-subduing toils" (schol. *ad Is.* 5.75a).

24 For ἔρδω meaning "succeed," see Slater 1969, Pi. *Ne.* 7.11, Ba. 18.43–4. Cleonicus was Lampon's father.

25 However διὰ δαίμονας is understood, the gnome emphasizes strength. Cf. Bury 1892.94 and Farnell 1932.365.

26 On the different perceptions of the role of skill in the different events, see Chapter 9.

27 Gildersleeve 1908.210, Farnell 1932.74, and Gerber 2002.66 take the οὐ with σκαιότερον rather than σεσιγαμένον.

28 The notion that Phylacidas' blows "held straight forward" (εὐθυπορῆσαι, 60) also taps into the aristocratic discourse that elevates natural and divinely

sanctioned ability over taught skills. One who fights straight fights by nature and according to the ways of his ancestors, and opposes those forces that threaten aristocratic power. Cf. Pi. *Ol.* 7.90–2 and *Ne.* 1.25.

29 *Is.* 4 names the trainer in connection with a youth victory; see Chapter 6.

30 Hippocleas, the youth victor of *Py.* 10, went on to win twice at Olympia (Moretti 1957.82, 84); Timodemus, of *Ne.* 2, went on to win at Olympia (1957.96–7): and Telesicrates, of *Py.* 9, later won a better event at Delphi, the stadion (schol. *ad Py.* 9, inscr. a, b). None commissioned a second ode.

31 Pi. *Ol.* 13 and *fr.* 122. Xenophon's father and cousin had probably also commissioned victory odes; see Barrett 1978.1–9.

32 *Is.* 5.56–8, *Is.* 6.10–13. Cf. [Pi.] *Ol.* 5.15–16, Pi. *Py.* 1.89–90, 5.103–7, *Is.* 1.41–5, 3/4.46–7. *Is.* 4 is for a pancratiast, but this passage discusses his family's expenditures on equestrian competitions. δαπάνα is regularly paired with πόνος or μόχθος, words more usually used for the sufferings of warriors or competitors in the combat sports, as at [Pi.] *Ol.* 5.15–16, Pi. *Is.* 1.41–5, 5.56–8, 6.10–13; and in [Pi.] *Ol.* 5.15–16 it is explicitly associated with danger. Stressing the size and risk of these expenditures is a way of representing them as belonging to some other transactional order than that of commodity exchange; see Kurke 1991.98–104.

33 See Chapter 7, n.67.

34 Pfeijffer 1995.319–21 and 1999.168–76, argues that Pytheas did have some local victories to his credit before his Nemean victory: in contrast to Carey 1989b.290–5, Bury 1890.94–6, Farnell 1932.278–9, and Race 1997.53, he understands Pi. *Ne.* 5.44–6 to refer to victories won by Pytheas. This is unlikely because it means that Euthymenes, who certainly has a Nemean victory at the time of Phylacidas' first win (*Is.* 6.60–2, Cole 1987.553–4; cf. Carey 1989b.290–5), won that victory after *Ne.* 5 was composed and very close to the time of *Is.* 6. This possibility is surely precluded, however, by the brevity of the victory notice in that ode. Pfeijffer in fact thinks that Euthymenes won two Isthmian victories and one Nemean victory between *Ne.* 5 and *Is.* 6, which surely would have called for more comment than *Is.* 6.60–2. See also n.19, this chapter.

35 τέκτων is used of skilled manual workers, particularly carpenters, whose products are easily defined and clearly owe their existence to their work. Such work was clearly commodified in the late archaic period; Svenbro 1976.185–93 argues that, by representing himself as an artisan, Pindar points to the fact that his work is a commodity.

36 As the scholia show (*ad Ne.* 5.87), the lines admit of a rather different translation: "Know that you won with luck a sweet requital for Menander's toils." This translation is less attractive than the one given here because it renders σὺν τύχᾳ somewhat otiose, breaks up the natural sense unit of Μενάνδρου σὺν τύχᾳ, and makes a genitive (Μενάνδρου) dependent on a dependent genitive (μόχθων). This second translation, still, however, renders Menander's relation with Pytheas as one of gift exchange.

37 On this absence, see Cole 1992.57.

38 Cole 1992.42, Race 1997.53, and Pfeijffer 1999.176. Bury 1890.96 recognizes the dative.

39 As Bury 1890.96.

40 Kurke 1991.192–4 argues that the focus in the term, and in the whole imagery of craft in Pindar's odes, is on the skill present in the object produced, not on the skillfulness of the producer. I would be less exclusive, and indeed Kurke allows that some craft imagery (as in *Ne.* 5.1–2) does serve to glorify the poet; see 1991.251.

41 *Ol.* 6.88, *Is.* 2.47.

42 On Themistius, see n.19, this chapter. Pindar may be addressing a chorus here, or even himself (Bury 1890.96 and Pfeijffer 1999.180–5), but Pytheas is the referent of ἐπαύρεο in the previous line, and nothing indicates a new addressee (cf. *Ol.* 6.87–8, *Ne.* 2.24, *Is.* 8.65b, but also *Is.* 5.62–3). Moreover, Pindar often addresses the victor in the second person at the end of an ode: cf. *Ol.* 7.92, *Ne.* 3.83, 4.90, 6.60, 8.46.

43 See Chapter 6, n.2.

44 Schol. *ad. Ne.* 5.1a.

45 Kirchner 1996.173–5.

46 For these events, see the works listed under n.11.

47 Schol. *ad Ne.* 5.89b; schol. *ad Ne* 5.89a also credits Theseus with the invention of boxing and pancration. Such traditions may not have spread beyond Athens, however: schol. *ad Ne.* 5.89b offers as his sources the second-century Polemon and the third-century Ister of Cyrene, both antiquarians who might be expected to root out the most local of myths, and Ba. 13 credits the more Panhellenic hero Heracles with inventing the pancration.

48 Bury 1890.96, Cole 1992.47n.24, and Race 1997.53 see the necessity lying in a verbal connection between Ἀθανᾶν and ἀεθλητᾶισιν, but this makes little sense. Pindar is not justifying the connection between athletes and Athens, but between trainers and Athens.

49 See *Od.* 8.493, Hes. *Op.* 429–31, *Hymn. Hom. Ven.* 12–15, *Hymn. Hom.* 20.2–4, Pi. *Ol.* 7.50–2, 13.17–22, 63–86, and, more generally, Detienne and Vernant 1978.177–258 and *LIMC* II.1.1019.

50 I cannot agree with Pfeijffer 1999.81–3 that Pindar is treating the Athenian trainer harshly here.

51 Campbell 1992.199–201. See also Jebb 1905.353, Maehler 1982.285, Burnett 1985.88, and Cole 1992.42.

52 See Smyth 1920.566, nos. 2517–18.

53 *Contra* Cole 1992.42–3.

54 Ba. 13.54–7.

55 Jebb 1905.337, Platter 1989.145; see *LIMC* II.1.1026, esp. no. 517, an amphora in Brescia (*ABV* 292/1).

56 Cf. Pi. *Py.* 3.113, 5.115, *Ne.* 7.17, *Is.* 9.4.

57 Cf. Pi. *Ol.* 2.86, 3.44, 7.31, 9.28, 14.7, *Py.* 2.88, 5.12, 9.50, *Ne.* 8.41, *Is.* 2.12.

58 Cole 1992.41–50 argues that Lampon supported an alliance with Athens and so required both poets to praise Athens, albeit gently. Yet a requirement that Athens be praised does not explain why the references to Athens in both odes come when the trainer is praised (*Ne.* 4, also for an Aeginetan, praises Athens in

a victory catalogue as "rich and famous," λιπαρᾶν / εὐωνύμων, 18–19) or why the trainer is represented so differently in the two odes.

59 Cole 1992.41–4 argues that Lampon commissioned two odes because he had the larger political purpose of endorsing a pro-Athenian foreign policy at a particularly pivotal moment in Aegina's relations with Athens. On Damophilus, see Introduction, n.54.

60 The only exceptions would be an ode by Bacchylides for Teisias (Ba. 12) and one by Simonides for Crius (Sim. 507). Pindar wrote at least 12 odes for Aeginetans.

61 See Pi. *Ol.* 1.9, *Py.* 3.113, 9.78, 10.22, *Is.* 1.45, 8.47, Ba. 10.39.

62 The precise description of the song is lost, but Jebb 1905 and Campbell 1992.200 make this supplement. πλέκω is used of garlands in Ba. 17.114, Pi. *Ol.* 13.33, and *Is.* 8.66.

63 See further Nicholson 2001.44–52.

64 *Ne.* 6.45–6, 53–4; the latter gestures to the link overtly, when Pindar describes himself as "taking care" (αὐτὸς ἔχων μελέταν). As Ba. 13.191, Pi. *Is.* 6.66, and also *Ol.* 9.107 suggest, μελέτα was a regular aristocratic euphemism for training.

65 *Ol.* 10.99–105; see Nicholson 1998.28–9.

66 On *Ne.* 5.44–6, see n.34, this chapter.

9. CHIRON AND ATHENA

1 At Olympia, dedications were regularly placed next to those of earlier family members or fellow citizens (Hyde 1921.352–3, Raschke 1988.41).

2 Paus. 6.10.3. On this anecdote, see further Chapter 6. The emphasis on skill in the memorial itself did not necessarily challenge the prevailing aristocratic discourse of victory, because (as Chapters 7 and 8 argue) skill was often thought of as an inherited ability. Note, however, that Simonides, who wrote an epinician for Glaucus, is sometimes seen as challenging aristocratic versions of events (Young 1984.174, Rose 1992.159–60).

3 There is no reliable indication of the date of the victory or the ode, which seems to have been performed some time after the victory (Instone 1993.14–15, 28–30, Pfeijffer 1999.197–8, 218–27). The ode may well mark a local political victory won long after Aristocleidas had ceased to compete in athletics, the elevation of Aristocleidas to an Aeginetan body, the "Thearion of Pythios" (*Ne.* 3.70). The ode would then parallel *Ne.* 11, which marked the installation of Aristagoras of Tenedos in his local prytaneion, while also celebrating his youthful athletic victories. On the Thearion, see schol. *ad Ne.* 3.122a, b, Bury 1890.59, and Farnell 1932.260.

4 1985.40–7.

5 Pfeijffer 1999.214, *contra* schol. *ad Ne.* 3.97a.

6 Young 1968.86n.2, Carey 1980a.159–60, Hubbard 1985.42–3, Instone 1993.22–3.

7 Pfeijffer 1999.211. As Pfeijffer notes, ἔναιρε (47) is more usually used of death in war.

8 Cf. Hubbard 1985.42.

9 βαθυμῆτα (53) also points to Chiron's implication in the use and transmission of technical knowledge, because μῆτις is used of the intelligence required for crafts (Detienne and Vernant 1978.1–54, 177–275).
10 On the continuing connection of gift and giver, see Mauss 1990.11–12 and cf. Kopytoff 1986.64–91 and Appadurai 1986.16–29.
11 Schol. *ad Ne.* 3.57, Apollod. 3.13.7, and Pfeijffer 1999.316. On the possibility that Heracles also had help in his travels, see Pfeijffer 1999.297n.104.
12 1999.212.
13 Instone 1993.22.
14 Erbse 1969.283–5 and Hubbard 1985.42 see a reference to athletic training here.
15 Pfeijffer 1999.272–3, 626–7. The manuscripts read τεάν / . . . κατ' αἶσαν, "through your dispensation," which is very awkward; the Muse is the obvious referent, but it would be unique if she were given the job of dispensing victory. Schol. *ad Ne.* 3.25 seems to understand a third-personal pronoun, but it is far from clear that it reads one in the text.
16 Pfeijffer 1999.201, 215–16.
17 ἑὰν could easily refer to Aegina (13).
18 Pfeijffer 1999.228–31.
19 See Williams 1977.108–27, Macherey 1978.136–56, 258–98, Macherey and Balibar 1981.82–9, Ryan 1989.202–6, and Eagleton 1991.45–7.
20 Pi. *Ol.* 7.15–17, 77–87.
21 Paus. 6.7.1–2, schol. *ad Ol.* 7 inscr.a, c; DP no.151; Moretti 1957.94–5.
22 Of his sons, Damagetus won the pancratium in 452 and 448, Acusilaos the boxing in 448, and Dorieus the pancratium in 432, 428, and 424; of his grandsons, Eucles the boxing and Peisirhodus the boys' boxing, both perhaps in 404. See Paus. 7.1–4, POxy. 222, and Moretti 1957.100, 102, 106, 111–12.
23 *Ol.* 13.1–2, 98–100, 106–7. Barrett 1978.1 thinks that the Oligaethidae won sixty victories at both the Isthmus and Nemea, but the figure surely represents the sum total for both; cf. Cole 1987.553–68. *Ol.* 13.95–100 implies that Pindar cannot vouch for the exact accuracy of the figure; see Stoddart 1990.46–9.
24 Moretti 1957.94.
25 *Ol.* 13.30–1.
26 Moretti 1957.94. Phayllos of Croton had won Pythian victories in the pentathlon and stadion (Paus. 10.9.2, Moretti 1953.26–7).
27 *Ol.* 13.32–4 and Cole 1987.563–4.
28 Pi. *fr.* 122, on which see Kurke 1996.68n.3. As Barrett 1978.5–9 shows, the family had probably commissioned two victory odes from Simonides for different victors.
29 A simple reference to χεῖρες is often used by Pindar to indicate combat sports (see Pi. *Ol.* 4.25, 8.75, 10.62, *Py.* 10.23, *Is.* 5.9; cf. Ba. 2.4), and πόνος is particularly used to designate the labor of combat sports (*Ne.* 6.24, 10.24, *Is.* 4.47, 5.25, 6.11, 8.8). Verdenius 1987.70 takes ἐπιχθονίων to be dependent on ἀριστοπόνοις, but κρατεῖν can govern the genitive and mean "conquer"; see LSJ II.3.
30 See n.10.
31 Dickson 1986.129; cf. Gernet 1981.

32 For Athena's association with magical tools, see Detienne and Vernant 1978.177–86.
33 On the Telchines, see Detienne and Vernant 1978.259–75. *Contra* Young 1968.86n.2, Pindar seems here to be claiming for the sons of Helios an ability more usually credited to the Telchines; see Farnell 1932.55 and Bowra 1964.339.
34 Hubbard 1986.28–33 demonstrates that Pindar has "augmented the degree of personal agency" assigned to Bellerophon by the traditions available to him. In particular, the story told in the cult of Athena Chalinitis, presumably that of Paus. 2.4.1, described how Athena bridled Pegasus before giving him to Bellerophon, whereas the version in Hesiod (*fr.* 43a M-W) related that Poseidon presented Pegasus to him.
35 Hubbard 1986.34.
36 Cf. Dickson 1986.124.
37 As Kurke 1991.197–8 argues, *Ol.* 13 makes a considerable effort to praise the city of Corinth, but it does so in aristocratic terms, by representing the city's successes as the results of innate excellence, rather than, say, a healthy civic structure. Corinth's record at the Olympics is not outstanding, but, as the Oligaethidae's record suggests, it may have dominated at the Isthmian games.
38 Young 1968.86n.2.
39 Cf. *Ol.* 2.86–8.
40 See Dickson 1986.124, 129–32, 135–6.
41 On the sequence of the events, see Golden 1998.69–73.
42 On Thessalos, see Pi. *Ol.* 13.35–40, schol. *ad Ol.* 13.51d, Moretti 1957.79, Barrett 1978.1–2. Barrett 1978.14–15 offers some evidence that Thessalos' cousin, Namertidas, also competed in the pentathlon, but running seems to be the family specialty. This would explain their lengthy victory record, because runners could win multiple victories at a single festival.
43 Pi. *Ol.* 12, 14, *Py.* 9–11, *Ne.* 8, Ba. 6–7 (for the same victory), 10.
44 Schol. *ad Py.* 9, inscr.a, b.
45 Schol. *ad Py.* 9, inscr.a, b. Like the date, this information must have been taken from the Pythian victory lists used by the scholia.
46 Given that Xenophon competed in at least two events (and possibly the *diaulos* as well), a number of athletes (or a few injuries) were probably needed to block his efforts to win at Delphi.
47 Schol. *ad Py.* 9, inscr.b; see Hyde 1921.161–4.
48 On Apollo's youth, see Woodbury 1972.561–73.
49 *Contra* Woodbury 1972, esp. 561–2, 572, who is followed by Robbins 1978.99.
50 Robbins 1978.94–6, Stoddart 1990.61–6, Dougherty 1993.146–7. This relationship may have been familiar from local Cyrenean legends (Chiron also plays a role in *Py.* 4.102–15) and, perhaps, Hesiod's catalogue of women.
51 ἔντυεν means both "armed" and "encouraged" (LSJ, s.v. ἐντύνω).
52 On the colonial concerns of *Py.* 9, see Calame 1990.300–7, 1996.116–28, and Dougherty 1993.136–56.
53 Philostr. *Gym.* 43. On Polymestor, Amesinas, whom Philostratus calls Alesias, and Polydamas, see Moretti 1957.67, 96, 110.

CONCLUSION

1 Pfeiffer 1968.130. Within each festival, the odes are arranged according to a basket of criteria, including the event, the victor, and the victor's age. Accordingly, not all odes for victories in the same event are grouped together: *Ol.* 7 and 10–11 celebrate boxers, *Py.* 1–2 and 4–7 chariot victories, *Ne.* 2–3 and 5 pancratiasts, and *Ne.* 4 and 6 wrestlers. The Bacchylides papyrus groups together odes for the same victor, while alternating long and short ones.

WORKS CITED

Alexander, Robert, ed. 1909. *The Knights of Aristophanes*. Cambridge: Cambridge University Press.

Althusser, Louis. 1971. "Ideology and Ideological State Apparatuses." In *Lenin and Philosophy and Other Essays*. Trans. B. Brewster. London: New Left Books. 121–73.

Appadurai, Arjun. 1986. "The Social Life of Things: Commoditization in Cultural Perspective." In *The Social Life of Things: Commodities in a Cultural Perspective*. Ed. A. Appadurai. Cambridge: Cambridge University Press. 3–63.

Arnold-Biucchi, Carmen. 1990. *The Randazzo Hoard 1980 and Sicilian Chronology in the Early Fifth Century B.C.* Numismatic Studies no. 18. New York: American Numismatics Society.

Barrett, W. S. 1978. "The Oligaithidai and Their Victories (Pindar, *Olympian 13;* SLG *339, 340*)." In *Dionysiaca: Nine Studies in Greek Poetry by Former Pupils Presented to Sir Denys Page on His Seventieth Birthday*. Ed. R. D. Dawe, J. Diggle, and P. E. Easterling. Cambridge: The Editors. 1–20.

Barringer, Judith. 2001. *The Hunt in Ancient Greece*. Baltimore: Johns Hopkins University Press.

Barron, John P. 1984. "Ibycus: Gorgias and Other Poems." *BICS* 31: 13–24.

Beazley, John Davidson. 1927. "The Antimenes Painter." *JHS* 47: 63–92.

Beazley, John Davidson. 1928. *Greek Vases in Poland*. Oxford: Oxford University Press.

Beazley, John Davidson. 1931/32. "Groups of Mid-Sixth-Century Black-Figure." *ABSA* 32: 1–22.

Beazley, John Davidson. 1951. *The Development of Attic Black-Figure*. Berkeley: University of California Press.

Beazley, John Davidson. 1953/54. "Ten Inscribed Vases." *Archaiologike Ephemeris* 92–3: 200–6.

Bell, J. M. 1978. "Κίμβιξ καὶ σοφός: Simonides and the Anecdotal Tradition." *QUCC* 28: 29–86.

Bell, Malcolm. 1995. "The Motya Charioteer and Pindar's *Isthmian 2*." *Memoirs of the American Academy in Rome* 40: 1–42.

Bergk, Theodor, ed. 1878. *Poetae Lyrici Graeci*. 4th ed. Vol. 1. Leipzig: B. G. Teubner.

Bicknell, Peter. 1970. "The Exile of the Alkmeonidai during the Peisistratid Tyranny." *Historia* 19: 129–31.

Bizard, Léon. 1920. "Fouilles du Ptoion." *BCH* 44: 227–62.

Blass, Friedrich. 1898. "Bacchylides' Gedicht auf Pytheas von Aigina." *RhM* 53: 283–307.

Bloch, Maurice, and Jonathan Parry, eds. 1989. *Money and the Morality of Exchange*. Cambridge: Cambridge University Press.

Blümel, Carl. 1936. *Der Sport der Hellenen*. Berlin: Staatlichen Museen.

Blundell, Mary Whitlock. 1989. *Helping Friends and Harming Enemies: A Study in Sophocles and Greek Ethics*. Cambridge: Cambridge University Press.

Boardman, John. 1974. *Athenian Black Figure Vases: A Handbook*. London: Thames and Hudson.

Boardman, John. 1989. *Athenian Red Figure Vases: The Classical Period: A Handbook*. London: Thames and Hudson.

Boardman, John. 2001. *The History of Greek Vases: Potters, Painters and Pictures*. London: Thames and Hudson.

Bode, Nina. 1993. "Die Statue von Mozia: Hamilkar als Heros." *AK* 36: 103–10.

Bowie, Ewen. 1986. "Early Greek Elegy." *JHS* 106: 13–35.

Bowra, C. Maurice, ed. 1947. *Pindari Carmina cum Fragmentis*. 2nd ed. Oxford: Oxford University Press.

Bowra, C. Maurice. 1964. *Pindar*. Oxford: Oxford University Press.

Braswell, Bruce Karl. 1988. *A Commentary on the Fourth Pythian Ode of Pindar*. Berlin: de Gruyter.

Brown, Christopher. 1984. "The Bridegroom and the Athlete." In *Greek Poetry and Philosophy: Studies in Honor of Leonard Woodbury*. Ed. Douglas E. Gerber. Chico: Scholars Press. 37–50.

Bulman, Patricia. 1992. *Phthonos in Pindar*. Berkeley: University of California Press.

Bundy, Elroy. 1986. *Studia Pindarica*. Berkeley and Los Angeles: University of California Press.

Burnett, Anne Pippin. 1985. *The Art of Bacchylides*. Cambridge, Mass.: Harvard University Press.

Bury, John Bagnell, ed. 1890. *The Nemean Odes of Pindar*. London: Macmillan.

Bury, John Bagnell, ed. 1892. *The Isthmian Odes of Pindar*. London: Macmillan.

Calame, Claude. 1990. "Narrating the Foundation of a City: The Symbolic Birth of Cyrene." In *Approaches to Greek Myth*. Ed. Lowell Edmunds. Baltimore: Johns Hopkins University Press. 277–341.

Calame, Claude. 1996. *Mythe et histoire dans l'antiquité grecque: La création symbolique d'une colonie*. Lausanne: Editions Payot.

Cameron, Alan. 1973. *Porphyrius the Charioteer*. Oxford: Oxford University Press.

Campbell, David A., ed. 1982. *Greek Lyric Poetry*. Bristol: Bristol Classical Press.

Campbell, David A., ed. and trans. 1991. *Greek Lyric III: Stesichorus, Ibycus, Simonides and Others*. Cambridge, Mass.: Harvard University Press.

Campbell, David A., ed. and trans. 1992. *Greek Lyric IV: Bacchylides, Corinna and Others*. Cambridge, Mass.: Harvard University Press.

Carey, Christopher. 1980a. "Three Myths in Pindar: *N.* 4, *O.* 9, *N.* 3." *Eranos* 78: 143–62.

Carey, Christopher. 1980b. "The Epilogue of Pindar's Fourth Pythian." *Maia* 32: 143–153.

Carey, Christopher. 1989a. "Prosopographica Pindarica." *CQ* 39: 1–9.

Carey, Christopher. 1989b. "Two Transitions in Pindar." *CQ* 39: 287–95.

Carnes, Jeffrey. 1996. "The Ends of the Earth: Fathers, Ephebes and Wild Women in *Nemean* 4 and 5." *Arethusa* 29: 15–55.

Carnes, Jeffrey. 1999. "The Tricker Tricked: A Reinterpretation of *Nemean* 4.57–58." *RhM* 142: 1–9.

Carson, Anne. 1982. "Wedding at Noon in Pindar's Ninth Pythian." *GRBS* 23: 121–8.

Chamoux, François. 1953. *Cyrène sous la monarchie des Battiades*. Paris: de Boccard.

Chamoux, François. 1955. *L'Aurige de Delphes*. Paris: de Boccard.

Cole, A. Thomas. 1987. "1+1=3: Studies in Pindar's Arithmetic." *AJPh* 108: 553–68.

Cole, A. Thomas. 1992. *Pindar's Feasts or the Music of Power*. Rome: Ateneo.

Crotty, Kevin. 1982. *Song and Action: The Victory Odes of Pindar*. Baltimore: Johns Hopkins University Press.

Crowther, Nigel. 1989. "Boy Victors at Olympia." *AC* 58: 206–10.

Crowther, Nigel. 1991. "The Olympic Training Period." *Nikephoros* 4: 161–6.

Crowther, Nigel. 1992a. "Second Place Finishes and Lower in Greek Athletics." *ZPE* 90: 97–102.

Crowther, Nigel. 1992b. "Rounds and Byes in Greek Athletics." *Stadion* 18: 68–74.

Crowther, Nigel. 1993. "Number of Contestants in Greek Athletic Contests." *Nikephoros* 6: 39–52.

Crowther, Nigel. 1994. "Reflections on Greek Equestrian Events. Violence and Spectator Attitudes." *Nikephoros* 7: 121–33.

Davies, John Kenyon. 1971. *Athenian Propertied Families*. Oxford: Oxford University Press.

Davies, John Kenyon. 1984. *Wealth and the Power of Wealth in Classical Athens*. Salem, N.H.: Ayer.

Detienne, Marcel, and Jean-Pierre Vernant. 1978. *Cunning and Intelligence in Greek Culture and Society*. Trans. Janet Lloyd. Sussex: Harvester.

Dickson, Keith. 1986. "Damasiphron Khrusos: Act, Implement and Tekhne in Pindar." *Ramus* 15: 122–42.

Dickson, Keith. 1988. "The Semiotics of Eidos in Olympian 8." *Helios* 15: 115–26.

Dickson, Keith. 1990. "Voice and Sign in Pindar." *Ramus* 19: 109–29.

Dougherty, Carol. 1993. *The Poetics of Colonization: From City to Text in Archaic Greece*. New York: Oxford University Press.

Drachmann, A. B., ed. 1903. *Scholia Vetera in Pindari Carmina*. Vol. 1. *Scholia in Olympionicas*. Leipzig: B. G. Teubner.

Drachmann, A. B., ed. 1910. *Scholia Vetera in Pindari Carmina*. Vol. 2. *Scholia in Pythionicas*. Leipzig: B. G. Teubner.

Drachmann, A. B., ed. 1927. *Scholia Vetera in Pindari Carmina*. Vol. 3. *Scholia in Nemeonicas et Isthmionicas; Epimetrum; Indices*. Leipzig: B. G. Teubner.

duBois, Page. 1991. *Torture and Truth*. New York: Routledge.

Dunbabin, Thomas J. 1968. *The Western Greeks: The History of Sicily and South Italy from the Foundation of the Greek Colonies to 480 B.C.* Oxford: Oxford University Press.

Eagleton, Terry. 1983. *Literary Theory: An Introduction*. Minneapolis: University of Minnesota Press.

Eagleton, Terry. 1991. *Ideology: An Introduction*. London: Verso.

Ebert, Joachim. 1972. *Griechische Epigramme auf Sieger an Gymnischen und Hippischen Agonen*. Abhandlungen der Sächsischen Akademie der Wissenschaften zu Leipzig, Philologisch-Historische Klasse, 63.2. Berlin: Akademie-Verlag.

Erbse, Hartmut. 1969. "Pindars dritte nemeische Ode." *Hermes* 97: 272–91.

Farnell, Lewis. 1930. *The Works of Pindar*. Vol. 1. *Translation in Rhythmical Prose with Literary Comments*. London: Macmillan.

Farnell, Lewis. 1932. *The Works of Pindar*. Vol. 2. *Critical Commentary*. London: Macmillan.

Fennell, Charles A. M., ed. 1899. *Pindar: The Nemean and Isthmian Odes*. Cambridge: Cambridge University Press.

Figueira, Thomas. 1993. *Excursions in Epichoric History: Aeginetan Essays*. Lanham: Rowman and Littlefield.

Fontenrose, Joseph. 1988. "The Cult of Apollo and the Games at Delphi." In *Archaeology of the Olympics: The Olympics and Other Festivals in Antiquity*. Ed. Wendy Raschke. Madison: University of Wisconsin Press. 121–40.

Freeman, Edward. 1891. *The History of Sicily from the Earliest Times. Vol. II*. Oxford: Oxford University Press.

Friedländer, Paul, and Herbert Hoffleit. 1948. *Epigrammata: Greek Inscriptions in Verse from the Beginnings to the Persian Wars*. Berkeley: University of California Press.

Frisk, Hjalmar. 1955. *Griechisches Etymologisches Wörterbuch*. Vol. I. Heidelberg: C. Winter.

Frow, John. 1986. *Marxism and Literary History*. Cambridge, Mass.: Harvard University Press.

Fumerton, Patricia. 1999. "Introduction: A New New Historicism." In *Renaissance Culture and the Everyday*. Ed. P. Fumerton and Simon Hunt. Philadelphia: University of Pennsylvania Press. 1–17.

Gallagher, Catherine, and Stephen Greenblatt. 2000. *Practicing New Historicism*. Chicago: University of Chicago Press.

Gardiner, Norman. 1910. *Greek Athletic Sports and Festivals*. London: Macmillan.

Gardiner, Norman. 1978. *Athletics of the Ancient World*. Chicago: Ares.

Gentili, Bruno. 1988. *Poetry and Its Public in Ancient Greece*. Trans. A. Thomas Cole. Baltimore: Johns Hopkins University Press.

Gerber, Douglas E. 1976. *Emendations in Pindar*. Amsterdam: Hakkert.

Gerber, Douglas E. 1982. *Pindar's Olympian One: A Commentary*. Toronto: University of Toronto Press.

Gerber, Douglas E. 1984. "Emendations in the Odes of Pindar: An Historical Analysis." *Entretiens Hardt* 31: 1–32.

Gerber, Douglas E. 1987. "Pindar's *Olympian* 4: A Commentary." *QUCC* 54: 7–24.

Gerber, Douglas E. 1999. "Pindar *Nemean* 6: A Commentary." *HSPh* 99: 33–91.

Gerber, Douglas E. 2002. *A Commentary on Pindar Olympian Nine*. Stuttgart: Franz Steiner.

Gernet, Louis. 1981. "Value in Greek Myth." In *Myth, Religion and Society*. Ed. Richard Gordon. Cambridge: Cambridge University Press. 111–46.

Gildersleeve, Basil. 1908. *The Olympian and Pythian Odes*. London: Macmillan.

Golden, Mark. 1990. *Children and Childhood in Classical Athens*. Baltimore: Johns Hopkins University Press.

Golden, Mark. 1998. *Sport and Society in Ancient Greece*. Cambridge: Cambridge University Press.

Gregory, Chris. 1982. *Gifts and Commodities*. London: Academic Press.

Grenfell, Bernard, and Arthur Hunt. 1899. *The Oxyrhynchus Papyri*. Vol. 2. London: Egypt Exploration Fund.

Grillet, Bernard. 1975. *Les femmes et les fards dans l'antiquité Grècque*. Lyon: Centre National de la Recherche Scientifique.

Gross, W. H. 1969. "Quas iconicas vocant. Zum Porträtcharakter der Statuen dreimaliger olympischer Sieger." *Nachrichten der Akademie der Wissenschaften in Göttingen*. Pt. 3. 61–76

Gzella, Stanislaw. 1971. "The Problem of the Fee in Greek Lyric." *Eos* 59: 189–202.

Gzella, Stanislaw. 1981. "Pindar and Aegina." *Eos* 69: 5–19.

Habicht, Christian. 1985. *Pausanias' Guide to Ancient Greece*. Berkeley: University of California Press.

Hamilton, Richard. 1972. "Olympian Five: A Reconsideration." *AJPh* 93: 324–9.

Hamilton, Richard. 1974. *Epinikion: General Form in the Odes of Pindar*. The Hague: Mouton.

Hansen, William. 2000. "The Winning of Hippodameia." *TAPhA* 130: 19–40.

Harrell, Sarah. 2002. "King or Private Citizen: Fifth-Century Sicilian Tyrants at Olympia and Delphi." *Mnemosyne*, 4th ser. 55: 439–64.

Harriott, Rosemary. 1969. *Poetry and Criticism before Plato*. London: Methuen.

Heath, Malcolm. 1988. "Receiving the κῶμος: The Context and Performance of Epinician." *AJPh* 109: 180–95.

Hitzig, Hermann, and Hugo Blümner, eds. 1984. *Pausaniae Graeciae Descriptio*. 3 vols. Hildersheim: Georg Olms.

Hodkinson, Stephen. 1999. "An Agonistic Culture? Athletic Competition in Archaic and Classical Spartan Society." In *Sparta: New Perspectives*. Ed. S. Hodkinson and Anton Powell. London: Duckworth. 147–87.

Hoppin, Joseph. 1917. *Euthymides and His Fellows*. Cambridge, Mass.: Harvard University Press.

Howard, Jean. 1986. "The New Historicism in Renaissance Studies." *English Literary Renaissance* 13: 13–43.

Hubbard, Thomas K. 1985. *The Pindaric Mind*. Leiden: Brill.

Hubbard, Thomas K. 1986. "Pegasus' Bridle and the Poetics of Pindar's *Thirteenth Olympian*." *HSPh* 90: 27–48.

Hubbard, Thomas K. 2002. "Pindar, Theoxenus, and the Homoerotic Eye." *Arethusa* 35: 255–96.

Hubbard, Thomas K. 2003. "Sex in the Gym: Athletic Trainers and Pedagogical Pederasty." *Intertexts* 7: 1–26.

Huxley, George. 1975. *Pindar's Vision of the Past*. Belfast: Author.

Hyde, Walter Woodburn. 1921. *Olympic Victor Monuments and Greek Athletic Art*. Washington, D.C.: The Carnegie Institution.

Instone, Stephen. 1993. "Problems in Pindar's Third Nemean." *Eranos* 91: 13–31.

Jacquemin, Anne. 1999. *Offrandes monumentales à Delphes*. Bibliothèque des écoles françaises d'Athènes et de Rome. Fasc. 304. Athènes: Ecole française d'Athènes.

Jameson, Fredric. 1981. *The Political Unconscious*. Ithaca: Cornell University Press.

Jebb, Richard, ed. 1905. *Bacchylides. The Poems and Fragments*. Cambridge: Cambridge University Press.

Jeffery, Lilian. 1961. *The Local Scripts of Archaic Greece: A Study of the Origin of the Greek Alphabet and Its Development from the Eighth to the Fifth Centuries B.C.* Oxford: Oxford University Press.

Jenkins, Kenneth. 1986. *Coins of Greek Sicily*. London: British Museum.

Jenner, E. A. B. 1986. "Further Speculations on Ibycus and the Epinician Ode." *BICS* 33: 59–66.

Jüthner, Julius. 1968. *Die Athletischen Leibesübungen der Griechen. II. Einzelne Sportarten*. Österreichischen Akademie der Wissenschaften, Philosophisch-Historische Klasse, 249.2. Ed. Friedrich Brein. Vienna.

Jüthner, Julius. 1969. *Philostratos über Gymnastik*. Amsterdam: E. J. Bonset.

Kirchner, Roderich. 1996. "Der Ringtrainer Melesias. Zur Prosopographica Pindarica." *Altertum* 41: 165–76.

Köhnken, Adolf. 1971. *Die Funktion des Mythos bei Pindar: Interpretationen zu sechs Pindargedichten*. Berlin: de Gruyter.

Kopytoff, Igor. 1986. "The Cultural Biography of Things: Commoditization as a Process." In *The Social Life of Things: Commodities in a Cultural Perspective*. Ed. Arjun Appadurai. Cambridge: Cambridge University Press. 64–91.

Kraay, Colin. 1976. *Archaic and Classical Greek Coins*. Berkeley: University of California Press.

Kroll, John, and Nancy Waggoner. 1984. "Dating the Earliest Coins of Athens, Corinth and Aegina." *AJA* 88: 325–40.

Krumeich, Ralf. 1997. *Bildnise griechischer Herrscher und Staatsmänner im 5. Jahrhundert v. Chr.* Munich: Biering und Brinkmann.

Kurke, Leslie. 1989. "Καπηλεία and Deceit: Theognis 59–60." *AJPh* 110: 535–44.

Kurke, Leslie. 1990. "Pindar's Sixth *Pythian*, and the Tradition of Advice Poetry." *TAPhA* 120: 85–107.

Kurke, Leslie. 1991. *The Traffic in Praise: Pindar and the Poetics of Social Economy*. Ithaca: Cornell University Press.

Kurke, Leslie. 1996. "Pindar and the Prostitutes, or Reading Ancient 'Pornography'." *Arion* 4: 49–75.

Kurke, Leslie. 1998. "The Economy of *Kudos*." In *Cultural Poetics in Archaic Greece: Cult, Performance, Politics*. Eds. L. Kurke and Carol Dougherty. New York: Oxford University Press. 131–63.

Kurke, Leslie. 1999. *Coins, Bodies, Games, and Gold: The Politics of Meaning in Archaic Greece*. Princeton: Princeton University Press.

Kurke, Leslie. 2003. "Aesop and the Contestation of Delphic Authority." In *The Cultures within Greek Culture: Contact, Conflict, Collaboration*. Eds. L. Kurke and Carol Dougherty. Cambridge: Cambridge University Press. 77–100.

Kyle, Donald. 1987. *Athletics in Ancient Athens. Mnemosyne*, Suppl. 95. Leiden: Brill.

Langlotz, Ernst. 1968. *Griechische Vasen in Würzburg*. 2 vols. Rome: L'Erma di Bretschneider.

Lattimore, Steven. 1988. "The Nature of Early Greek Victor Statues." In *Coroebus Triumphs: The Alliance of Sport and the Arts*. Ed. Susan Bandy. San Diego: San Diego State University Press. 245–56.

Lefkowitz, Mary. 1976. *The Victory Ode: An Introduction*. Park Ridge, N.J.: Noyes Press.

Lefkowitz, Mary. 1985. "Pindar's Pythian V." In *Pindare*. Fondation Hardt pour l'étude de l'Antiquité Classique, Entretiens 31. Geneva: Olivier Reverdin et Bernard Grange. 33–69.

Lefkowitz, Mary. 1991. *First-Person Fictions: Pindar's Poetic 'I'*. Oxford: Oxford University Press.

Macherey, Pierre. 1978. *A Theory of Literary Production*. Trans. Geoffrey Wall. London: Routledge and Kegan Paul.

Macherey, Pierre, and Etienne Balibar. 1981. "On Literature as Ideological Form." In *Untying the Text; A Post-Structuralist Reader*. Ed. R. Young. Boston: Routledge and Kegan Paul. 79–99.

Mader, Walter. 1990. *Die Psaumis-Oden Pindars (O.4 und O.5): Ein Kommentar.* Commentationes Aenipontanae 29. Innsbruck: Universitätsverlag Wagner.

Maehler, Herwig. 1982. *Die Lieder des Bakchylides. Part 1: Die Siegeslieder, vol. 2, Kommentar. Mnemosyne*, Suppl. 62. Leiden: Brill.

Maehler, Herwig, post Bruno Snell, ed. 1987. *Pindari Carmina cum Fragmentis.* Leipzig: Teubner.

Maehler, Herwig, ed. 1989. *Pindari Carmina cum Fragmentis, Pars II.* Leipzig: Teubner.

Malkin, Irad. 1987. *Religion and Colonization in Ancient Greece.* Studies in Greek and Roman Religion 3. Leiden: Brill.

Malkin, Irad. 1994. *Myth and Territory in the Spartan Mediterranean.* Cambridge: Cambridge University Press.

Mann, Christian. 2001. *Athlet und Polis im archaischen und frühklassichen Griechenland.* Göttingen: Vandenhoeck und Ruprecht.

Mauss, Marcel. 1990. *The Gift: The Form and Reason for Exchange in Ancient Societies.* Trans. W. D. Halls. New York: W. W. Norton.

Miller, Andrew. 1983. "*N.* 4. 33–43 and the Defense of Digressive Leisure." *CJ* 78: 202–20.

Miller, Stephen. 2000. "Naked Democracy." Ed. Pernille Flensted-Jensen, Thomas H. Nielsen, and Lene Rubinstein. Copenhagen: Museum Tusculanum. 277–96.

Mitchell, B. M. 1966. "Cyrene and Persia." *JHS* 86: 99–113.

Montrose, Louis. 1989. "Professing the Renaissance: The Poetics and Politics of Culture." In *The New Historicism.* Ed. H. Aram Veeser. New York: Routledge. 15–36.

Moretti, Luigi. 1953. *Iscrizioni agonistiche greche.* Rome: Angelo Signorelli.

Moretti, Luigi. 1957. "Olympionikai: i vincitori negli antichi agoni olimpici." *MAL* (ser. 8) 8.2: 55–198.

Moretti, Luigi. 1987. "Nuovo supplemento al catalogo degli Olympionikai." *MGR* 12: 67–91 (Studi pubblicati dell'Istituto italiano per la storia antica, 39).

Morris, Ian. 2000. *Archaeology as Cultural History: Words and Things in Iron Age Greece.* Malden: Blackwell.

Most, Glenn. 1985. *Measures of Praise: Structure and Function in Pindar's Second Pythian and Seventh Nemean Odes.* Göttingen: Vandenhoeck und Ruprecht.

Mullen, William. 1982. *Choreia: Pindar and Dance.* Princeton: Princeton University Press.

Murray, Oswyn. 1993. *Early Greece.* 2nd ed. Cambridge, Mass.: Harvard University Press.

Nagy, Gregory. 1990. *Pindar's Homer: The Lyric Possession of an Epic Past*. Baltimore: Johns Hopkins University Press.

Nash, Laura. 1990. *The Aggelia in Pindar*. New York: Garland.

Neer, Richard. 2002. *Style and Politics in Athenian Vase-Painting: The Craft of Democracy, ca. 530–460 B.C.E.* Cambridge: Cambridge University Press.

Nicholson, Nigel. 1998. "The Truth of Pederasty: A Supplement to Foucault's Genealogy of the Relation between Truth and Desire in Ancient Greece." *Intertexts* 2: 26–45.

Nicholson, Nigel. 2000. "Pederastic Poets and Adult Patrons in Late Archaic Lyric." *CW* 93: 235–59.

Nicholson, Nigel. 2001. "Pindar *Nemean* 4.57–58 and the Arts of Poets, Wrestlers and Trainers." *Arethusa* 34: 31–59.

Nisetich, Frank. 1977. "Convention and Occasion in *Isthmian* 2." *CSCA* 10: 133–56.

Norwood, Gilbert. 1956. *Pindar*. Berkeley: University of California Press.

Peek, Werner. 1958. "Ein Delphisches Weihgedicht." *Philologus* 102: 43–59.

Pellizer, Ezio. 1990. "Outlines of a Morphology of Sympotic Entertainment." In *Sympotica: A Symposium on the Symposium*. Ed. Oswyn Murray. Oxford: Oxford University Press. 177–84.

Pfeiffer, Rudolf. 1968. *History of Classical Scholarship from the Beginnings to the End of the Hellenistic Age*. Oxford: Oxford University Press.

Pfeijffer, Ilja. 1995. "The Date of Pindar's Fifth *Nemean* and Bacchylides' Thirteenth ode." *CQ* 45: 318–32.

Pfeijffer, Ilja. 1998. "Athletic Age Categories in Victory Odes." *Nikephoros* 11: 21–38.

Pfeijffer, Ilja. 1999. *Three Aeginetan Odes of Pindar: A Commentary on Nemean V, Nemean III, and Pythian VIII*. Leiden: Brill.

Platter, Charles. 1989. "Veil and Sign: Bacchylides and the Limits of Praise." Ann Arbor: University Microfilms.

Pleket, Henri. 1975. "Games, Prizes, Athletes and Ideology." *Stadion* 1: 49–89.

Poliakoff, Michael. 1982. *Studies in the Terminology of the Greek Combat Sports*. Königstein/Ts.: Hain.

Poliakoff, Michael. 1987. *Combat Sports in the Ancient World*. New Haven: Yale University Press.

Poralla, Paul. 1985. *Prosopographie der Lakedaimonier bis auf die Zeit Alexanders des Grossen*. Chicago: Ares.

Race, William. 1990. *Style and Rhetoric in Pindar's Odes*. Atlanta: Scholars Press.

Race, William, ed. and trans. 1997. *Pindar*. Vol 2. Cambridge, Mass.: Harvard University Press.

Raschke, Wendy. 1988. "Images of Victory: Some New Considerations of Athletic Monuments." In *Archaeology of the Olympics: The Olympics and Other Festivals in Antiquity*. Ed. W. Raschke. Madison: University of Wisconsin Press. 38–54.

Raubitschek, Antony. 1949. *Dedications from the Athenian Acropolis: A Catalogue of the Inscriptions of the Sixth and Fifth Centuries B.C* Cambridge, Mass.: Archaeological Institute of America.

Rawson, Elizabeth. 1981. "Chariot Racing in the Roman Republic." *PBSR* 49: 1–16.

Redfield, James. 1975. *Nature and Culture in the Iliad: The Tragedy of Hector.* Chicago: University of Chicago Press.

Redfield, James. 1982. "Notes on the Greek Wedding." *Arethusa* 15: 181–201.

Richter, Gisela, and Marjorie Milne. 1973. *Shapes and Names of Athenian Vases.* Washington, D.C.: McGrath.

Robbins, Emmet. 1978. "Cyrene and Cheiron: The Myth of Pindar's Ninth Pythian." *Phoenix* 32: 91–104.

Robbins, Emmet. 1986. "The Broken Wall, the Burning Roof and Tower: Pindar, *Ol.* 8.31–46." *CQ* 36: 317–21.

Robinson David, Cornelia Harcum, and John Iliffe. 1930. *A Catalogue of the Greek Vases in the Royal Ontario Museum of Archaeology, Toronto.* Toronto: University of Toronto Press.

Rolley, Claude. 1990. "En regardant L'Aurige." *BCH* 14: 285–97.

Rose, Peter. 1974. "The Myth of Pindar's First Nemean: Sportsmen, Poetry and Paideia." *HSPh* 78: 145–75.

Rose, Peter. 1992. *Sons of the Gods, Children of the Earth: Ideology and Literary Form in Ancient Greece.* Ithaca: Cornell University Press.

Ruck, Carl. 1968. "Marginalia Pindarica." *Hermes* 96: 129–42.

Rutter, N. Keith. 1997. *The Greek Coinages of Southern Italy and Sicily.* London: Spink.

Ryan, Michael. 1989. "Political Criticism." In *Contemporary Literary Theory.* Eds. G. Douglas Atkins and Laura Morrow. Amherst: University of Massachusetts Press. 200–13.

Sahlins, Marshall. 1972. *Stone Age Economics.* Chicago: University of Chicago Press.

Scanlon, Thomas. 2002. *Eros and Greek Athletics.* Oxford: Oxford University Press.

Schachter, Albert. 1997. "The Politics of Dedication: Two Athenian Dedications at the Sanctuary of Apollo Ptoieus in Boeotia." In *Ritual, Finance, Politics: Athenian Democratic Accounts Presented to David Lewis.* Eds. Robin Osborne and Simon Hornblower. Oxford: Oxford University Press. 291–306.

Schein, Seth. 1987. "Unity and Meaning in Pindar's Sixth Pythian Ode." *Metis* 2: 235–47.

Schwartz, Jacques. 1960. *Pseudo-Hesiodeia: Recherches sur la composition, la diffusion et la disparition ancienne d'oeuvres attribuées à Hésiode.* Leiden: Brill.

Seltman, Charles. 1924. *Athens: Its History and Coinage before the Persian Invasion.* Cambridge: Cambridge University Press.

Sergent, Bernard. 1986. *Homosexuality in Greek Myth*. Trans. Arthur Goldhammer. Boston: Beacon Press.

Sewell, William. 1999. "The Concept(s) of Culture." In *Beyond the Cultural Turn: New Directions in the Study of Society and Culture*. Eds. Victoria Bonnell and Lynn Hunt. Berkeley: University of California Press. 35–61.

Shear, Julia. 2003. "Prizes from Athens: The List of Panathenaic Prizes and the Sacred Oil." *ZPE* 142: 87–108.

Simpson, Michael. 1969. "The Chariot and the Bow as Metaphors for Pindar's Poetry." *TAPhA* 100: 471–2.

Slater, William. 1969. *Lexicon to Pindar*. Berlin: de Gruyter.

Slater, William. 1984. "*Nemean One*: The Victor's Return in Poetry and Politics." In *Greek Poetry and Philosophy: Studies in Honor of Leonard Woodbury*. Ed. Douglas E. Gerber. Chico: Scholars Press. 241–64.

Smyth, Herbert. 1920. *A Greek Grammar for Colleges*. New York: American Book Company.

Stehle, Eva. 1997. *Performance and Gender in Ancient Greece*. Princeton: Princeton University Press.

Steiner, Deborah. 1998. "Moving Images: Fifth-Century Victory Monuments and the Athlete's Allure." *ClAnt* 17: 123–49.

Stern, Jacob. 1970. "The Myth of Pindar's Olympian Six." *AJPh* 91: 332–40.

Stoddart, Robert. 1990. *Pindar and Greek Family Law*. New York: Garland.

Sutton, Robert F. 1981. "Interaction of Men and Women on Attic Red Figure." Ann Arbor: University Microfilms.

Sutton, Robert F. 1992. "Pornography and Persuasion on Attic Pottery." In *Pornography and Representation in Greece and Rome*. Ed. Amy Richlin. Oxford: Oxford University Press. 3–35.

Svenbro, Jesper. 1976. *La parole et le marbre: aux origines de la poétique grecque*. Lund: Studentlitteratur.

Svenbro, Jesper. 1988. *Phrasikleia: anthropologie de la lecture en Grèce ancienne*. Paris: La Découverte.

Tandy, David. 1997. *Warriors into Traders: The Power of the Market in Early Greece*. Berkeley: University of California Press.

Thompson, Homer. 1956. "Activities in the Athenian Agora: 1955." *Hesperia* 25: 46–68.

Thompson, Homer. 1961. "The Panathenaic Festival." *AA* 76: 224–31.

Thummer, Erich. 1968. *Pindar: Die Isthmischen Gedichte*. Vol. 1. Heidelberg: Carl Winter.

Toynbee, Jocelyn. 1948. "Beasts and Their Names in the Roman Empire." *PBSR* 16: 24–37.

Treu, Georg. 1966. *Olympia: Die Ergebnisse der von dem Deutschen Reich veranstalteten Ausgrabung*. Vol. 3. *Die Bildwerke von Olympia in Stein und Thon*. Ed. Ernst Curtius and Friedrich Adler. Amsterdam: Hakkert.

Turyn, Alexander, ed. 1952. *Pindari Carmina cum Fragmentis*. Cambridge, Mass.: Harvard University Press

Ure, Percy. 1922. *The Origin of Tyranny*. Cambridge: Cambridge University Press.

Vanoyeke, Violaine. 1990. *La prostitution en Grèce et à Rome*. Paris: Belles Lettres.

Verdenius, Willem Jacob. 1987. *Commentaries on Pindar, Volume I. Mnemosyne*, Suppl. 97. Leiden: Brill.

Vernant, Jean-Pierre. 1983. *Myth and Thought among the Greeks*. London: Routledge and Kegan Paul.

von Reden, Sitta. 1995a. *Exchange in Ancient Greece*. London: Duckworth.

von Reden, Sitta. 1995b. "Deceptive Readings: Poetry and Its Value Reconsidered." *CQ* 45: 30–50.

Wade-Gery, Henry. 1932. "Thucydides the son of Melesias." *JHS* 52: 205–27.

Waele, Jos de. 1971. *Acragas Graeca, Die historische Topographie des griechischen Akragas auf Sizilien*. Archeologische studiën van het Nederlands Instituut te Rome. Staatsuitgsverij: 's-Gravenhage.

Webster, Thomas B. L. 1972. *Potter and Patron in Classical Athens*. London: Methuen.

West, Stephanie. 1970. "Chalcenteric Negligence." *CQ* 20: 288–96.

West, Stephanie. 1988. "Archilochus' Message-Stick," *CQ* 38: 42–8.

White, Allon, and Peter Stallybrass. 1986. *The Politics and Poetics of Transgression*. Ithaca: Cornell University Press.

Wilamowitz-Moellendorff, Ulrich von. 1922. *Pindaros*. Berlin: Weidmann.

Willcock, Malcolm M. 1995. *Pindar: Victory Odes: Olympians 2, 7, 11; Nemean 4; Isthmians 3, 4, 7*. Cambridge: Cambridge University Press.

Williams, Frederick. 1976. "A Critical Edition of Nemean Odes 1–4 of Pindar." Ann Arbor: University Microfilms.

Williams, Raymond. 1977. *Marxism and Literature*. Oxford: Oxford University Press.

Woloch, Michael. 1963. "Athenian Trainers in the Aeginetan Odes of Pindar and Bacchylides." *CW* 56: 102–4, 121.

Woodbury, Leonard. 1955. "The Tongue and the Whetstone." *TAPhA* 86: 31–9.

Woodbury, Leonard. 1968. "Pindar and the Mercenary Muse: Isthm. 1.32ff." *TAPhA* 99: 527–42.

Woodbury, Leonard. 1972. "Apollo's First Love: Pindar, *Pyth.* 9.26ff." *TAPhA* 103: 561–73.

Young, David C. 1968. *Three Odes of Pindar: A Literary Study of Pythian 11, Pythian 3, and Olympian 7*. Leiden: Brill.

Young, David C. 1983a. "Professionalism in Archaic and Classical Greek Athletics." *AncW* 7: 45–51.

Young, David C. 1983b. "Pindar *Pythians* 2 and 3: Inscriptional ποτέ and the 'Poetic Epistle'." *HSPh* 87: 31–48.

Young, David C. 1984. *The Olympic Myth of Greek Amateur Athletics*. Chicago: Ares.

INDEX